821.70°

He

D1491766

The Active Universe

Pantheism and the concept of Imagination in the English Romantic poets

by

H. W. PIPER

Emphatically such a being lives
An inmate of this active *universe.*

The Prelude

UNIVERSITY OF LONDON

THE ATHLONE PRESS

1962

Published by
THE ATHLONE PRESS
UNIVERSITY OF LONDON
at 2 *Gower Street, London* wc1
Distributed by Constable & Co. Ltd
12 *Orange Street, London* wc2

U.S.A.
Oxford University Press Inc
New York

© *H. W. Piper,* 1962

CENTRAL RESOURCES
LIBRARY

HERTFORDSHIRE
COUNTY LIBRARY
821.7'09 PiP
2349933

H23 425 057 5

B 62-14435

2043

Printed in Great Britain by
WESTERN PRINTING SERVICES LTD
Bristol

ACKNOWLEDGEMENTS

I am grateful for the advice and assistance in my researches which I received from Professor Pons and Professor Carré of the University of Paris, Professor G. Bullough of King's College, London, and Professor K. Coburn of the University of Toronto, and for the facilities made available by the authorities of the Bibliothèque Nationale and the Archives Nationales, Paris, the British Museum, the Barr-Smith Library of the University of Adelaide, the Public Library of South Australia and the Dixson Library of the University of New England. I am also grateful to Professor A. N. Jeffares of the University of Leeds, Mr D. C. Muecke of Newcastle University College, and Dr K. A. McKenzie and Mr C. Clarke of the University of New England for criticism of my manuscript; to Professor D. R. Grey of the University of New England, and Professor J. J. C. Smart of the University of Adelaide for similar criticism from the philosophical point of view, and to Dr C. B. Martin, also of the University of Adelaide, for most helpful suggestions in connection with the Epilogue to the book. I am particularly indebted to Professor Coburn and to Dr C. J. Holloway of the University of Cambridge for criticism and suggestions which enabled me to revise properly my first draft.

H.W.P.

CONTENTS

ABBREVIATIONS

DNB	*Dictionary of National Biography*
ELH	*English Literary History*
E & S	*Essays and Studies*
JEGP	*Journal of English and Germanic Philology*
JHI	*Journal of the History of Ideas*
MLN	*Modern Language Notes*
MP	*Modern Philology*
OED	*Oxford English Dictionary*
PMLA	*Publications of the Modern Language Association of America*
PQ	*Philological Quarterly*
RES	*Review of English Studies*
SP	*Studies in Philology*

Introduction

This book is a study of 'Romantic Pantheism' and its part in the development of the Romantic theory of the Imagination.

The new vision to be found in *The Ancient Mariner* and *Tintern Abbey* was not the result of a lucky hit or a chance turn: it came from deliberate thought about the Imagination which had occupied the minds of Wordsworth and Coleridge before 1798 and which did so for many years afterwards. But this deliberate thought did not occur in an historical vacuum. Contemporary philosophical speculation—particularly speculation determined by emergent *scientific* ideas—influenced both Coleridge and Wordsworth. Moreover these ideas (scientific as well as philosophical) tended to be entertained by men whose political opinions were of a radical cast. Coleridge's unitarianism and Wordsworth's association with the sympathizers with the French Revolution placed them in a current of thought which between 1750 and 1800, in England and in France, swept away the Newtonian mechanical 'universe of death' and brought a new conception of life, development and purpose in the natural world. In the eighteenth century the poets had seen the universe as the beautiful handiwork of God; the Romantics were able to see it as full of human significances and full of a life which answered to man's.

I begin with an account of certain strands of radical thought in the later eighteenth century. In the perspective of history, figures such as Priestley and the elder Darwin are smaller than they once were, but in the seventeen-nineties they were the two most distinguished English sympathizers with the French Revolution. Their importance in the formation of a young radical can only be realized when one recaptures the state of

B

1

mind that led Coleridge to place Priestley alongside Newton, and to call Erasmus Darwin 'the first literary character in Europe'. Odd though such a state of mind may seem, it is from it that one must begin any study of the origin of *Lyrical Ballads*.

The deliberations of Wordsworth and Coleridge issued in two rather different concepts of the Imagination which were set forth in *The Excursion* and in *Biographia Literaria*. I am principally concerned here with the Wordsworthian notion of the Imagination as the power to communicate with the life in natural objects. It cannot be stressed too strongly that the concept of Imagination which energized the greatest English Romantic poetry was an integral part of a comprehensive philosophical view, the theory of an 'active universe'.

From *The Excursion* Wordsworth's theory passed to Shelley and Keats like a gift of tongues. The early poems and letters which were the germs of the younger poets' full flower—*Mont Blanc*, the *Hymn to Intellectual Beauty*, and Keats' letters on the Imagination—were all first inspired by *The Excursion*, and from Shelley and Keats this influence, mingled with that of Coleridge, passed on to Victorian poetry.

In short, the crucial point in the history of English Romanticism came when the concept of the 'active universe' met the developing theory of the Imagination. In its leading sense, Imagination meant full response to, and implication with, the living qualities of natural objects. That is why it was able to assimilate and transform contemporary theories of merely passing interest into an important poetic approach to the universe.

1

The Two Universes

═══════════

As Alchemy went before Chemistry, and Astrology before Astronomy, so in all countries of civilized Man has Metaphysics outrun Common Sense. The creed of true Common Sense is composed of the *Results* of Scientific Meditation, Observation and Experiment, as far as they are *generally* intelligible. It differs therefore in different countries and in every different age of the same country. The Common Sense of a People is the moveable *index* of its average judgment and information. Without Metaphysics Science could have had no language and Common Sense no materials.

S. T. Coleridge, *Aids to Reflection*

One of the most prominent features of English Romantic thought is the belief that the universe was a living unity which could be known through the imagination. This was something much more than the age-old belief in an *animus mundi*: as M. H. Abrams has pointed out:

The mere postulation of an animate universe was no novelty; Isaac Newton's ubiquitous God, constituting duration and space and sustaining by his presence the laws of motion and gravitation, and the World-Soul of the ancient Stoics and Platonists, are often to be found dwelling amicably together in the nature-poetry of the eighteenth century.[1]

[1] *The Mirror and the Lamp*, p. 64. He remarks further (p. 55), 'The habitual reading of passion, life and physiognomy into the landscape is one of the few salient attributes common to most of the major romantic poets.'

3

What was new was not so much pantheism as the Romantic animism, the belief that this life could be found in each natural object and that, through the imagination, a real communication was possible between man and the forms of nature.

The world-soul was, in itself, no novelty to the readers of Pope and Thomson: the Romantic view was new to contemporary readers and a few sentences from early reviews of *The Excursion*, the first published work to give a long and closely-reasoned account of this view, will make the point clear. Though not published until the second decade of the century, the central books of *The Excursion* contain the ideas which Wordsworth and Coleridge had developed in 1798 and which had informed the former's poetry from *Lyrical Ballads* onwards. Favourable and unfavourable reviews were in complete agreement as to what the newness of these ideas was; they differed only in their reactions to it. The *Quarterly* was sympathetic:

To a mind constituted like that of Mr. Wordsworth, the stream, the torrent and the stirring leaf—seem not merely to suggest associations of deity, but to be a kind of speaking communication with it. . . . In his poetry nothing in Nature is dead. Motion is synonymous with life. . . . From such a creed we should expect unusual results; and . . . more touching considerations than from the mouth of common teachers. . . . The general tendency of the argument (which we might almost affirm to be the leading moral of the poem) is to abate the pride of the calculating *understanding*, and to reinstate the *imagination* and the *affections* in those seats from which modern philosophy has laboured but too successfully to expel them. . . . The causes which have prevented the poetry of Mr. Wordsworth from attaining its full share of popularity are to be found in the boldness and originality of his genius.[1]

The *Monthly Review* was hostile to the poem for those exact reasons which made the *Quarterly* sympathetic.

The prevailing doctrine of Mr. Wordsworth's poetical system is that of a soul animating and informing all nature; and, not content

---

[1] *The Quarterly Review*, XII (Lamb's review which was altered by Gifford).

with this generalized exposition of the creed in question, he extends it to every individual object, with such constant and unvarying minuteness that not a stream sparkles in the sun, not a leaf trembles to the breeze, not a torrent descends from the hills, not a cloud settles on the brow of a mountain, but stream, sun, leaf, breeze, torrent, hill, cloud and mountain's brow are sure to be animated at once, as with the touch of harlequin's wand, and endued with powers of sensation and reflection equal to those that are enjoyed by the poet, or by the most refined and intellectual of his readers. . . . Mr. Wordsworth disdains metaphor and fable. That which he describes is set forth in the colours of reality, not fiction;—in the language of a devout and sincere believer;—like the honest Swedenborgian who would stop short in the middle of the street in order to make a bow to St. Paul. . . . It is most unfortunate to the reader who is not prepared by a similar process of conversion for a similar reach of mysticism. . . . So intimately is this mystic principle connected with, and so closely does it pervade, the whole structure of the poem, that it is scarcely possible to turn to any one of the subjects to which it refers without finding it introduced in some form, and, generally speaking, with as little variety as can well be imagined. . . . Neither mysticism nor enthusiasm is the best conductor of misguided mortals back to the precincts of a calm and rational religion. The originality of Mr. Wordsworth is assumed by a certain class of critics as a matter out of all question . . . but . . . almost all that is not too mystical to be comprehended is too commonplace to be tolerated.[1]

The reviewers were less disputing poetical than philosophical differences; a world of inanimate natural objects, however much part of a universe imbued with a generalized world-soul, against a living nature endued with powers of sensation and communication, and, with this, rational deism or theism against imaginative animism, are the questions which here divide the critic who thinks Wordsworth's poetry affected or nonsensical from the critic who approves it. The assumptions of the *Monthly's* reviewer were those which had been taken as commonsense for more than a century and his angry bewilderment is understandable. Nevertheless those assumptions were not eternal truths; they were metaphysical ideas based on

[1] *The Monthly Review*, LXVI.

Newtonian science, and the ideas which here challenged them sprang originally from a rejection of that metaphysical system.

Both Wordsworth and Coleridge were quite conscious that their views were here opposed to those of the preceding century, which Coleridge regarded as those of 'Newton and the other materialists'[1] and which Wordsworth, more favourably disposed to Newton himself, called 'a universe of death'.[2] This reaction was, in fact, not uncommon among Radical or Revolutionary writers at the end of the eighteenth century. It is noteworthy that quite early in their careers the two poets arrived at very similar doctrines of Nature quite independently of each other: when Wordsworth in 1794 was writing the Windy Brow alterations to *An Evening Walk* which embodied so many of his leading ideas,[3] he had not met Coleridge, and when the latter in 1795 was writing *Joan of Arc*, Book II and *The Eolian Harp* he had not met Wordsworth, nor could he have read the lines written at Windy Brow. The apparent coincidence is easily explained: what Coleridge and Wordsworth had in common at this time was the background of late eighteenth-century radicalism, and it is here that the immediate origins of their ideas are to be sought. As will appear later, there were at this period a number of influential writers, particularly amongst those of a radical and scientific turn, who taught quite seriously the theory that such natural forms as the 'stream, sun, leaf', of the reviewer were, as organized bodies, 'endued with powers of sensation and reflection equal to those that are enjoyed by the poet'. To these qualities they would have added purposiveness, and they would have regarded all these as forming parts also of a world-soul which differed from the generalized world-soul of the ancients in that it was constituted by an infinite system of perceptions and sensibilities. Such a theory is the first step (and the step made by the two poets in 1794 and 1795) towards the characteristic Romantic concept, the second step being taken when this set

[1] '*Notizbuch aus den Jahren 1795–8*' in *Archiv* 98 (1896); (hereinafter noted as *Gutch Memorandum Book*), p. 29 (a).

[2] *The Prelude* (1805), XIII. 141.

[3] *Poetical Works*, ed. E. de Selincourt, i, pp. 10, 12–13.

of ideas was brought together with the developing theory of the Imagination.

Though these new doctrines of nature were quasi-scientific in form and were first argued in connection with developments in the natural sciences, yet at least part of their attraction for those who adopted them lay in the political and religious deductions which could be drawn, for the purpose which these theories read into nature was most usually evolutionary, and in all their various forms the doctrines tended to level man with other natural objects. Obviously this carried important consequences for early nineteenth-century thought generally.

The revelation by seventeenth-century science of a mathematical order controlling nature, and the complete explanation by the abstract science of mechanics of certain aspects of natural phenomena, profoundly shaped the eighteenth-century world view and the poetry which expressed the eighteenth-century mind. The Newtonian universe was a world planned and set going by God in accordance with the immutable laws of motion, and to know it meant to know its design. It was

A mighty maze but not without a plan![1]

This idea of perfect physical plan mingled with much older ideas of moral plan to produce eighteenth-century 'optimism' —the belief that the world was as good as God could make it, given the limits He imposed by logic on his omnipotence. Eighteenth-century 'optimism' held that, despite the seeming contradictions which these limitations caused, the divine hand which had shaped the mathematical perfection of the heavens had also ordered the present world as the best possible expression of His benevolence and His desire for rich fullness in His creation.

This belief in the goodness (could we but know it) of the existing world was stoical rather than 'optimistic' in its modern sense, and it contrasts clearly with the nineteenth-century belief that the world is imperfect but perfectible and that its goodness is a growing thing whose fullness lies in the

[1] *Essay on Man*, I. 6.

future. Each belief drew strength from its idea of the natural world, the one from the Newtonian picture of an unchanging world ruled by unchanging law,

> The gen'ral ORDER, since the whole began
> Is kept by Nature, and is kept in Man.[1]

and the other from the ideas of growth and development which supplanted it.[2] These were represented not only by the evolutionary theories of the later eighteenth century, which obviously favoured a belief in progress, but also by the most important of the alternative explanations of the development of species. Catastrophism, the ruling theory of the early nineteenth century,[3] held that a series of cataclysms, the last of which was Noah's flood, had destroyed all living things on the earth's surface and that after each cataclysm there had been a fresh creation which included progressively higher orders of organized being. From this popular scientific works[4] were able to draw the nineteenth-century moral that progress was the law of the world. Changing views of the nature of the physical world supported changing notions of the divine plan, and, with Wordsworth, Shelley and Keats at least, the connection between the poet's view of Nature and his beliefs as to man's destiny was, as we shall see later, very close.

Another principle of seventeenth- and eighteenth-century science which affected thought in quite distant fields was the sharp distinction which it drew between life and mind on the one hand and matter on the other. Earlier natural philosophy had given matter powers of self-movement and qualities which it shared with living beings:

[1] id., I. 171–2.

[2] Historically speaking, that is: logically the two are not completely incompatible. For the accelerated rate of change in ideas (of which this change formed part) in the 1780s and 1790s see A. O. Lovejoy, 'The Meaning of Romanticism for the Historian of Ideas' in *J.H.I.*, II (1941).

[3] See K. A. Von Zittel, *History of Geology and Palaeontology*, p. 141.

[4] See Hugh Miller, *Old Red Sandstone*, 7th ed. (Edinburgh, 1854), pp. 244, 271; Robert Hunt, *The Poetry of Science*, 3rd ed. (London, 1854), pp. 355–6; James McCosh and George Dickie, *Typical Forms and Special Ends in the Creation* (Edinburgh, 1856), pp. 386–7.

> Yea plants, yea stones, detest
> And love.[1]

Newton's First Law of Motion stated that 'A body must continue in its state of rest or uniform motion in a straight line, unless acted upon by some external force.' It can be seen in this definition that the concept of motion has become disconnected from that of matter. Indeed matter was interpreted as absolutely inert, and, seen in this way, it had nothing in common with either life or mind. The material universe became a collection of bodies colliding like billiard balls and acting upon one another only by impact. Certainly there was action at a distance in the force of gravitation, but this was partly explained by assuming the existence of a very fine aether, pervading all space, through which this force was transmitted.

The place of mind and life in this universe of dead matter was to vex succeeding philosophers, but the simplicity of the system and its apparent certainty in matters of physics made its acceptance rapid and complete. Its effects were far-reaching. It broke down the authority of those analogies that had linked the man of the sixteenth century to nature and to God. The life of nature had been to the Elizabethans something akin to the life of man, and it had entwined with and sustained their poetic thought as the music does a song. In the eighteenth century this kinship with nature was inevitably lost. The new Newtonian universe was complex, surprising and beautiful in its order, and by its origins and by the witness it bore to its Planner it was divine, but in it man with his thinking mind must always be an observer and a stranger. It bore no more intimate relationship to him than did the watch to which it was so often compared. Here again the nineteenth century differed from the eighteenth. Whether the later views took the form of thorough-going materialism or of beliefs that the natural world was essentially spiritual (and the two alterna-

---

[1] J. Donne, *A Nocturnal upon Saint Lucies Day*, ll. 33–4. For a discussion of the way in which Newtonian atomic theory destroyed the older conception of natural process, see J. Gregory, 'The Animate Model of Physical Process' in *Science Progress*, xx (1926).

tives were not in fact very different[1]), in both cases they attempted to bring mind and matter on to the one plane where, from the poet's point of view, they were capable of intimate relationship and, from a more general point of view, they were capable of being explained by the same laws.

The eighteenth-century view of the relation of the physical universe to God and to man produced a feeling for the unity and divinity of external nature which helped the growth of romanticism, but it was a view which was ultimately opposed to that of the Romantic poets we are to consider. This is true also of such a variant as the view of God's relation to creation expressed by Newton in his theory of the aether, which may have influenced Wordsworth.[2] Newton conceived the aether as a fine fluid penetrating through invisible pores into solid bodies and bringing God's energy in the force of gravitation. Thus the aether was the medium of God's direct action on matter—the means by which His mathematical laws were applied to the universe—and His relationship to inert matter was that of the soul to the body.

> All are but parts of one stupendous whole
> Whose body Nature is, and God the soul;[3]

The sense of mathematical law ordering and unifying all things certainly touched Wordsworth as

> An image not unworthy of the one
> Surpassing Life, which out of space and time,
> Nor touched by welterings of passion, is
> And hath the name of God.[4]

and in phrases like those here he sometimes suggests a conception of God close to Newton's. Nevertheless Wordsworth's conception of the Life in nature as well as out of it goes beyond

[1] See p. 35 below.
[2] See S. G. Dunn, 'Wordsworth's Metaphysical System' in *Essays and Studies* (1932). The article is, of course, more concerned with resemblances between Wordsworth and Newton than with the differences which are the point here.
[3] *Essay on Man*, I. 267–8.
[4] *The Prelude* (1805), VI. 154–7.

Newton's conception to the point of contradicting its central assumption, the inertness of matter, while Coleridge in his Unitarian days as well as later opposed Newton's ideas vigorously. Newton's conception of the relationship finds God in nature, but it stresses His transcendence and virtually excludes the immanence stressed by Wordsworth and Coleridge. Matter itself remains inert and mechanical, and there is no room here for Wordsworth's 'moral life' in natural objects or Coleridge's 'Monads of the Infinite Mind'. As far as the relationship of man to nature is concerned, the theory of the aether left it unaltered; the dichotomy which set matter against life and mind remained, and the mathematical reason was left supreme as the only way of approaching and understanding the external world.

The popularization of the mechanical view of the universe and of 'Newtonian' metaphysics had, of course, more direct effects upon poetry than those which have just been discussed. On the one hand, by directing a vivid and reverent attention to the beauty and complexity of the physical world, it was responsible for much of the popularity of 'Nature poetry' in the period: on the other hand, it affected and altered the ways in which men spoke of and valued their aesthetic experience of nature.

The 'Nature poetry' of the period had as its principal themes the greatness and the beauty of the natural world. To admire the greatness of the universe was to admire it as the handiwork and visible testament of the Creator it declared. Eighteenth-century aesthetics found a place for this feeling of religious awe either among the pleasures of the Imagination, as when Addison wrote of the pleasure to be derived from the contemplation of the great, 'when the soul grasps at that which is beyond its capacity',[1] or as part of the theory of the sublime, as when Burke wrote of the emotion inspired by power, vastness and infinity,[2] but the varying explanations allowed the recognition of the ultimate source in the greatness of God, and the discovery of God in nature is the theme of much eighteenth-

[1] *Spectator*, 412.
[2] E. Burke. *Works* (London, 1889), i, pp. 100–2.

century poetry. It is easy to see here the likenesses to much Romantic poetry, and it has been pointed out by a recent scholar[1] that, in seeking God in nature, the *Lines written above Tintern Abbey* were in no way revolutionary, and were in fact accepted by many readers as one more example of a prevailing mode. Nevertheless the differences are more important and more fundamental than the likenesses: both the way in which Wordsworth conceived God to exist in Nature and the means by which he found him there imply a new theory of Nature and the Imagination, which makes the imaginative experience of nature more immediate and more significant than that to be found in eighteenth-century poetry. It is this which makes the poem a 'seminal poem in the literary revolution'[2] and which relates it more closely to *The Ancient Mariner* and *Prometheus Unbound* than to *The Seasons*.

The poetic expression of the second theme, the beauty of nature, needed a rather more complicated explanation, and this was provided by the Imagination or Fancy. The two words, synonymous to Addison, had stood in medieval psychology for two distinct internal faculties, the faculty of forming images of absent objects and the faculty of altering or recombining images. They now came to stand for part of the means by which mind apprehended the world of matter, though what the Imagination apprehended was not the 'real' world but a mental appearance. Those aspects of the natural world which could be used by the reasoning mind in mechanics (that is, extension and mass, the primary or objective qualities) were distinguished from those which could not, and only the former were considered 'real'. Colour, scent and the like became 'secondary' or 'subjective' qualities. The results can be seen in Addison's essays on Imagination.

Things would make but a poor Appearance to the Eye, if we saw them only in their proper Figures and Motions: And what Reason can we assign for their exciting in us many of those Ideas

[1] R. D. Mayo, 'The Contemporaneity of the Lyrical Ballads' in *PMLA* (1954).

[2] id. Mayo recognizes that the poem is fundamentally different from the poems with which contemporary readers might have classed it.

which are different from any thing that exists in the Objects themselves, (for such are Light and Colours) were it not to add Supernumerary Ornaments to the Universe, and make it more agreeable to the Imagination? . . .

I have here supposed that my Reader is acquainted with that great Modern Discovery, which is at present universally acknowledged by all the Enquirers into Natural Philosophy: Namely that Light and Colours, as apprehended by the Imagination, are only Ideas in the Mind, and not qualities that have any Existence in Matter.[1]

The pleasures which arose from the contemplation of natural objects were pleasures of the Imagination, and the Imagination could also delight in the contemplation of Ideas when the objects which had produced them were absent, and could 'enlarge, compound and vary them at her own pleasure'. It was peculiarly the task of poetry to produce these secondary pleasures of the Imagination. 'It is this Talent of affecting the imagination, that gives an Embellishment to good Sense, and makes one Man's compositions more agreeable than another's. It sets off all Writings in general, but it is the very Life and highest Perfection of Poetry.'[2]

It can be seen from this that even in its first sense, that of apprehending external objects, the Imagination could not be trusted to discover real qualities:

In short, our Souls are at present delightfully lost and bewildered in a pleasant Delusion, and we walk about like the enchanted Hero of a Romance, who sees beautiful Castles, Woods and Meadows; and at the same time hears the warbling of Birds, and the purling of Streams; but upon the finishing of some secret Spell, the fantastic Scene breaks up, and the disconsolate Knight finds himself on a barren Heath, or in a Solitary Desert.[3]

Hence in its sense of compounding and enlarging ideas for use in literary composition the Imagination was even more simply a power of illusion.

In the course of the century there were some developments at both levels of meaning. The dominant position of the deductive reason in the understanding of the world was shaken by the philosophies of Berkeley and Hume, though the concept

[1] *Spectator*, 413. [2] id., 421. [3] id., 413.

of the Imagination was not an immediate beneficiary of this.[1] At the other level, where the word meant the power of conceiving poetic works or more generally the power of 'conception of feeling, incident, circumstance',[2] some of the writers of the mid-century gave greater importance to the Imagination than Addison had, but these claims came far short of the Romantic claim of 'the Truth of the Imagination'. When Reynolds said that 'the imagination is here a residence of truth'[3] the word 'here' is a clear warning to look to the context. In context this is simply a claim that the visual artist ought to aim at 'the known first effect produced by objects on the imagination'. Similarly when Reynolds claimed that in art and in life men can arrive at right conclusions 'by what *appears* a kind of intuition',[4] he is not claiming that there is in fact any power superior to deductive reason; his next sentence makes it clear that what he is referring to is the result of long experience, in which though the original deductive steps 'in process of time are forgotten, the right impression still remains fixed in his mind'. Similarly, the high value set by certain mid-century writers on the poetic Imagination or Fancy, while it shows a growing impatience with the control of the 'Judgement', does not seem to imply any specific new claim for the powers of the Imagination.[5]

Certainly developments in the eighteenth century tended 'to abate the pride of the calculating understanding' and to

[1] Wilma L. Kennedy, *The English Heritage of Coleridge of Bristol, 1798*, p. 11.

[2] id., pp. 52–3, 58. [3] id., p. 70. [4] id., p. 70 (my italics).

[5] Wilma L. Kennedy (id., p. 55) writes of the *Ode on the Poetical Character*, that:

> William Collins . . . discerned the true kinship of 'Heav'n and Fancy' in the weaving of 'the godlike gift' of the poetic genius: 'cest of amplest power' (on few bestowed); 'band' 'wove on that *creating* day' with 'laughing earth' and 'tented sky', and like them 'call'd with thought to birth' . . .

However, this reading ignores the important points that the band was not said to be woven on the same day that earth and sky were born (not 'woven'), but later, and that the earth and sky were not the product of the marriage between Heaven and Fancy but either the product of an earlier marriage between Heaven and Thought or produced by Heaven

promote a sense of the innate value of imaginative literature, thus preparing the way for the later theories, but the steps taken by the Romantic poets were long ones. Nowhere before the last years of the century do we find any sign of what was to be the leading sense of the word Imagination for Wordsworth and Coleridge in 1797, and for Wordsworth for much longer; that is, as meaning a power operative in man's experience of the external world and enabling him to recognize

alone, with thought. Indeed the syntax of 'When He, who call'd with Thought to birth, Yon tented Sky . . . Long by the lov'd *Enthusiast* woo'd, Himself in some Diviner Mood, Retiring, sate with her alone . . .' makes it clear that Thought was excluded from this bridal chamber! In these circumstances it is impossible to be sure just what Collins meant by saying that Wonder and Truth sat near the bridal gift (H. W. Garrod remarks, in *Collins* (Oxford, 1928), p. 68, 'there are characteristic obscurities here') but it seems clear that this 'association of imagination with truth' claims less than Dr Kennedy thinks it does. Dr Kennedy's further points, that weaving is not combining, and that threads are not fixed nor definite, also seem difficult to credit. Other mid-century writers, particularly William Duff and Edward Young, made high claims for the importance of the imagination in literature, and M. Kallich, 'The Association of Ideas and Akenside's *Pleasures of Imagination*' in *MLN* (1947), has argued that for Akenside the laws of association could be consciously employed by the poet. Nevertheless all this is very far from the 'creativeness' and 'truth' of the Imagination as the Romantics understood it. The general influence of Plato's *Ion* on the Romantic theory of the Imagination should not be overlooked. H. N. Fairchild (*Religious Trends in English Poetry*, i, pp. 205 and *passim*) finds the Platonic doctrine of poetic inspiration, which he regards as essentially the same as the doctrine of the truth of the Imagination held by Wordsworth, Coleridge, Shelley and Keats, present in the poetry of Ken, Norris, Mrs Rowe, Watts, Blackmore, Dennis and Samuel Say, and he traces it through Toland, Thomson, Aaron Hill, Akenside, Young and others down to the later Romantics. While it is clear that the poet's age-old claim to inspiration from a higher source of truth is reflected in the Romantic concept of the Imagination, nevertheless the latter is a much more specific claim. R. D. Havens ('Discontinuity in Literary Development' in *SP*, 1950) quite rightly takes the view that the Romantic theory of the Imagination is a case of *dis*continuity in development, as does C. M. Bowra (*The Romantic Imagination*, p. 1), while M. H. Abrams (*The Mirror and the Lamp*, p. 158) regards any eighteenth-century anticipations of the theory as unimportant compared to the Romantic developments.

sensibility, purpose and significance in natural objects. Nor is there any substantial anticipation of Coleridge's later and more generalized theory in which the primary and the secondary Imagination were in effect one power, working first to create the external world in its totality and then to create, from that material, fresh creations which would have in them the same life and truth.

Thus when the *Monthly*'s reviewer was faced by an explicit statement of the views of Nature and Imagination which informed Wordsworth's poetry (and of the kind of views which had informed Coleridge's),[1] it was natural that he should appeal to commonsense as evidence against Wordsworth's poem. The themes and tasks of the poetry which he knew best had been decided by commonsense—that is to say, by the underlying assumptions as to the nature of things which men of the eighteenth century had made—and by these lights the reviewer was right, for however much English Romantic poetry is part of a general movement of taste it is here also the embodiment of a new system of assumptions. It is now time to go back and trace that system from its immediate origins in the second half of the eighteenth century to its propagandists of the early seventeen-nineties and later to the early poetry of Coleridge and Wordsworth.

The account of that aspect of the reaction against 'Newtonianism' which concerns us can begin in mid-eighteenth-century France. The corresponding German reaction can be omitted: neither Wordsworth nor Coleridge had much acquaintance with German thought in 1797, much less in 1794 and 1795,[2] and if such earlier German thought as Leibniz's *Monadology* influenced the French writers about to come under discussion (which is very doubtful[3]) then it was very much altered in

[1] See Chapters III and IV below.

[2] Coleridge placed his reading even of Leibniz after his Berkeleyan period (*Biographia Literaria*, i, 93). For a discussion of the Monads of Joan of Arc see p. 39, n. 4 below.

[3] P. Hazard, *European Thought in the Eighteenth Century*, p. 304, finds the influence of Leibniz in the theory of de Maupertuis (see p. 19 below) and R. Latta, in his edition of *The Monadology and Other Philosophical Writings*, p. 198, finds it in the 'molecules organiques' of

transmission. On the other hand Wordsworth may well have met the French tradition through Beaupuy or in Revolutionary Paris, while Priestley, whose Unitarianism certainly influenced Coleridge, first met the new ideas in Paris.[1]

Buffon, both of which belong to the tradition about to be described. On the other hand W. H. Barber, *Leibniz in France*, pp. 94, 144, 158–9, 174, x, describes the controversy with Voltaire and the Leibnizians into which de Maupertuis' views on elementary particles led him, records the hostility of Diderot to Leibniz, and finds Leibnizian influence on this tradition only in the work of Charles Bonnet, who differed in believing in preformed seeds (see Appendix A below and Latta, op. cit., pp. 260, 414) and in a pre-established harmony between seeds and the conditions for their germination (C. Bonnet, *Œuvres* (Neufchatel, 1779), vol. xv, p. 269). It would seem that the tradition is Leibnizian in its belief in the activity of matter and in its belief in the importance of organization (cf. Latta, op. cit., p. 198) but anti-Leibnizian in attributing intelligence to matter (cf. Latta, op. cit., p. 400), in believing in a world-soul (cf. Latta, op. cit., p. 34) of which the active molecules are *components* (cf. Latta, op. cit., pp. 109–10), and in believing that the molecules act upon one another (cf. Latta, op. cit., p. 219). An account of this tradition from a slightly different point of view will be found in Wilson L. Scott, 'The Significance of "Hard" Bodies in the History of Scientific Thought' in *Isis* (1959). Scott suggests (p. 203) that de Maupertuis was attempting a synthesis of Newtonian and Leibnizian views. Earlier (p. 199) he describes the Newtonian doctrine of 'hard' atoms ('Newton added the concept of indivisibility to Descartes' concept of brittle, inelastic hardness') which was scientific orthodoxy down to Dalton and beyond, and contrasts it with the anti-Newtonian doctrine as follows:

> Two kinds of elastic atoms were advanced in the eighteenth century, the one by Boscovitch in Rome and the other by Smeaton in England, whose theories were popularized by Priestley, Davy, Rennie, Joule, Maxwell and Clausius, and later developed by J. J. Thomson and Bohr into the planetary atom. The point forces in today's atoms represent a direct heritage from Boscovitch; absolute hardness in the Newtonian sense is now denied existence even as an idea.

Scott is concerned with the implications of this doctrine for 'chemistry, physics and engineering': the present study is concerned rather with the implications which its earlier forms had for biology, politics and religion and hence the names which will figure more prominently are those of de Maupertuis, Diderot, d'Holbach, Buffon, Robinet, Volney, Cabanis, Priestley and Erasmus Darwin.

[1] *DNB*, xvi, pp. 360–1.

Paul Hazard, in *European Thought in the Eighteenth Century*, places the origin of the new theories in a chance remark of Locke's: 'We have the ideas of *matter* and *thinking*, but possibly shall never be able to know whether any mere material being thinks or no.' Locke was simply illustrating the limits of the knowable, but the remark was taken up by Voltaire to embarrass the Christians, and then by pantheists and atheists to embarrass the Deists[1] and developed by them into a system. At the same time the reaction was also partly the result of the progress of the sciences, particularly the biological sciences. These had produced innumerable facts for which mechanics had no possible explanation. The phenomena of growth, reproduction, crystalline structure, chemical action and electricity were all objects of investigation during the century and in each the facts seemed to contradict the assumption that matter was inert. Towards the end of the century the Scottish philosopher, Dugald Stewart, described the state of knowledge thus:

The most profound discoveries which are placed within the reach of our researches lead to a confession of human ignorance; for when they flatter the pride of man . . . by enabling him to trace the simple and beautiful laws by which physical events are regulated, they call his attention at the same time, to those general and ultimate facts . . . which by evincing to him the operation of powers, whose nature must remain for ever unknown, serve to remind him of the insufficiency of his faculties to penetrate the secrets of the universe. Wherever we direct our enquiries: whether to the anatomy and physiology of animals, to the growth of vegetables, to the chemical attractions and repulsions, or to the motions of the heavenly bodies: we continually perceive the effect of powers that cannot belong to matter.[2]

In this state of affairs it was natural to turn to a new worldview in which the system of inert matter was replaced by a system of forces, of which matter itself might be only an effect.

[1] P. Hazard, *European Thought in the Eighteenth Century*, pp. 119–29. See also D. Mornet, *La Pensée française au XVIIIe siècle*, pp. 42–3, 102–4.

[2] D. Stewart, *Elements of the Philosophy of the Human Mind*, i, pp. 88–9.

The new belief can first be seen clearly in Diderot, the moving spirit of the *Encyclopédie*, whose works formed a great storehouse of ideas for the later thinkers of the French Enlightenment. Diderot took up the new faith most boldly in his then unpublished *Rêve d'Alembert*, but it appeared, if rather more circumspectly, in his published works, particularly in *De l'Interprétation de la Nature* (1754). This book, written after four volumes of the *Encyclopédie* had appeared and when Diderot had fully formed his opinions, was an expression of his belief that the reign of mathematics was over and that that of biological sciences and experimental physics was beginning, as well as an attempt to point out the direction that speculation and hypothesis in those sciences ought to take. That direction, as more than one contemporary noted, was more metaphysical than physical.

Much of the discussion in the book springs from a treatise published in the name of a Dr Baumann of Erlangen, but which was in fact written by the French scientist de Maupertuis. Diderot takes up the ideas of this treatise and draws their logical conclusions.

The author begins by showing briefly the ideas of those who have preceded him, and the inadequacy of their principles for the general development of phenomena. Some have postulated only *extent* and *movement*. Others have thought it necessary to add to extent, *impenetrability, mobility*, and *inertia*. . . . *Attraction* has been admitted in proportion to mass and in inverse proportion to the square of the distance. The simplest operations of chemistry, or the elementary physics of small bodies, have made it necessary to have recourse to *attractions* which follow other laws; and the impossibility of explaining the formation of a plant or an animal by attractions, inertia, mobility, impenetrability, movement, matter or extent has led Baumann to suppose still other properties in nature. Dissatisfied with *plastic natures* . . . with *intelligent subordinate substances* . . . with the *simultaneity* of the creation and the formation of substances and with their *extemporaneous production* . . . he has concluded that all these unphilosophic systems would never have arisen but for the ill-founded fear of attributing well-known modifications to something whose essence, being unknown to us, may, for this very reason, be very compatible with these modifications. . . . This something is material substance [L'être corporel]; the modifications are *desire, aversion, memory and intelligence*; in a word all those qualities which we recognise in animals, and which the Ancients comprehended under the name of the *sensitive soul*, and which Doctor Baumann admits, in due proportion to their forms and their masses, as much in the smallest particle of matter as in the largest animal. If there were, says he, any danger in giving molecules of matter some degree of intelligence this danger would be just as great in supposing it in an elephant or a monkey as in a grain of sand. . . .

What is there to prevent these intelligent and sensitive elementary particles from varying infinitely from the order which constitutes the species? Thence an infinite number of species of animal sprung from the first animal; an infinite number of beings sprung from a first being; a single act in nature.

But will each particle, in accumulating and combining, lose its little degree of feeling and perception? Not at all. . . . From these individual perceptions, gathered and combined, there will result a single perception; and this system of perceptions . . . will be the soul of the animal.

It is here that we are surprised that the author either has not seen the terrible consequences of his hypothesis, or having seen the consequences, has not abandoned the hypothesis. I ask if the universe, or the whole collection of feeling and thinking molecules, forms a whole or not. If he replies that it does not, he shakes with that word the foundations of belief in the existence of God, by introducing disorder into nature. . . . If he agrees that it is a whole . . . he must admit that in consequence of this universal amalgamation, the world, like a huge animal, has a soul; and that, as the world may be infinite, this soul of the world, I do not say is, but may be an infinite system of perceptions, and the world may be God. . . .

Doctor Baumann's hypothesis may very well unveil, if he wishes it, the most incomprehensible mystery of nature, the formation of animals, or more generally of all organized bodies; it will come to grief on the universal aggregation of phenomena and the existence of God.

But although we may reject the ideas of the doctor of Erlangen, we shall very ill conceive . . . the fecundity of his hypothesis . . . and the difficulty of rebutting his conjectures with success, if we do not regard them as the fruit of profound meditation, a bold attempt on the universal system of nature, and the sketch of a great philosophy.[1]

This theory in which the 'soul of the world' is a system of individual perceptions and sensibilities in matter is very different from Newton's 'ubiquitous God constituting duration and space' who appears as the world-soul of Pope and Thomson; Diderot, of course, was making an indirect attack on Deism. Even so, the 'universal system of nature' thus expounded had two faces: it made the universe altogether material and, since matter had the qualities of spirit, wholly spiritual. By changes of emphasis it could be made to appear one or the other. The book which most flaunted its materialism, and which became the symbol of materialistic and atheistic philosophy, was Baron d'Holbach's *Système de la Nature* (1770). In it d'Holbach acknowledged the latent pantheism of the system and argued against this aspect of it, but his chief emphasis was on the sufficiency of this new materialism to explain the world. 'Physicists', he wrote, 'have preferred to suppose an imaginary external cause, rather than to suppose that bodies find their power of movement in their own natures.'[2] All action was a manifestation of this power under the different names of attraction and repulsion, sympathy and antipathy, affinity or relationship, and, in men, love or hate. The earth and all its products, including man, could be explained as the result of these forces, responding and adapting themselves to changes in climate.

D'Holbach was opposed to any idea of a universal spirit modelled after the human spirit. The body needed no spirit to explain its workings and therefore neither did the universe. But the society in which he moved seems to have taken a more metaphysical view. Garat, who survived the Revolution, the Consulate and the Empire to serve the restored Bourbons, gives a detailed account of the salons and their opinions in his life of his fellow-Revolutionist Suard. The salons which Suard frequented met at the houses of M. Watelet, M. de Saint Lambert and M. Necker, and the group included d'Holbach,

[1] D. Diderot, *Œuvres complètes*, ii, pp. 45–9 (my translation).
[2] P. H. D. d'Holbach, *Système de la Nature*, p. 21 (my translation).

Helvetius, Condorcet, Buffon, Malesherbes, Morellet, d'Alembert and Delille. Of the conversation in these salons Garat wrote (in the tone becoming to an ex-Jacobin in the service of the Most Christian Monarch),

These *interpretations of nature*, sprung from conversation, returned to it after they had become more dangerous in books written with talent; for, indeed, they tried to join the authority of a Swedish metaphysician to that opinion which supposes in matter an underlying sensibility [sensibilité sourd] which can only develop in favourable organisations. These have been presented with eloquence by that blind man Saunderson, who decomposes and explains the light of the sun. These doctrines carry, in society and in the depths of souls, more terror than doubt. The Universe, transformed into an Eternal Being, can never replace for man that Father which he believes he will have beyond the perishable world.[1]

The French salons under Louis XVI were by no means as devout as Garat became under Louis XVIII, and, far from bringing terror and doubt, the new doctrines brought new and, for radicals, welcome cosmologies. These exploited one or, more often, both of the two possibilities which Diderot had noticed in 'Dr Baumann's' hypothesis, explaining the development of organized bodies, and replacing God by the sum of nature.

This pantheism was at the root of several systems which set out to show that the spirit of the universe took a providential interest in mankind. Thus Volney, whose book *Les Ruines* (1791) was immensely popular during the Revolution, taught that 'the secret power which animates the universe' had made man the architect of his own destiny through his sensibility to pleasure and pain, and that man must necessarily become happy. Another system of the same kind which will be dis-

[1] D. J. Garat, *Memoires sur la vie de M. Suard*, p. 203 (my translation). The Swedish metaphysician is presumably Swedenborg, but I have found no mention of him in the 'books written with talent'. Saunderson is the subject of Diderot's *Lettres sur les Aveugles* (1749) in which these doctrines are hinted. The phrase 'sensibilité sourd' seems to be an echo of 'sensibilité obtus et sourd' in the passage just quoted from Diderot's *De l'Interprétation de la Nature*.

cussed in a later chapter was that of the eccentric priest of nature, 'Walking' Stewart.

In their simplest form the theories of evolution took no account of providence. As we have seen in d'Holbach's *Système de la Nature*, evolution was explained as the response of natural forces to climate. This seems to have been the view of Buffon in his evolutionist period, when he wrote in *Epoques de la Nature* (1779) of the animals as being produced by the forces of the earth in the different climates (*ceux que cette même terre a pu produire par ses propres forces*)[1] and when, according to Herault de Séchelles, he remarked, 'I have always spoken of the Creator: but one has only to erase that word and put in its place "the power of nature" which results from the two great laws of attraction and repulsion'. Wordsworth, though he showed little interest in the topic, expresses this 'climatic' view of evolution in *The Prelude*:

> Should the whole frame of earth by inward throes
> Be wrenched, or fire come down from far to scorch
> Her pleasant habitations and dry up
> Old Ocean, in his bed left singed and bare,
> Yet would the living Presence still subsist
> Victorious, and composure would ensue,
> And kindlings like the morning—presage sure
> Of day returning and of life revived.[2]

But the most interesting theories were those which explained evolution, not as an adjustment to environment, but as a purposeful development of the spirit in nature, and which looked to the inevitable progress of this universal force to bring perfection (and, if the writer's mind ran that way, Utopia).[3] These writers include Diderot himself, the biologist Robinet, Erasmus

---

[1] G. L. L. de Buffon, *Epoques de la Nature*, p. 128.

[2] *The Prelude*, v. 30–7. For parallels to Wordsworth's ideas see d'Holbach's *Système de la Nature*, p. 82, and Condorcet's *Esquisse d'un tableau historique des progrès de l'esprit humaine*, p. 3.

[3] G. F. Cuvier, the greatest of the early nineteenth-century biologists, who opposed the evolutionary theories of his day, regarded them all as off-shoots of pantheism. See *Les Ossements fossiles*, pp. 135–7 and also p. 32 (in the Eloge by his collaborator M. C-L. Laurrillard).

Darwin in his earlier work, and, in a rather peculiar fashion, Joseph Priestley.

Diderot's belief in evolution and the transformation of species appears in *De l'Interprétation de la Nature*, where he traces it from the elements of life in matter, through life, movement, sensation and thought, to sounds, language, laws, science and arts. In the *Rêve d'Alembert* he starts from the same premise of life in nature, which he describes in almost Wordsworthian terms, 'Each form has the happiness and the unhappiness which is proper to it. From the elephant to the flea, from the flea to the living, sensitive molecule there is not a point in all nature which does not suffer and rejoice.' In the same paragraph he describes individuals and species as purposive forces within the whole. 'There is only a single great individual, and that is the whole. . . . What is a being? the sum of a certain number of tendencies. Can I be anything but a tendency? No, because I am going towards a goal. And the species? The species are only tendencies towards a particular common goal.'[1]

A clearer theory of this purposiveness was given by Robinet, in *Considérations philosophiques de la gradation naturelle des formes de l'être* (1768).

All matter is organic, living and animal. . . . In some aspects, the active power seems to reside in matter and to be an essential quality in it, though in other ways activity seems to be the substance, and matter only an instrument which this substance uses to deploy its energy. . . . We do not realise that the material or visible world is an assemblage of phenomena, and nothing else; that there must necessarily be an invisible world which is the foundation of the visible, and in which we must seek the source of whatever is real and substantial in nature. This invisible world is the aggregate of all the forces which continually strive to ameliorate their existence, and do so, in fact, by ceaselessly extending and perfecting their action, in the proportion appropriate to each. There is a gradation of forces in the invisible world, as there is a gradation of forms in the extended or visible world. The active forces propagate themselves in their manner as the material forms do. One might well say that material forms only proceed from

[1] D. Diderot, *Œuvres complètes*, i, pp. 139–40 (my translation).

one another because a certain degree of force from one has animated the other, and so on. . . . The necessary progress of these two elements fills the universal scale of nature. . . .

The whole of nature thus offers to our contemplation two great objects, the progression of forces and the development of forms.[1]

In this gradation certain successively higher classes of organization and 'powers' of force became generally recognized. Robinet agrees with Charles Bonnet (and with the German Herder) in giving the stages of organization as unorganized matter, the crystal, the vegetable, the insect, the animal and the human. Cabanis and Erasmus Darwin list the forces of gravitation, the attractions of chemistry, the spirit of vegetation and that of animation.

Thus the ideas that all matter was living, organic and animal, that all natural objects, as organized forms of matter, had their own life and sensibility, and that the whole organization of the natural world was capable of intelligent purpose (whether expressed in evolution or in a provident interest in mankind) were all widely diffused in pre-Revolutionary France. But though the ideas can be found with a radical emphasis in Volney's *Les Ruines* (1791), Carra's *Système de la Raison* (3rd ed., 1791) and, very fully, in Cabanis' *Rapports du Physique et du Morale* (1802) (published as separate memoirs 1790–6),[2] yet they never became the tenet of a particular party or sect. In England the ideas, in differing forms, were held by Erasmus Darwin and by James Hutton, the father of modern geology, but their chief exponent was Joseph Priestley, whose position as a Unitarian leader gave their diffusion a rather different course from that which it had in France. Priestley used his scientific theories as a weapon in religious controversy, and thus, though the theories were neither essential to Unitarianism nor peculiar to it, they were closely associated with it.

Priestley's influence spread in many directions. As a religious controversialist he provided the Unitarians with their

[1] J. B. R. Robinet, *Considerations philosophiques de la gradation naturelle des formes de l'être*, pp. 8–10 (my translation).

[2] For the subsequent history of this tradition in French thought see H. Maret, *Essai sur le panthéisme dans les sociétés modernes*.

philosophical arguments. As a scientist he was known in France, where he dined and disputed with d'Holbach. Later, he became the best-known English sympathizer with the French Revolution, in which his son and his nephew took active parts, and he was made an honorary citizen of France. In England he was, of course, an important figure in science. In addition he was a member of the Birmingham Lunar Society, a group of friends which met at one another's houses and which included Erasmus Darwin, James Watt the engineer, and Josiah Wedgwood.

It is interesting to notice the contacts between the members of the Lunar Society and Wordsworth and Coleridge. Both the poets were early admirers of Darwin. Wordsworth, as Legouis has shown, modelled his early couplet style on his poetry, while Coleridge borrowed ideas and images from it for his own early poems. Coleridge, as a Unitarian, was a disciple and admirer of Priestley, and, as a Pantisocrat, nearly joined Priestley's Susquehanna settlement scheme. He knew both the geographical and the philosophical writings of Thomas Cooper, Priestley's agent for the scheme.[1] Wordsworth, when he arrived in Paris in 1792, was shown the city by Cooper's co-delegate from the Manchester Constitutional Society, James Watt junior, and when he returned to London in 1793 his chief friend was the former agent of the Wedgwoods, William Nicholson. Among the two poets' friends in Bristol were Beddoes and Davy, of the Pneumatical Institute financed by Tom Wedgwood and Gregory Watt. Finally it was the Wedgwoods who provided Coleridge's annuity. Almost every one of these men was a Unitarian, a radical and a scientist,[2] and the

[1] See M. W. Kelley, 'Thomas Cooper and Pantisocracy' in *MLN* (1930).

[2] All were interested in science. Priestley, Cooper, the Wedgwoods and Nicholson were Unitarians (see Index to R. V. Holt, *The Unitarian Contribution to Social Progress*) as, probably, was James Watt jnr. (see p. 65 below). Watt senior was either a Unitarian or a Deist (see A. Carnegie, *James Watt*, pp. 136–7). Darwin and Beddoes were sceptics (*Collected Letters of S. T. Coleridge*, i, p. 178, and H. W. Donner, *Thomas Lovell Beddoes*, p. 53) but Darwin at least supported Priestley's views as to the nature of matter (*Zoonomia* (1794) Sec. 13 and 14) as did Davy.

list gives some impression of the way in which the doctrines of Priestley must have been spread by personal contact as well as by his published works.

The theories of Priestley and Darwin will be discussed in more detail in the next chapter, but they may be outlined now. Both believed in the active force of matter, and both suggested that 'such inorganic systems as plants' may have some power of feeling, but beyond this common agreement their theories are more or less complementary to each other. The essence of Priestley's metaphysical belief was that there was no such thing as matter. What did exist was active force, and the apparent solidity of matter was only the resistance of this force. Thus the whole universe was spiritual force, and all action the direct action of God. Though such a system can only be distinguished from pantheism by Priestley's assertions that God, as well as being everything, was also additional to the sum of things, yet Priestley was a devout believer. He looked to this divine force for the fulfilment of the apocalyptic prophecies and the coming of the Millennium, and he saw the French Revolution as the first stage in this process.

On the other hand, Darwin, though he shared Priestley's belief in the active force of matter, was a sceptic in matters of religion. Further, though he welcomed the Revolution as the culmination of human enlightenment, he was less interested in the future than the past. He is, of course, best known for his theory of evolution, which he conceived to be the result of the progressive action of natural forces, and he personified these forces in his poetry as the spirits of the elements. There was nothing of the mystic in Darwin, and the

For the general radicalism of Unitarians at this time see H. Gow, *The Unitarians*: 'These men and women were united, not merely by theological belief, but by a political and social ideal. They were on the side of emancipation from civil and religious bonds.' For the radicalism of Priestley, Darwin, Cooper and James Watt jnr., see Chapters II and III below, for that of Beddoes see the *DNB*, for that of Thomas Wedgwood see R. B. Litchfield, *Tom Wedgwood* (London, 1903); Nicholson attended the chapel of the very radical Unitarian preacher Fawcett, to which he took Wordsworth (see *Poetical Works of William Wordsworth*, v, p. 374).

sense of divine purpose which fills Priestley is wholly missing from his work. On the other hand, his poetry is full of the natural world and all the variety of natural processes, while in Priestley's arid philosophical works the living universe which is their subject often seems no more alive than the hypothetical John Doe and Richard Roe of a law-suit.

In the early years of the last decade of the century the two friends who thus gave complementary emphases to the new theory were the two most distinguished English sympathizers with the French Revolution, one the leading biologist and leading poet of England, the other perhaps the leading chemist and certainly the best-known theologian. It is not surprising that Coleridge's early radical sympathies should have brought him strongly under the influence of both.

2

Coleridge:
The Unitarian Poet
1794–6

Until 1794 Coleridge, for all his lively interest in out-of-the-way ideas, remained sufficiently orthodox to contemplate a career in the established church, but in that year came his conversion to Unitarianism, an event which was to change the whole pattern of his life and of his ideas. Two years earlier his support of the Unitarian Dr Frend, whose trial before the Vice-Chancellor's court at Cambridge Coleridge had followed closely, had brought him into sympathetic contact with the creed, but his own conversion to it was as sudden as it was complete. It meant, of course, the end of his career at Cambridge but it meant also an end to the sudden vacillations and erratic changes of direction which had marked that career. For the next three years Coleridge was to be an energetic and devoted propagandist for the ideas which he had now adopted.

At first sight these ideas may seem a jumble of contradictions. Coleridge was at one and the same time 'a Unitarian Christian and an Advocate for the Automatism of man'[1] and also a firm opponent of materialism,[2] a believer in the

[1] *Collected Letters*, i, p. 147.
[2] e.g. *The Destiny of Nations*, ll. 27–35 and note (in *Joan of Arc* only).

29

corporeality of thought[1] and also an admirer of Baxter's
Immateriality of the Soul,[2] a follower of Hartley and yet an
anti-Newtonian,[3] a poet who wrote that we are

> Placed with our backs to bright Reality,
> That we may learn with young unwounded ken
> Things from their shadows.[4]

and then, thirteen lines later,

> But Properties are God.[5]

These apparent contradictions can be resolved only when it is
realized that Coleridge was simply being 'right orthodox in the
heterodoxy of Unitarianism'[6] and that these were all ideas
that he could have learned, and presumably did learn, from
Joseph Priestley, the founder of that system.[7]

Coleridge's enthusiasm for Priestley at this time is well
evidenced in his letters and poems; indeed, it was presumably
because of it that his radicalism took the form of Pantisocracy

---

[1] *Collected Letters*, i, p. 137.   [2] *Notebooks*, i, p. 188 n.
[3] See p. 38 below, and p. 133, n. 1 below.
[4] *The Destiny of Nations*, ll. 21–3 and app. crit.   [5] id., l. 36.
[6] *Collected Letters*, i, p. 153. Unless this point is grasped it is possible
to fall into the sort of confusion in which R. L. Brett (*Essays and
Studies*, 1949) quotes, from the opening paragraph of *The Destiny of
Nations*, lines which he imagines were written 'as early as 1797' as an
example of Coleridge's reaction against Hartley when, of course, they
were actually written for *Joan of Arc* in early 1795, Coleridge's most
Hartleyan period. In much the same manner, Brett considers that there
can be little doubt that Coleridge was led to read Cudworth by the
appearance of the latter's name in a list, in Burnet, of divines who had
saved 'the esteem over the nation' of the Church of England. When
one remembers the sacrifices which Coleridge was making in 1795
because of his attitude to the established church, then this concern for
the esteem of those whom Coleridge was, even in 1796, to call 'the
moloch priests' seems rather mis-dated. As will appear, it was more
probably his Unitarianism which led him to Cudworth, but it is important to realize that he had written of the 'Monads' before he drew
Cudworth from the Bristol library.
[7] For Priestley's position as the originator of Unitarianism see
Encyclopaedia of Religion and Ethics, art. 'Unitarianism', and *Table
Talk*, June 23, 1834. A fuller account will be found in E. M. Wilbur's
A History of Unitarianism, pp. 293–315.

—the plan for a democratic community which should form part of the settlement on the Susquehanna that Priestley was promoting.[1] Coleridge went so far as to hope that his religious leader would become one of the Pantisocrats. 'He [Dyer] is intimate with Dr Priestley and doubts not that the Doctor will join us', he wrote to his fellow-Unitarian, Southey, in September 1794.[2]

To the same cause can probably be attributed his introduction to David Hartley's *Observations on Man* and the attachment to its doctrines which later led him to christen his first son Hartley. The system of psychology set out in that book, which explained the development of complex ideas from sense-impressions by the principle of association and which suggested that both sense-impressions and ideas were carried by vibrations in nervous tissue, formed an essential part of Priestley's demonstration that all phenomena, including mental ones, were manifestations of energy. Hartley, it is true, had still kept a distinction between mind and matter, but Priestley, in his edition of the *Observations on Man*, added a preface showing that the mind, as an immaterial principle, could be eliminated and suggesting that thought is simply a form of vibratory movement.[3]

In an early draft of *Religious Musings* Coleridge introduced Hartley as 'he first who marked the ideal tribes Roll subtly surging' and went on to describe Priestley as 'pressing on his steps'. This may have been meant literally, but if it is metaphorical it describes exactly Priestley's intellectual position.

Coleridge soon made Hartley, as amended by Priestley, part of his creed. In December 1794 he proclaimed himself 'a Unitarian Christian and an Advocate for the Automatism of man' and in the same month he made, in significant terms, his first reference to Hartley. 'I am a complete Necessitarian and understand the subject as well almost as Hartley himself, but I go farther than Hartley and believe the corporeality of

[1] See J. R. MacGillivray, 'The Pantisocracy scheme' in *Toronto Studies in English* (1931).
[2] *Collected Letters*, i, p. 98.
[3] J. Priestley (ed.), *Hartley's Theory of the Human Mind*, p. xix.

31

thought, namely, that it is motion.'[1] This suggests that Coleridge had been reading Hartley in Priestley's edition, or at least that he knew and accepted Priestley's interpretation of the theory. In any case the letters make it clear that, for Coleridge, Hartley's doctrines were part of Unitarian Christianity.

Coleridge accepted also the metaphysical system by which Priestley supported his religious views, and this metaphysical system formed the ground work of the two long ambitious poems which Coleridge attempted in this period, *Joan of Arc* Book II (revised as *The Destiny of Nations*) and *Religious Musings*. As Coleridge's sonnet to Priestley makes clear, the latter's authority for him was threefold, as a democrat, as a theologian and as a scientist, and he wrote as late as 1798, 'I regard every experiment that Priestley made in chemistry as giving *wings* to his more sublime theological works'.[2] The same relationship would have seemed good to Priestley himself: his hopes for society were derived from his religious faith and that in turn rested on his beliefs about the physical world. Both the religious and the scientific beliefs are summed up in the lines from *Joan of Arc*

> Glory to Thee, Father of Earth and Heaven!
> All-conscious Presence of the Universe!
> Nature's vast ever-acting Energy!
> In will, in deed, Impulse of All to All![3]

These lines Coleridge himself later explained as Unitarian doctrine:

Tho' these Lines may bear a sane sense, yet they are easily and more naturally interpreted with a very false and dangerous one. But I was at that time one of the *Mongrels*, the Josephidites [Josephides=the Son of Joseph], a proper name of distinction from those who believe *in*, as well as believe Christ the only begotten Son of the Living God before all Time.[4]

This note clearly acknowledges that Coleridge thought of this form of pantheism as the product of his Unitarianism while the

[1] *Collected Letters*, i, p. 137.
[2] id., p. 372.
[3] *The Destiny of Nations*, ll. 459–62.
[4] id., note to l. 461.

complicated word-play on 'Joseph' points to its source in the ideas of Joseph Priestley as well as to beliefs about the paternity of Christ, with which the passage would otherwise have no obvious connection.

The longest and clearest exposition of these ideas of Priestley's is in his *Matter and Spirit* (1777). There is no proof that Coleridge read this particular work (for he never named any of the books in which he read Priestley's 'divine theology') but two copies of it (one of 1777 and one of 1782) were in the Green and Gilman sales lists which included parts of Coleridge's library, and the second edition formed the first volume of Priestley's work on philosophical necessity, which a Unitarian preacher given to discoursing on that subject would be likely to study thoroughly. Between 1794 and 1796 Coleridge read many of the authors cited in this work—Baxter's *Immateriality of the Soul* (whose criticism of Newton was Priestley's point of departure), Russel's *Essay on the Nature and Existence of the Material World*, Mosheim's *Ecclesiastical History*, Cudworth's *Intellectual System*, Ramsay's *Philosophical Principles* and possibly Giordano Bruno.[1] He drew much from these, and may have met pantheism before in his Cambridge reading of the neo-platonists or in other sources, but a study of his poetry from 1794 to 1796 confirms what the note just quoted says, and what we should in any case expect from a Unitarian preacher, that the view of the world which his reading was used to supplement and amplify was learned from his religion. Certainly when Lamb received *Religious Musings* and the *Destiny of Nations* he welcomed them as Unitarian poems and assumed that Coleridge had read Priestley on Necessity.[2]

Priestley's system originated in a criticism of Andrew Baxter's *Immateriality of the Soul*. In this book (read by Coleridge in 1795) Baxter rejected Newton's theory of the aether, that very fine fluid which was postulated to transmit the force of gravitation, and set out to show that it involved impossible mathematical contradictions. As Baxter continued

[1] See p. 39, n. 4 below.
[2] *Works of Charles Lamb*, ed. W. MacDonald, ix, pp. 9–12, 15.

to regard inactivity as a fundamental property of matter, he argued that some other source than the aether must be found for its gravitational and other movements, and he found this source in the direct action of spirit on matter. Priestley concurred in rejecting the aether[1] but he pointed out that Baxter's hypothesis made solid matter quite unnecessary:

This scheme of the mutual penetration of matter first occurred to Mr. Michell on reading *Baxter on the immateriality of the Soul.* He found that the author's idea of matter was, that it consisted, as it were, of bricks cemented together by an immaterial mortar. . . . He began to perceive that the bricks were so covered with this immaterial mortar that if they had any existence at all, it could not be perceived, every effect being produced . . . by the immaterial, spiritual and penetrable mortar.[2]

In Priestley's view, Baxter's theory was far from supporting any absolute distinction between spirit and matter: instead it led logically to the elimination of one or the other of them:

Mr. Baxter . . . acknowledges that *powers of resistance and cohesion* are essential to matter, and absolutely to make it a solid substance. But asserting as he does that these powers are the immediate agency of the Deity himself, it necessarily follows, that there is not any such thing as *matter* distinct from *the Deity* and his *operations.* An opinion in which Mr. Baxter's hypothesis necessarily terminates.[3]

Priestley was led therefore 'to adopt the hypothesis of Mr. Boscovitch . . . that matter . . . consists of physical points only, endued with powers of repulsion and attraction'.[4] For the apparent solidity of matter Priestley substituted power of resistance. In his system every atom was a point of force acting by attraction and repulsion on its neighbours: these centres of force were established by the Deity himself, all action was his action, and the physical world was made up of his energy.[5]

[1] J. Priestley, *Disquisitions concerning Matter and Spirit* (2nd ed., 1782), p. 30.
[2] id., pp. 26–7.　　　　　　　　[3] id., p. 14.
[4] id., p. 24.　　　　　　　　　[5] id., p. 41.

This system had important implications. If there was no solidity in Nature, but only energy, then the barrier between the physical and the mental or spiritual disappeared, for both were the same thing: 'If they say that on my hypothesis there is no such thing as matter and that everything is spirit, I have no objection. . . . The world has been too long amused by mere names.'[1] Coleridge himself summed up the argument very clearly many years later in *Biographia Literaria*:

For since impenetrability is intelligible only as a mode of resistance; its admission places the essence of *matter* in a mode of power which it possesses in common with *spirit*; and body and spirit are therefore no longer absolutely heterogeneous, but *may* without any *absurdity* be supposed to be different modes, or degrees of perfection, of a common substratum. . . . But as soon as materialism becomes intelligible it ceases to be materialism. In order to explain *thinking*, as a material phenomenon, it is necessary to refine matter into a mere modification of intelligence. . . . Even so did Priestley. . . . He stript matter of all its material properties; substituted spiritual powers.[2]

This makes it clear why Coleridge, in his Priestleyan period, used the term materialist for the Newtonians who believed in the existence of matter distinct from spirit.

From this position Priestley went on to deduce the important features of his theology. One deduction concerned the nature of man.

The whole argument for an immaterial thinking principle in man, on this supposition, falls to the ground; matter, destitute of what has hitherto been called *solidity*, being no more incompatible with sensation and thought, than that substance, which, without knowing anything about it, we have been used to call *immaterial*.[3]

For Priestley matter was not only endowed with feeling and intellect but merged with the divinity. God, as a spirit was superior to, but not different in kind from matter, that is to say energy,[4] and this natural energy is what we know of God. 'If then our ideas concerning matter do not go beyond the

---

[1] id., p. 33.　　　　　　　　　[2] *Biographia Literaria*, i, pp. 88, 91.
[3] J. Priestley, *Matter and Spirit*, p. 23.　　　　[4] id., p. 173.

powers of which it is possessed, much less can our ideas go beyond powers, properties or attributes with respect to the Divine Being.'[1] All nature was simply an extension of the Divine Being. 'Matter is, by this means, resolved into nothing but the divine *agency* exerted according to certain rules.'[2] Priestley quoted Giordano Bruno to summarize his position. 'All the motions that strike our senses, the resistance which we find in matter, are the effects of the immediate action of God. . . . There is no active force in nature but that of God . . . an immense spring which is in continual action.'[3]

Thus Coleridge, in the note quoted earlier, was right in describing as Unitarian his lines apostrophizing God as

> Nature's vast ever-acting Energy!
> In will, in deed, Impulse of All to All![4]

and the fear which he expressed that they might be taken as pantheistic was quite natural.[5] Nevertheless Priestley gave even the pantheistic aspects of his system a strong biblical colouring:

The Divine Being and his energy are absolutely necessary to that of every other being. His power is the very *life and soul* of everything that exists; and, strictly speaking, *without him we* ARE, as well as *can* DO *nothing*.[6]

In fact the system now held out to the public, taken in its fullest extent, makes the Divine Being to be of as much importance in the system, as the apostle makes him, when he says, *In him we live,*

---

[1] id., p. 140. [2] id., p. 39.
[3] id., p. 15. [4] *The Destiny of Nations*, ll. 461–2.
[5] Coleridge made an isolated expression of dissatisfaction with Priestley on this point as early as March, 1796, in a letter to the Rev. T. Edwards (*Collected Letters*, i, pp. 192–3) in which he complained that for Priestley God does and is everything, 'an eating, drinking, lustful God'. The fit must have been momentary, for in the poem he was then publishing he twice described God as 'omnific' (*Religious Musings*, ll. 106, 415; the word is also used by Priestley in *Matter and Spirit*, p. 317) and he wrote that the Elect 'dare know of what may seem deform the Supreme Fair sole operant'. A glance at the rest of the letter will perhaps explain Coleridge's momentary doubts.
[6] J. Priestley, *Matter and Spirit*, p. 42. Cf. *The Eolian Harp*, ll. 44–8, quoted p. 43 below.

and move, and have our being. . . . Every other system of philosophy is discordant with the scriptures.[1]

Priestley himself did not regard his system as pantheistic; for in it, though God was all forces and all intelligences, he and they had also separate existences and consciousnesses:

Nor indeed is making the deity to *be*, as well as to *do* everything, *in this sense* anything like the system of Spinoza, because I suppose a source of infinite power and superior intelligence, from which all inferior beings are derived; that every inferior being has a consciousness distinct from that of the supreme being.[2]

This supposition connected Priestley's physical theories to revealed religion and enabled him to give explanations of such matters as providence, prophecy and the resurrection of the dead.

It was to this theological and metaphysical system that Coleridge was converted in 1794 and inevitably the system became a major theme in his poetry. Between the beginning of 1795 and the end of 1796 Coleridge made three attempts at a long Miltonic poem which should embody his new philosophy and present his own justification of the ways of God to man. The poems, *Joan of Arc* Book II, *Religious Musings* and *The Destiny of Nations* (which was a revision of the first poem) were failures, and it was not until he had thought more deeply about the poetic imagination that he was able to write *The Ancient Mariner*. Nevertheless that poem bears important traces of his Unitarian concept of nature and it was in the course of working out the implications of the Unitarian philosophy and of trying to give poetic form to its ideas that Coleridge began to develop something of the symbolic scheme and some of the images that give power to the later poem.

Coleridge began to pour his new ideas into poetry in 1795 when he was writing the 250 lines which he contributed to the second book of Southey's epic poem *Joan of Arc*. The title of this book was 'Preternatural Agency' and the Agencies supplied by Southey were such personifications as Cruelty, Superstition and Murder which Coleridge quite sufficiently described

[1] id., p. 149. Cf. Coleridge's letter quoted p. 140 below.
[2] J. Priestley, *Matter and Spirit*, p. 42.

as 'images imageless, Small-Capitals constituting themselves Personifications'. His own remedy was to replace them by those natural forces which his religion taught him to see as 'the divine agency' and so he plunged at once into a recapitulation of Priestley's arguments. After an opening which can be taken as Platonic or Unitarian[1] or both, he began his second paragraph with an attack on the Newtonians:

> themselves they cheat
> With noisy emptiness of learned phrase,
> Their subtle fluids, impacts. essences. . . .[2]

Here he added a long footnote attacking Newton's theory of the aether. This note has been taken by editors as an example of his ingenuity, but it is, in fact, condensed from the still longer note of Baxter's[3] which was crucial to the argument against a mechanical universe. Coleridge was not punctilious about acknowledging borrowed footnotes but he does, at one point in this note, mention Baxter by name. Like Priestley, and unlike Baxter, Coleridge did not go on to prove the immateriality of the soul, but to prepare the ground for a belief in the divine activity of 'matter'. This belief he expounds in the next section of the poem and, though he

[1] *The Destiny of Nations*, ll. 15–23 and app. crit. Line 21 is an obvious reference to Plato's cave, but the general theme of the passage is equally Unitarian. (Lamb commented on a similar passage, *Religious Musings*, ll. 395–8, 'I thank you for these lines in the name of a necessarian'.) (*Works*, ed. W. MacDonald, ix, p. 15.) Cf. Priestley, *Matter and Spirit*, p. 148:

> The idea which the scriptures give us of the divine nature is that of a being, properly speaking, *everywhere present*, constantly supporting, and, at pleasure, controlling the laws of nature, but not the object of any of our senses: and that, out of condescension, as it were, to the weakness of human apprehension, he chose, in the early ages of the world, to signify his peculiar presence by some *visible symbol*, as that of a supernatural bright cloud.

With this compare also Coleridge's idea (at this time) of how God educated primitive peoples (*The Destiny of Nations*, ll. 60–88) and the discussion of symbols on pp. 57–8 below.

[2] *The Destiny of Nations*, ll. 30–2.

[3] A. Baxter, *An Enquiry into the Immateriality of the Soul* (1745), i, pp. 34–50.

professes to suspend judgement, he makes it the machinery
of his poem.

> But Properties are God: the naked mass
> (If mass there be, fantastic guess or ghost)
> Acts only by its inactivity.
> Here we pause humbly. Others boldlier think
> That as one body is the aggregate
> Of atoms numberless, each organized;
> So by a strange and dim similitude
> Infinite myriads of self-conscious minds
> Form one all-conscious Spirit, who directs
> With absolute ubiquity of thought
> All his component Monads, that yet seem
> With various province and apt agency
> Each to pursue its own self-centering end.[1]

It is important to realize that at this date the word 'Monad'
did not necessarily or predominantly have Leibnizian conno-
tations.[2] The word was ordinarily used to mean an atom and
though Priestley himself does not use the word, it was used
by one of his critics[3] to describe the 'points of force'. Coleridge's passage, with its Monads which are not sealed cells but
forms of energy and which are *components* of the all-conscious
Spirit, is quite contrary to Leibniz's doctrine[4] but it is a

---

[1] *The Destiny of Nations*, ll. 36–47. The second line was added in
revision, presumably in 1796. I have left it in for the sake of clarity.
With the first line of the quotation compare Priestley, *Matter and Spirit*
p. 140 (pp. 35–6 above).

[2] See *O.E.D.* 'Monad' sense 2. The suggestion by L. Hansen, *The Life
of S. T. Coleridge: the early years*, p. 148 (probably following Alois
Brandl) that Coleridge got his system of monads from Hartley is
not tenable. Despite the prominence of the Hartley quotation in the
O.E.D. he only used the word twice, both times in the singular to mean
a unity. On the other hand Hartley's use of the word for the human
soul may have given Coleridge his clue to extend it to all of Priestley's
'inferior beings' each of which has 'a consciousness'.

[3] (Russel), *An Essay on the Nature and Existence of a Material World*
(1781), p. 53: 'The one of two doctrines is submitted to our choice;
either the infinite divisibility of matter or the hypothesis of monads
or uniform particles which are themselves indivisible.'

[4] For the nature of the differences between these Monads and those
of Leibniz see p. 16, n. 3 above. Coleridge's Monads seem closer to

recognizable statement of Priestley's Unitarianism. The Monads are the units of 'Nature's vast ever-acting Energy', each having its own province as part of the 'Divine Agency'.

Coleridge was engaged in Miltonic imitation and these Monads must have seemed to him a credible and serious substitute for the angelic hosts of *Paradise Lost*, reconciling (just as the angels had) the Marvellous with the Probable. But, like the angels, the Monads were immaterial and immateriality, as Dr Johnson observed, supplies no images. To learn how to present them in poetry he turned to the work of Erasmus Darwin who agreed with Priestley's views as to the nature of the material world and the qualities of life and energy to be found in it (though not with Priestley's faith in revealed religion) and who had already attempted to present natural forces in poetic dress.

The first pages of the *Gutch Memorandum Book*, the note-book that Coleridge was using at this time, show that he had been reading Darwin's poem *The Botanic Garden* with an eye to subjects for his own poetry.[1] Now Erasmus Darwin's theory of evolution,[2] as it appeared in that poem, was that the world

Giordano Bruno's—see R. Latta, *Leibniz: The Monadology etc.*, p. 34:

> The term was used by Giordano Bruno, whose Monads were ultimate spherical points, regarded as possessing both spiritual and material characteristics. There are some parts of the philosophy of Bruno with which the doctrine of Leibniz has affinity, as, for instance, Bruno's contention that there is nothing, however little or valueless, that does not contain in it life or soul. But Leibniz repeatedly attacks the doctrine of a world soul, which is Bruno's central conception. Thus, in adopting the term 'Monad', Leibniz may be said to have taken from Bruno little more than the name.

There is some positive evidence that Coleridge had not read Leibniz (*Biographia Literaria*, i, p. 93; *Collected Letters*, i, p. 590) but there is no evidence that he had read Bruno either.

[1] *The Gutch Memorandum Book* 1 (a) to 4 (a). Notes on 3 (b) and 4 (b) show that Coleridge was working on *Joan of Arc*.

[2] See Appendix A for a discussion of whether or not Coleridge at this period accepted the idea of evolution in time. This question has little bearing on his view of nature for he still regarded the world as the result of natural forces which he variously identified with the Monads, the plastic spirits, Blumenbach's *nisus formativus* and Hunter's *vis plastica*.

had developed gradually as a result of the action of natural forces which he represented as the spirits of the elements. 'The Rosicrucian doctrine of Gnomes, Sylphs, Nymphs and Salamanders affords a proper machinery for a philosophic poem: as it is probable that they were originally the names of the hieroglyphic figures of the elements, or of Genii presiding over their operations.'[1] Each of the four cantos of the first part of Darwin's poem is addressed to the spirits of one of the four elements and describes their activities. The nymphs of fire

> chase the shooting stars
> Or yoke the vollied lightning to their cars.

Those of earth, among other duties, produce diamonds, while those of water bring 'the genial shower' for the roots of plants.[2]

Coleridge identified the Monads with these spirits. The passage in *Joan of Arc* continues

> . . . All his component Monads, that yet seem
> With various province and apt agency
> Each to pursue its own self-centering end.
> Some nurse the infant diamond in the mine:
> Some roll the genial juices through the oak;
> Some drive the mutinous clouds to clash in air,
> And rushing on the storm with whirlwind speed
> Yoke the red lightning to their volleying car.
> Thus these pursue their never-varying course,
> No eddy in their stream. Others more wild,
> With complex interests weaving human fates,
> Duteous or proud, alike obedient all,
> Evolve the process of eternal good.[3]

These are clearly Darwin's spirits, though Coleridge has added a class concerned with human fates and merged the spirits of air and fire.[4]

In the passages that follow, Coleridge tried to show the Monads at work on 'the process of eternal good'. He began

[1] *The Botanic Garden*, Note to i. i. 73.

[2] id., i. i. 115–16; i. ii. 228; i. iii. 522–4.

[3] *The Destiny of Nations*, ll. 61–81.

[4] In this he was probably following Priestley; see pp. 99–100 below.

with the spirits of the shooting stars and northern lights, which he rather confusingly described as rebellious—presumably to show that apparent rebellion was really part of divine purpose. The spirits lead the Lapps to superstition, but superstition is the first step to religion.

<blockquote>
Yet these train up to God

.   .   .   .

[The Lapp] marks the streamy banners of the North,
Thinking himself those happy spirits shall join
Who there in floating robes of rosy light
Dance sportively. For Fancy is the power
That first unsensualises the dark mind.[1]
</blockquote>

That all sense impressions are meant to train up to God, is, of course, Hartley's thesis, but Hartley thought of the process as taking place in the life of each individual. Coleridge, with his characteristic passion for producing new systems, was here trying to show it as a process in history and a stage in the development of the world.

This system of education through superstition could not carry the poem beyond the primitive ages, and so, to reach Joan of Arc, Coleridge introduced one of the beings concerned with human fate, the Guardian Angel of France. The Spirit's task is to show Joan the history of the world in a series of visions. The first, a vision of the creation drawn partly from *The Botanic Garden*[2] shows that Coleridge, like Darwin, thought of that event as a victory over Chaos. The progeny of Chaos had since become 'monarchs o'er mankind', and the poem leads up to the vision in which Joan sees their overthrow in the French Revolution.

By this point Coleridge had lost touch with his first theme. The preternatural agencies in this latter part of the poem are the Southeyan personifications which Coleridge said he was forced to introduce to preserve the connection with Southey's machinery[3] but which would probably have been forced on

[1] *The Destiny of Nations*, ll. 61–81.

[2] Cf. *The Destiny of Nations*, ll. 283–91 with *The Botanic Garden*, I. i. 101–4.

[3] *The Destiny of Nations*, note to ll. 421–3.

him in any case by his lack of any very clear idea of how
'Nature's vast ever-acting Energy' did work out His purpose
for men. Certainly 'the process of eternal good', as it is
organized by Oppression, Envy and Justice, is both confused
and confusing.

Nevertheless the poem shows that, for poetical purposes at
least, Coleridge did have a clear theory of the nature of the
world. The qualification is a necessary one, for when he next
described the theory, later in the year in *The Eolian Harp*,

> Or what if all of animated nature
> Be but organic Harps diversely fram'd,
> That tremble into thought, as o'er them sweeps
> Plastic and vast, one intellectual breeze,
> At once the Soul of each, and God of all?[1]

he still did not commit himself completely to the idea, though
clearly the main purpose of the poem was to express it. Indeed
the word 'Plastic' in this passage is an indication[2] that these
beliefs would have received fresh reinforcement between *Joan
of Arc* and *The Eolian Harp*, for in May 1795 Coleridge had
drawn Cudworth's *Intellectual System* from the Bristol library.

[1] *The Eolian Harp*, ll. 44–8.

[2] Though the word 'plastic' strongly suggests Cudworth's influence, it
by no means proves it, and the central idea of the passage quoted does
not derive from him. The lines reached this form at some time between
October 1795 and March 1796: in the draft preserved in the Rugby
School MS, pp. 27, verso-28 recto, reads (in part):

> That tremble into thought while through them breathes
> One infinite and intellectual breeze . . .
> Thus *God* would be the universal Soul,
> Mechaniz'd matter as the organic harps,
> And each one's Tunes be that, which each calls *I*.—

which is not at all like Cudworth. The word 'plastic' was common
property, even Darwin referring to 'Nature's plastic power' (*The
Botanic Garden*, I. iv. 59). In 1796 Coleridge (*Collected Letters*, i, p. 294)
wrote of Monro's belief in a 'plastic nature' though in the passage presumably referred to (A. Monro, *Observations on . . . the Nervous System*,
p. 104) Monro speaks only of 'a living principle pervading the universe'.
The passage illustrates affinities between Unitarianism and Neo-
platonism but the idea that God is 'the soul of each' is Unitarian and
is not Cudworth's.

43

Cudworth was one of the seventeenth-century Cambridge Platonists and the absorption of Platonic or neo-platonic (or even Berkeleyan) doctrines into the concept of an active and living universe proved surprisingly easy. The fundamental doctrine of Unitarianism, and of the new quasi-pantheism generally, was that God's energy was the reality in the natural world, and no doubt Platonism, omnipresent in Western thought, had its influence here: the Platonic doctrine of the One who is behind all the appearances of the natural world and who draws all things by love must have played its part in shaping the Unitarian conception of a God who is beyond as well as being the natural world, and who impels all things. There are fundamental differences here as well as likenesses, but whether the reality in Nature is the Divine thought, as in Platonism (and Berkeleyanism), or the Divine energy, Nature in both systems is a shadow of the Divine—in Platonism because it is imperfect, and in Unitarianism because though it is all we know (except by revelation) of the Divine, it is less than the whole reality.

In Romantic poetry concerned with the 'active universe' careful reading is sometimes needed to distinguish between the core of doctrine and the Platonic colouring which came so easily. Thus when Shelley writes in *Queen Mab*:

> Through all this varied and eternal world
> Soul is the only element . . .

the reader could understandably prepare himself for a Platonic or Berkeleyan thesis. It is only when Shelley goes on:

> The moveless pillar of a mountain's weight
> Is active, living spirit. Every grain
> Is sentient both in unity and part,
> And the minutest atom comprehends
> A world of loves and hatreds.[1]

that it becomes clear that the doctrine being expounded is that of the French 'materialists'![2] Such a passage makes clear how

[1] *Queen Mab*, iv. 139–46.
[2] cf. p. 20 above.

44

it was possible for Shelley's thought to become more and more Platonic without ever losing touch with his earlier ideas.[1]

Suggestions of Platonism can be found early in Coleridge's poetry. In *Joan of Arc* he used Plato's cave to introduce the statement that man's task is to learn to know 'The substance from the shadow'. Certainly this is Platonic but it can equally echo Priestley's belief that God may manifest himself as a natural appearance or 'symbol'[2] and when Coleridge repeated the same idea in *Religious Musings*[3] it was in a much more Unitarian context, and it was Hartley, not Plato, that he quoted on the ecstasy of knowing God.[4] Similarly towards the end of *Religious Musings* there occurs a passage beginning 'Life is a vision shadowy of truth'[5] which the reader might well take for Platonic but which another Unitarian, Lamb, welcomed as a necessarian[6] though this did not deter Coleridge from claiming it as Berkeleyan a year later after he had adopted that philosophy.

In 1795 Cudworth's neo-platonic 'plastic natures' entered into that process of blending by which the Monads of *Joan of Arc*, already identified with Darwin's spirits who control natural processes, became the spirits of *The Ancient Mariner*, where they retain much of their old character even though they can be described in the gloss as Platonic spirits. In Cudworth, Coleridge would have read:

Aristotle himself held the world's animation or a mundane soul, forasmuch as he plainly declares himself concerning it elsewhere, saying, *We commonly think of the Heavens as nothing else but Bodys and Monads, having only a certain order, but altogether inanimate: whereas we ought on the contrary to conceive of them as partaking of life and action*; that is as *Simplicius* rightly expounds the place as being endu'd with a rational or intellectual life. . . . by the *Heaven*, as in many other places of *Aristotle* and *Plato*, is to be understood the whole world.

[1] For this continuity see A. M. D. Hughes, *The Nascent Mind of Shelley*.

[2] *Matter and Spirit*, pp. 148, 176.   [3] *Religious Musings*, ll. 45–53.

[4] id., note to l. 43.   [5] id., ll. 396–401.

[6] *Works*, ed. W. MacDonald, ix, p. 15.

. . . the *Plastick Nature* essentially depends upon *Mind* and *Intellect*, and could not possibly be without it; for which reason the *Philosopher* joins *Mind* and *Nature* both together.[1]

There is nothing here completely incompatible with Unitarianism. Cudworth's 'plastic natures' are unlike Coleridge's Monads and Priestley's units of the Divine energy in that they are created spirits, not parts of the Divinity or 'Monads of the Infinite Mind', but as natural forces and agents of the divine purpose they are easily assimilated to the Unitarian system: in *Matter and Spirit* Priestley had suggested that neo-platonic doctrines of the soul, and particularly Cudworth's doctrine of the world-soul, supported his own views[2] and it was possibly this that sent Coleridge to the *Intellectual System*. Nevertheless this represents a broadening of Coleridge's interest in the subject and perhaps it foreshadows the many changes which were to take place in the foundations which supported his enduring belief in the 'One Life'.

At the beginning of 1796 these changes were still in the future and the natural forces in *Religious Musings* are still those of *Joan of Arc*. In *The Eolian Harp* Coleridge seems to imply a distinction between 'animated' nature and inanimate, but there is no warrant for this in either of the longer poems (nor for that matter in Cudworth). In both poems the Monads were natural forces at work in the physical world and endowed with self-consciousness and purpose, parts of the Infinite Mind whose intentions they were carrying out. The problem which such a system raises, and which Coleridge failed to solve in *Joan of Arc*, is that of the existence of evil. God was omnific and benevolent; he performed all the actions in the world and all had goodness as their end. Why then did evil exist?

The question is not an easy one even in orthodox theology but it was of special importance to Unitarians. Priestley had written, 'The origin and existence of evil can only be accounted for on the supposition of its being ultimately *subservient to good*, which is a more immediate consequence of the system of

[1] R. Cudworth, *True Intellectual System of the Universe* (2nd ed., 1743), p. 169.

[2] *Matter and Spirit*, pp. 235–6.

necessity than of any other.'[1] The difficulty lay in demonstrating that evil *was* subservient to good, particularly as Coleridge was simultaneously engaged in vigorous protests against corruption in religion and injustice in politics. In *Joan of Arc* he had made two suggestions, one that superstition was the first step to religious belief, and the other, later in the poem, that pain corrects error,[2] but he did not push either very far. His continuing interest in the subject is indicated by the fact that he drew Balguy's *Divine Benevolence Asserted* from the Bristol Library in May 1795 and by the fact that in January 1796 he had an argument with Erasmus Darwin himself on this question of 'whether we be the outcasts of a blind idiot called nature, or the children of an all-wise and infinitely good god' though Darwin remained obstinately infidel.[3] His next long poem was largely a fresh and more thoroughly worked-out attack on the problem.

The sub-title of *Religious Musings* states that the poem was 'written on the Christmas Eve of 1794' and some part of the poem may have been in existence in 1795, but Coleridge added to it very greatly in 1796 and did not finish it until some weeks after the printing of the rest of his first volume of poems had been completed in February or March. The poem itself falls into two parts, the difference being indicated by the note to line 192 stating that 'In this paragraph the Author recalls himself from his indignation against the instruments of Evil, to contemplate the *uses* of these Evils in the great process of divine Benevolence.' The first half of the poem, down to line 191 does consist of religious musings, or rather religio-political preachings, largely drawn from a Unitarian pamphlet,

[1] *Matter and Spirit*, pp. 178–9.

[2] *The Destiny of Nations*, ll. 130 f., app. crit. ll. 124–7.

[3] *Collected Letters*, i, pp. 177, 178. Darwin's attitude can be seen in a note to *The Botanic Garden*, i. i. 278:

> The benevolence of the great Author of all things is greatly manifest in the sum of his works as Dr. Balguy has well evinced . . . but . . . lions preying upon lambs, these upon living vegetables, and mankind upon them all, would appear to be a less perfect part of the economy of nature than those before mentioned, as contributing less to the sum of general happiness.

Gilbert Wakefield's *The Spirit of Christianity compared with the Spirit of the Times* (1794).[1] This pamphlet was an attack on the government for declaring war on France and its chief points were that Christ, 'the meek and lowly Nazarene', is the Prince of Peace (cf. *Religious Musings*, ll. 161, 169); that if one member of a community suffers, all suffer (cf. *Religious Musings*, ll. 119–21); that the Duke of Portland's speech, claiming that the war was in defence of religion, was unchristian (cf. *Religious Musings*, ll. 159–69); that the government supported the 'royal banditti' in their dismemberment of Poland (cf. *Religious Musings*, ll. 170–3) and also supported the slave trade (cf. *Religious Musings*, ll. 135–41); and that the clergy preaching war in their Fast-Day sermons were 'heathen ministers' and 'worshippers of Baal' (cf. *Religious Musings*, l. 185 'moloch priest') who 'call forth their congregations to desolate the globe with torrents of human blood' (cf. *Religious Musings*, ll. 185–92). When *Religious Musings* reaches this point, the subject matter changes: the second half of the poem turns abruptly away from present political issues to sketch the history of the world from the primeval age to the Millennium, and it attempts, by ideas drawn from Darwin and Priestley, to show the hand of God in the French Revolution.

Darwin, though politely sceptical of divine benevolence, believed in progress and sympathized with the Revolution. In *The Botanic Garden* his spirits of the elements take an interest in human affairs and lead various great scientists, among them Benjamin Franklin, to their discoveries. After describing Franklin's electrical discoveries, Darwin told how Franklin stabbed the young vultures of tyranny in the New World, and lit 'the patriot flame' which travelled back to rouse 'the sleeping giant' in France. A panegyric on the Revolution followed.[2]

The Botanic Garden was written before the Terror. By 1796 Coleridge could no longer defend the Revolution except as a stage towards goodness, but he adopted Darwin's scheme in

---

[1] Coleridge contemplated writing a sonnet to Wakefield (*Collected Letters*, i, p. 201).

[2] *The Botanic Garden*, i. ii. 361–94.

part. After an account, on the lines of Rousseau's *Second Discourse*, of how primitive simplicity gave way to avarice and war, he claimed that,

> From Avarice thus, from Luxury and War
> Sprang heavenly Science; and from Science Freedom.
> O'er waken'd realms Philosophers and Bards
> Spread in concentric circles.[1]

These philosophers and bards admire the triumphs of the Patriot-Sage, Franklin, and, sympathizing with the Revolution in spite of its excesses,

> Shall watch the mad careering of the storm;
> Then o'er the wild and wavy chaos rush
> And tame the outrageous mass, with plastic might
> Moulding Confusion[2]

to those perfect forms which they dreamt of in their solitary reveries.

But Coleridge could offer more reasons than these for believing that the evils of the Revolution would turn out well. The reference in the poem to the Thousand Years of the Millennium and the lines on Priestley,

> Him from his loved native land
> Statesmen blood-stained and priests idolatrous
> By dark lies maddening the blind multitude
> Drove with vain hate. Calm, pitying he retired,
> And mused expectant on these promised years.[3]

show that the poet had been reading either Priestley's *The Present State of Europe Compared with Ancient Prophecies* (1794) or his *Conclusion to Hartley's Observations* (1794), both of which gave the writer's reasons for leaving England and his views on the Millennium. In them the French Revolution was interpreted as the beginning of those events prophesied in Revelations which were to follow the opening in heaven of the fifth seal and which were to be followed in turn by the beginning of the Millenium. Both quoted interpretations of scriptural prophecy by Newton and Hartley in support of this

[1] *Religious Musings*, ll. 224–7.   [2] id., ll. 244–7.   [3] id., ll. 372–6.

theory and hence both Newton and Hartley appear alongside Priestley in *Religious Musings*.

It was in the light of this theory that Coleridge saw the French Revolution. In Darwin's poem the sleeping giant

> Starts up from earth, above the admiring throng
> Lifts his colossal form and towers along.[1]

In Coleridge's the Revolution is portrayed as

> The Giant Frenzy
> Uprooting empires with his whirlwind arm
> Mocketh high Heaven; burst hideous from the cell
> Where the old Hag, unconquerable, huge,
> Creation's eyeless drudge, black Ruin, sits
> Nursing the impatient earthquake.[2]

When the Revolution and the earthquakes had done their work, the biblical Millennium was to arrive, not only metaphorically through the intervention of 'Philosophers and Bards', but also literally in a general resurrection in which 'the mighty dead rise to new life'.[3] The mighty dead named were the four Christian inspirers of the poem (all of whom could have been claimed as Unitarians)—Milton, Newton (who is described in a figure similar to 'one auspicious and one drooping eye' as raising his serener eye to heaven; that is, he was to be raised as the interpreter of prophecy, not as the physicist who believed in the aether), Hartley and Priestley (though the last was still alive).

This method of demonstrating divine benevolence even in 'Creation's eyeless drudge, black Ruin' seems curious now, but interpretations of history were popular at the time— indeed they still are. Coleridge's was no worse than the nearly contemporary interpretations and prophecies of Volney, Godwin or Chateaubriand and he had the authority of scripture for his general scheme. What is interesting is that, though at the beginning of the passage dealing with the Apocalypse he seems to be taking the prophecies as figurative:

[1] *The Botanic Garden*, I. i. 387–8.
[2] *Religious Musings*, ll. 317–22.
[3] id., ll. 361–2.

> The Kings and the Chief Captains of the World,
> With all that fixed on high like stars of Heaven
> Shot baleful influence, shall be cast to earth . . .[1]

yet later in the passage the earthquakes seem meant to be taken literally. This is even clearer in the manuscript of an early draft of the poem[2] which continues

> black *Ruin* sits
> Nursing the impatient earthquake, and with dreams
> Of shatter'd cities and the promis'd day
> Of central fires thro' nether seas upthundering
> Soothes her fierce solitude.

it is also made clear later in the poem:

> How the black-visaged, red-eyed Fiend outstretched
> Beneath the unsteady feet of Nature groans,
> In feverish slumbers—destined then to wake,
> When fiery whirlwinds thunder his dread name
> DESTRUCTION![3]

In interpreting the fall of stars as the fall of the great Coleridge was following well-known rules for the allegorical interpretation of biblical prophecies[4] but when he reached the earthquakes he rejected the allegorical interpretation in favour of actual volcanic disturbances.

The reason for this can be seen in the *Gutch Memorandum Book* which shows Coleridge gathering scientific evidence for the possibility of the fulfilment of these prophecies by natural forces. The relevant pages are 16(b) to 18(b) which seem to mark a re-reading of *The Botanic Garden*. On the first of these pages is an unfavourable criticism of Darwin's poetry, but this does not necessarily show any lack of enthusiasm for his type of subject, for a list of projected works a few pages on included a *Hymn to Dr. Darwin in the manner of the Orphics* and *Hymns to the Sun the Moon and the Elements*.[5] Like many other

---

[1] id., ll. 310–12.
[2] B.M. MSS. Add. 35, 343.
[3] *Religious Musings*, ll. 388–92.
[4] Isaac Newton, *Opera*, v, pp. 305–9.
[5] *Gutch Memorandum Book* 24 (b).

entries in this book, the criticism of Darwin seems to have been written with an eye to Coleridge's own projects. 'Dr. Darwin's poetry . . . arrests the attention too often and so prevents the rapidity necessary to pathos—it makes the great little.' The next page shows him selecting these potentially great subjects from *The Botanic Garden*. The first note on it reads:

Millennium or History of as brought about by progression in natural philosophy or science of airs and winds.

This refers to *The Botanic Garden*, I. iv. 307–20.

> Oh, Sylphs! disclose in this inquiring age
> One Golden Secret to some favoured sage;
> Grant the charm'd talisman, the chain, that binds
> Or guides the changeful pinions of the winds;
>
> .   .   .   .
>
> Autumn and Spring in lively union blend,
> And from the skies the Golden Age descend.

and to the notes on the passage which suggest that the Millennium (in its secular sense) may be brought about by advances in meteorology and which direct the reader to an *Additional Note on Winds*. To this I shall return when I reach *The Ancient Mariner*.

That Coleridge had been paying attention to some of Darwin's other notes on winds is indicated by the fact that one of his notes to *Religious Musings*, that on the simoom, is adopted bodily from Darwin's note on the same subject.[1] He must therefore have also known Darwin's general theory that hot and, as he thought, poisonous winds such as the Simoom, the Harmattan and the Tornado, were in origin volcanic vapours and that their noxious qualities and the intense heat which accompanied them were the result of this origin.[2] Such a theory would fit very well with certain passages in the *Apocalypse*:

---

[1] *The Botanic Garden*, note to I. iv. 65 (noted by J. L. Lowes in *The Road to Xanadu*).

[2] *The Botanic Garden*, notes to I. iv. 65; I. iv. 29; II. iv. 328.

And he opened the bottomless pit; and there arose a smoke out of the pit as the smoke of a great furnace; and the sun and the air were darkened by reason of the smoke of the pit.[1]

And the fourth angel poured out his vial upon the sun; and power was given unto him to scorch men with fire. And men were scorched with great heat.[2]

Such a scheme had obvious attractions for one who believed that all natural forces were the action of God and, indeed, Darwin in his capacity as a poet had ascribed moral purposes to these winds in the passage immediately preceding that on the Millennium. Besides helping sages, Darwin's spirits carried out vengeance against tyrants and this passage describes such a punishment, beginning,

> Sylphs! your bold hosts, when Heaven with vengeance dread
> Calls the red tempest round the guilty head,
> Fierce at his nod assume vindictive forms
> And launch from airy cars the vollied storms[3]

and going on to describe the destruction of Sennacharib by

> Contagious vapours and volcanic gales.[4]

Such natural explanations of biblical story presumably inspired Coleridge's further notes on this page of the memorandum book, which read:

Quere—might not a commentary on the Revelations be written from the late philosophical discoveries.

> And cauldrons the scooped earth a boiling sea!
> Rush on my ear a cataract of sound
> The guilty pomp consuming while it flares.

The lines of verse contain echoes of Darwin's descriptions of volcanic action in an earlier canto[5] and the whole page of

---

[1] Revelations 9.2. [2] Revelations 16.8.
[3] *The Botanic Garden*, I. iv. 263–6. [4] id., I. iv. 294.
[5] id., I. iii. 149–58:

> with bellowing sound
> Fierce Giesar roared, and struggling shook the ground;
> Poured from red nostrils with her scalding breath
> A fiery deluge o'er the blasted heath;

notes appears to be a project for a poem showing the arrival of the Millennium through advances in the science of airs and the fulfilment of the prophecies of Revelations by natural volcanic forces.

Darwin's suggestion that control of the winds will make possible the equalization of the earth's climate, and hence the Millennium, duly appears in *Religious Musings*:

> While as to solemn strains,
> The THOUSAND YEARS lead up their mystic dance
> Old OCEAN claps his hands! the DESERT shouts!
> And soft gales wafted from the haunts of spring
> Melt the primaeval North![1]

The earthquakes, the fiery whirlwinds and perhaps the waning sun (for Darwin has accounts of the sun obscured by volcanic mist)[2] apparently represent the other parts of this scheme.

It is an interesting illustration of the incongruity between Coleridge's poetic method at this time and his religious faith (or perhaps a sign of certain crudities in both) that he should have had to represent the agent of an 'infinitely good god' as a 'red-eyed fiend', even though the description of the Apocalypse ends with an apostrophe to the Monads:

> Contemplant Spirits! . . .
> And ye of plastic power, that interfused
> Roll through the grosser and material mass
> In organising surge! Holies of God!
> (And what if Monads of the infinite mind?)[3]

Nevertheless, as a statement of Unitarian doctrine, the poem impressed Charles Lamb, while Coleridge himself wrote, 'I build all my poetic pretensions on the Religious Musings. . . . I have studied the subject widely and deeply.'[4]

> And wide in air, in misty volumes hurled
> Contagious atoms o'er the alarmed world
> . . .
> Where with soft fires in unextinguished urns,
> Cauldroned in rock, innocuous lava burns. . . .

[1] *Religious Musings*, ll. 359–61 and app. crit.
[2] *The Botanic Garden*, note to ii. iv. 328.
[3] *Religious Musings*, ll. 402–8.   [4] *Collected Letters*, i, p. 205.

Coleridge's next attempt at a long Miltonic poem came towards the end of 1796, when he began to revise his contribution to *Joan of Arc* with the idea of expanding it into an independent poem which he called variously *The Progress of Liberty* or *Visions of the Maid of Orleans*. His new theory of an apocalypse which was to complete the progress of liberty as well as to show God's action in nature leading through apparent evil to final benevolence would have made the obvious climax of the visions if the poem had progressed far enough. That this was Coleridge's intention is indicated by the *Gutch Memorandum Book* where, alongside notes eventually incorporated into the revision, the following scrap of blank verse appears:

> Like a mighty giantess
> Seized in sore travail and prodigious birth
> Sick nature struggled; long and strange her pangs
> Her groans were horrible; but O! most fair
> The twins she bore—equality and peace.[1]

Thus in the revised version of the poem the climax would have been an apocalypse involving convulsions of nature instead of the political revolution of the earlier version. But the poem did not reach this point: under Lamb's merciless criticism the revision was given over, these lines were rhymed for use in *The Departing Year* and the same poem saw Coleridge's last reference to the volcanoes which were to carry out God's mercies

> Strange-eyed Destruction! who with many a dream
> Of central fires through nether seas up-thundering
> Soothes her fierce solitude; yet as she lies
> By livid fount, or red volcanic stream,
> If ever to her lidless dragon-eyes,
> O Albion! thy predestin'd ruins rise,
> The fiend-hag on her perilous couch doth leap,
> Muttering distemper'd triumph in her charmed sleep.[2]

After this the overt treatment of this theme, along with the overt attempt to justify the ways of God to man, vanishes from Coleridge's poetry.

---

[1] *Gutch Memorandum Book* 27 (b).
[2] *Ode to the Departing Year*, ll. 141–8.

This whole period of Coleridge's poetic career was indeed marked by 'turgid odes and tumid stanzas' but it had its importance as an apprenticeship in ideas. Conceptions, themes and symbols that appear here in crude and unconvincing forms were to reappear as subtle and beautiful in his later thought and poetry. The early poems might easily enough lead one to think that Coleridge was bent on developing only the oddities of Unitarianism but a closer examination will make it clear that he was trying steadily to refine these theories and to reinforce them from older philosophies. We have already seen how Coleridge in 1795 drew on Cudworth's plastic natures and this led to a further development towards the end of 1796 when Coleridge, having again drawn Cudworth from the Bristol library, wrote away for the works of Iamblichus[1] to whom Cudworth had referred as an authority on neoplatonic spirits. The differences between the Monads and the spirits of *The Ancient Mariner* are some measure here of the development of Coleridge's thought.

The same sort of continuous development can be seen in his conversion to the philosophy of Berkeley towards the end of 1796. Coleridge must have become acquainted with criticisms of Priestley from the Berkeleyan point of view by the end of 1795, when he drew from the Bristol library Russel's *Essay on the Nature and Existence of a Material World*. In 1796 he drew a volume of Berkeley's works and later drew Russel's book again, this time calling it 'The Nature and Existence of an External World'. However it was not until some months after this, and after he had named his first son Hartley, that he declared himself a Berkeleyan.[2] This seems to have made no difference to his allegiance to Priestley's 'divine theology' and in 1797 he attached a note to *Religious Musings* claiming as Berkeleyan a passage which could not have been so when it was written and which Lamb had welcomed as a necessarian.[3] There was no real reason why he should not have done so, for Berkeley's *animus mundi* fitted well enough with Priestley's

---

[1] *Collected Letters*, i, p. 262.   [2] id., i, pp. 245, 278.
[3] *Religious Musings*, ll. 395–401, and *Works of Charles Lamb*, ed. W. MacDonald, ix, p. 15.

theology and Coleridge had already learned from the latter to accept the Infinite Mind as the ultimate substratum of the material world.[1]

For Coleridge, the teacher whom Berkeley replaced was Hartley: what was changed was Coleridge's view of the relationship between Nature (or God in Nature) and the human mind. Here what was important was Berkeley's conception of the external world as a perception originating in the divine mind or as, in effect, the language of God. The passage of *Religious Musings* which Coleridge *later* claimed as Berkeleyan begins

> Believe thou, O my soul,
> Life is a vision shadowy of Truth;[2]

and the next poetical passage which he was to note as specifically Berkeleyan is one in which 'the wide view' seems 'a living thing that acts upon the mind'.[3] But this idea of the natural world as communication between God and man was not wholly new to Coleridge and his formal adherence to Berkeley's philosophy came only when his thought had reached a point where it was needed. As early as *Joan of Arc* he had written

> For all that meets the bodily sense I deem
> Symbolical, one mighty alphabet
> For infant minds.[4]

Priestley had allowed that God might 'signify his peculiar presence by some *visible symbol* as that of a supernatural bright cloud, or some other appearance which could not but impress their minds with the idea of a real local presence'. In *Religious Musings* Coleridge's example of a symbol is a little similar but much subtler:

> Yet thou more bright than all that Angel Blaze,
> Despised GALILEAN! Man of Woes!
> For chiefly in the oppressed Good Man's face

[1] J. Priestley, *Matter and Spirit*, p. 23, and e.g. *Religious Musings*, ll. 49–56, 105–6.

[2] *Religious Musings*, ll. 395–6.

[3] *Collected Letters*, i, p. 335.   [4] *The Destiny of Nations*, ll. 18–20.

> The Great Invisible (by symbols seen)
> Shines with peculiar and concentred light,
>
> . . . . . .
>
> Who thee beheld thy imag'd Father saw.[1]

This is the only example Coleridge gives of what he means by a symbol: from it, it would seem that to him a symbol was a natural appearance designed to impress man's minds with the presence of God. Here the symbol is 'peculiar and concentred' but the earlier passage indicates that he thought of all Nature as consisting of symbols intended presumably to impress men with God's presence in nature.

It is in the light of this that Coleridge's apocalyptic ideas must be seen. For Priestley the coming horrors may have been merely acts of divine wrath in 'the great and terrible day of the Lord' but Coleridge insisted that by means of them

> Terror, Mercy's startling prelude
> Uncharm'd the Spirit spell-bound with earthly lusts,[2]

and that he was narrating 'the transfiguration of Fear into holy Awe'.[3] Thus, even before his Berkeleyan period, when Coleridge thought of God as 'Nature's vast ever-acting Energy' he thought of that Energy as acting always to influence men's minds and, when he adopted Priestley's theories about the coming Apocalypse, he thought of it in terms of the psychology of religious conversion.

At this point it is possible to summarize the scheme on which Coleridge was trying to build his most ambitious poetry of this period. It began with God who was 'Nature's vast ever-acting Energy', whose 'thoughts are acts'[4] and whose acts, the appearances of Nature, are symbols designed to bring men to knowledge of him. In Nature, God acted through his 'component Monads', the forces of Nature, and through these forces Coleridge expected a decisive manifestation of God in history. Taking his general cue from Priestley and from Revelations, but basing himself more closely on the contemporary natural science which he learned from Erasmus Darwin,

[1] *Religious Musings*, app. crit. to ll. 1–23, ll. 16–27.
[2] id., ll. 33–4, app. crit.　　　　　　　　　　　　　[3] id., note to l. 89.
[4] *The Destiny of Nations* (Draft I), l. 53.

he expected those forces of Nature which he personified as 'the Fiend Destruction' to produce volcanic earthquakes, poisonous vapours and intense heat which would bring men from their 'earthly lusts' through terror to holy awe. Then soft winds, altering the world's climate, would welcome the Millenium to the renovated earth.

Eight months after the last statement of this scheme in the turgid stanzas of *The Departing Year* Coleridge wrote *The Ancient Mariner*. The grandiose theory of divine intervention in history became a story of individual salvation; the 'science' which showed nature as God working to establish Pantisocracy and the rule of the Saints gave way to the magic which showed it as God caring for man; versified preaching gave way to poetry. The background to this change was the concept of the Imagination which he began to develop during his conversations with Wordsworth in the latter half of the year. Before we go on from Coleridge's early poems to *The Ancient Mariner* we must examine the beliefs about Nature and the experience of imaginative communion with Nature which Wordsworth brought to the discussions at Alfoxden and Nether Stowey.

3

Wordsworth
and the Religion
of Nature 1791–7

Studies of the early development of Wordsworth's philosophy
give most of their attention to his supposed reading of seven-
teenth- and eighteenth-century metaphysics, and such studies
usually contain the implied premise that he read these books
early in his poetic career. Little reason for reading of this kind
is offered by his other interests and friendships of the time and,
though his friendship with Beaupuy had a decisive effect on
his political opinions, one finds little suggestion in Wordsworthian studies that there was, before his period of close
intimacy with Coleridge, any similar period of stimulating
exchanges directing Wordsworth's attention to new positions
in philosophy. Certainly in the years immediately before 1797
Wordsworth did lead a retired life, but there was at least one
period, his sojourn in Revolutionary France and immediately
afterwards in London, when Wordsworth was in a state of
intellectual excitement and intensely receptive to new ideas.
During this time he was continually in the company of men
who not only shared his new political beliefs but who are
known to have held, or may reasonably be assumed to have
held, beliefs about the physical world of the kind described in
the first chapter. It is not surprising that Wordsworth's

'pantheism' first appeared when he first returned to poetry after this period, nor is it surprising that it appeared then in forms and phrases that point to the theories held by these men rather than to more remote and scholarly origins.

It should be said at once that Wordsworth's own account of his intellectual history in *The Prelude* gives no importance in this respect to his stay in France and that it places the development of his ideas much earlier in his life, during his youth and childhood. Nevertheless it can be shown easily enough that such an account is contradicted by the evidence of poems and letters written at the time. *The Prelude* was, of course, intended to illustrate a theory of Wordsworth's development which he adopted long after the period with which it deals; autobiographers often pre-date their opinions, if only for emotional reasons, and in Wordsworth's case there is the further consideration that his very theories demanded that he place the growth of his beliefs as far back into early youth as possible.[1] Hence they would make him emphasize notions and fancies which did not become seriously held beliefs until much later. Certainly the surviving letters and poems show that, whatever may have been passing in his head, he did not set his ideas to paper until he had spent some time among men who held similar beliefs.

According to *The Prelude*, Wordsworth in his early youth fancifully attributed life to natural objects and this paved the way to the recognition of a real life there. This full recognition took place in his seventeenth year.

> In all things now
> I saw one life, and felt that it was joy.[2]

At Cambridge this belief took a more reasoned form.

[1] The earliest material for *The Prelude* (except the Preamble) was written in 1798 as part of *The Ruined Cottage* (see *The Prelude*, ed. E. de Selincourt, p. xxxiii). There this material described the development of the character of the Pedlar and, as Wordsworth was bound by theory alone, the beliefs were made to appear much earlier in life than they do in *The Prelude*—as early, apparently, as the Pedlar's ninth summer.

[2] *The Prelude* (1805), ii. 429–30.

> A track pursuing not untrod before,
> From deep analogies by thought supplied,
> Or consciousnesses not to be subdued,
> To every natural form, rock, fruit or flower,
> Even the loose stones that cover the high-way,
> I gave a moral life, I saw them feel,
> Or linked them to some feeling. The great mass
> Lay bedded in a quickening soul, and all
> That I beheld respired with inward meaning.[1]

If this was so, nothing of it showed in his letters or his poetry before his return from France. Wordsworth's mysticism alone would not account for his discoveries, for mystical experiences seem to express themselves in terms of the mystic's ordinary religious faith.[2] Thus Wordsworth's letters in 1791 describe his experience in the Simplon Pass in the language of eighteenth-century Christianity, and it was only in 1799 that he remembered it as pantheistic. Similarly, an examination of the early poems shows that, though *Descriptive Sketches* contains what may be a description of a state of ecstasy,[3] yet in the early autumn of 1792, when he was finishing that poem by the banks of the Loire the beliefs that moved him to verse do not seem to have gone beyond simple Rousseausim. On the other hand, when he next wrote verse, early in 1794,[4] he had acquired some of his most characteristic beliefs and his opinions then were almost exactly those which *The Prelude* ascribes to his Cambridge days. It seems tolerably certain that

---

[1] id., III. 121–9.

[2] See E. Aegerter, *Le Mysticisme*, a comparative study of Christian, Moslem and Indian mysticism.

[3] *Descriptive Sketches* (1793), ll. 541–55. The description of ecstatic states here, in the additions to *An Evening Walk*, and in the *Lines left upon a Seat in a Yew-Tree*, negates the suggestion by L. Lemonnier, *Les Poètes romantiques anglais*, and M. Sherwood, *Coleridge's Imaginative Concept of Imagination*, that Wordsworth derived his knowledge of such states from Plotinus via Coleridge. For a suggestion that Coleridge himself got them from Hartley rather than Plotinus, see H. N. Fairchild, 'Hartley, Pistorius and Coleridge' in *PMLA* (1947).

[4] In the corrections to *An Evening Walk. Poetical Works*, ed. E. de Selincourt, i, pp. 10–12.

he actually adopted these beliefs between October 1792 and April 1794.

The usual accounts[1] of how he acquired these ideas give as their sources English metaphysical or theological works of the seventeenth or early eighteenth century—those leather-bound folios which adorned Wordsworth's library when he died a pillar of the Anglican Church sixty years later. It seems most unlikely that the young revolutionary of 1792 to 1794 would either have possessed them or been attracted by them; indeed it is difficult even to imagine him reading them in a period spent in Revolutionary Paris, among Unitarians and radicals in London, and in solitary walking tours of the English countryside. On the other hand a close examination of the circles in which Wordsworth moved during this period will show that they were pervaded by pantheistic or quasi-pantheistic ideas of the kind which he was to adopt and that, moreover, when Wordsworth first came to set down those ideas the form they took and the phrases in which they were expressed were close to those of the circles he had not long left: it was much later that his doctrine came to resemble more closely that of the English divines. In 1794 all the probabilities are on the side of France and radicalism.

With this in mind it is worth examining both the people among whom Wordsworth moved in London and Paris and the ideas which they held. There is always a current of ideas in Paris but in 1792 it was a torrent. The Revolution attracted men with new or odd ideas, and M. Mathiez, in his study *La Révolution et les Etrangers*, considers that it was the interest of the Girondins in philosophic and literary ideas that attached

[1] J. W. Beach, *The Concept of Nature in Nineteenth Century English Poetry*, allows the possible influence of certain French writers (see below) but he puts more weight on such earlier English writers as Cudworth, Berkeley and Hale. S. G. Dunn, 'Wordsworth's Metaphysical System' in *Essays and Studies* (1932), argues for the influence of Newton's ideas; the resemblance between these and certain aspects of Wordsworth's later pantheism or panentheism is strong, but the resemblance is much less when we consider the 1794 corrections to *An Evening Walk* (discussed below) with their strong animistic belief in the life of natural objects.

the English and Americans in Paris to that party.[1] Besides the Irish republicans, American democrats and South American nationalists who brought their causes to Paris, there were foreign vegetarians, rationalists, Unitarians and Children of Nature. Priestley's friends and followers were especially active, and Thomas Cooper, James Watt Junior, Hurford Stone, James Macintosh, William Priestley and his cousin Thomas Christie were all mentioned in British Foreign Office despatches.[2] The best known of the prophets of Nature was David Williams, but a rather different philosophy was represented by 'Walking' Stewart, the 'first man of nature'. Stewart, the Unitarians, and many of the Girondins held, in differing forms, a common philosophy of Nature and with these Wordsworth himself was in contact.

Though this was one of the formative periods of Wordsworth's life, a period when he was eagerly and intensely receptive of new ideas, it is not easy to reconstruct the effect of this atmosphere on the poet. In particular there is not much contemporary documentary evidence for either his opinions or his acquaintance at this time because, during the years when Pitt was prosecuting (and sometimes hanging) radicals, most of them burned their correspondence, and when an acquaintanceship was recalled in later years, the acquaintances were no longer interested in their early opinions. An anecdote from Muirhead's *Life of James Watt* illustrates this.

'I went over to Paris'—said the late poet Wordsworth to us, in one of those hours which his presence and converse winged with unfailing delight—'at the time of the Revolution in 1792 or 1793, and so was *pretty hot in it*; but found Mr. J. Watt there before me and quite as warm in the same cause. We thus both began life as

[1] A. Mathiez, *La Révolution et les Etrangers*, p. 46.

[2] W. Eden, Lord Auckland, *The Journal and Correspondence of William, Lord Auckland*, p. 437. Auckland confused the Priestleys. The Wilson mentioned as Watt's friend and companion is presumably John Wilson of Ainsworth, another Unitarian chemist interested in dyeing (see R. V. Holt, *The Unitarian Contribution to Social Progress*, pp. 50–1). Wilson's name disappeared from the membership list of the Manchester Literary and Philosophical Society, along with the names of Cooper and Watt, at this time.

thoughtless radicals; but we have both become in the course of our lives, *as all sensible men, I think, have done,* good soberminded Conservatives!'[1]

The J. Watt here mentioned was the engineer's son, James Watt Junior,[2] who was one of Wordsworth's three known acquaintances in Paris. What light there is to be had on this period of Wordsworth's life must come from identifying these acquaintances, discovering their opinions, noting anything relevant to Wordsworth in the 'climate of opinion' of the Girondist circles in which he is also said to have moved, and attempting from this to form some picture of Wordsworth's life in the revolutionary capital.

Wordsworth presumably owed his introduction to Watt to the Unitarian poetess Miss Charlotte Smith, whom he met in Brighton when he was on his way to Paris and she returning. She gave him a number of letters to her friends in Paris, the only one of which the address is known being to another Unitarian poetess, Helen Maria Williams.[3] He missed her but he met Watt who showed him over the city and took him to the Jacobin Club, of which Watt was a member, and to the National Assembly. Watt was, as far as one can tell,[4] another Unitarian, and like so many of them, he was deeply involved in the Revolution. With Thomas Cooper, he was a delegate to the National Assembly from the Manchester Constitutional

[1] J. P. Muirhead, *Life of James Watt*, p. 480.

[2] *DNB*, xx, p. 973.

[3] *Early Letters of William and Dorothy Wordsworth*, ed. E. de Selincourt, pp. 66–7.

[4] Watt was the friend and follower of Thomas Cooper, the Unitarian materialist, in both the Manchester Literary and Philosophical Society and the Manchester Constitutional Society (D. Malone, *The Public Life of Thomas Cooper* (1926), pp. 9, 27–31). Unfortunately the records of the former society, in which Cooper's materialism was debated acrimoniously, have been destroyed, and so it is impossible to get clear proof of Watt's opinions, but he certainly supported Cooper in the disputes leading up to the formation of the Constitutional Society, in which Cooper's Unitarianism was again a point of attack, and his long harmonious association with an active propagandist for Unitarianism and materialism makes it reasonable to assume that these were his own beliefs. See also p. 64, n. 2.

Society, and in later years he claimed to have been intimate with the leading French revolutionary politicians—so much so as to have dissuaded Danton and Robespierre from fighting a duel. Wordsworth could have had little time with him in 1791, but he intended to renew the acquaintance when he returned to the city in 1792.

Whether in fact he met Watt again is uncertain, for a letter preserved in the French Archives[1] shows that the latter left France for Naples 'in the autumn' of 1792, and this may have been before or after Wordsworth's arrival there in October. Watt's account was that he left because he had incurred the hostility of Robespierre, and this would suggest November, the period of the attacks on Robespierre by the Rolandists and Brissotins and of Robespierre's expulsion of these enemies from the Jacobin Club.

It is interesting that another of Wordsworth's acquaintances, Thomas Bailie, recounted that at about this time he warned Wordsworth of the danger he ran from his political connections,[2] and that the poet's nephew wrote that if Wordsworth had remained in Paris he would have perished with the Brissotins, with whom, wrote Christopher Wordsworth, he was intimately connected.[3] A further indication that Wordsworth may have moved in the same circles as Watt, may be provided by the facts that on the poet's return to London his chief friend was William Nicholson,[4] who was, like Watt, a

[1] Archives Nationales, Carton F7-4774(31), communicated to me by Mr J. Cobb.

[2] A. A. Watts, *Alaric Watts*, ii, p. 286. M. Moorman, *William Wordsworth*, i, p. 203, states, without discussion, that Wordsworth's only certain acquaintance in Paris was Watt. As the evidence for Watt is that reported by Muirhead (see p. 65, n. 1), the direct and unequivocal report by De Quincey is at least as strong for Stewart also. (Moorman's lack of discussion makes it difficult to know whether she was aware of this evidence.) Bailie's claim rests on his own statement to Alaric Watts, but Stewart's apparent acquiescence would strengthen the claim, in which there is nothing inherently improbable. Watts met Bailie in 1814 at Stewart's house in London.

[3] C. Wordsworth, *Memoirs of William Wordsworth*, i, pp. 76–7.

[4] *Poetical Works of William Wordsworth*, ed. E. de Selincourt, v, p. 374.

radical, a Unitarian and a chemist, and who was also the former agent of Watt's friends the Wedgwoods; that he there attended a Unitarian Chapel;[1] and that his poems were published by the leading Unitarian printer, Joseph Johnson[2]—all of which would point to introductions obtained in Paris. The exact nature of Wordsworth's connections with the Girondists will probably remain forever a mystery, but the connection with Watt offers some explanation of how an unknown youth like Wordsworth could find himself in touch with important political circles, and perhaps makes the lines of *The Prelude* in which Wordsworth says that he contemplated plunging into politics and offering himself as a leader just a little less absurd.

Thomas Bailie,[3] whom Wordsworth presumably met at Stewart's house in Paris, is a figure of less importance hitherto only known as a mis-spelt surname in Alaric Watts' memoirs, where he is described simply as 'an old republican'. He was, in fact, an Irish republican who fled to France after the arrest of General O'Connor in 1798 and on that occasion it was not he but his companion Hamilton who was known to the politicians of the Directorate. There is no extant evidence concerning Bailie's activities in France in 1792, and the only hint of his political connections is a family tradition[4] that his second son, Thomas Maubourg Bailie, born in 1797, was named after French friends. This would point to a connection with the Latour-Maubourgs and so with the Lafayette group. In any case his warning to Wordsworth implied that his political connections were different from Wordsworth's, and more moderate, for he called Wordsworth's friends 'the mountain'.

[1] id., pp. 374–5, and H. McLachlan, *The Unitarian Movement*, p. 275.

[2] H. McLachlan, *The Unitarian Movement*, p. 173.

[3] See p. 66, n. 2 above. The only further information about Bailie is to be found in the Archives Nationales, Cartons F7/6152, F7/3564, F7/6463 and Register A B/355, and in G. A. Bailie, *History of the Family of Bailie etc.* where he appears in a family tree. He was imprisoned in the Temple in 1804 for suspected espionage and deported to America in 1807.

[4] Communicated to me by Mrs C. W. H. Bailie of Manderstone, Berwickshire.

The third acquaintance was less important politically than Watt, but he may have been more important to Wordsworth's development. Whether or not Wordsworth moved much in Girondist circles, he certainly spent some time with 'Walking' Stewart and, De Quincey tells us, was 'captivated by his eloquence'.[1] Stewart was a notable eccentric, given to long walking tours of Asia, Europe and America, but despite his oddnesses he had some powers of mind: he was a Fellow of the Royal Society[2] and he was later to hold the friendship of such men as Robert Owen the socialist and Thomas Taylor the Platonist, who attended his lectures and soirées in London. Stewart's whole history[3] suggests that he was not much interested in politics (he was in Paris because he had invested his money in French securities) and the fact that it fell to his friend Bailie to warn Wordsworth of political dangers would seem to bear this out. Stewart's master-passion was his 'religion of Nature', which will be described later but which can be summarized as being a pantheistic creed involving a living, active universe of the kind described in the first chapter of this book. Stewart devoted his life to the propagation of this religion and it formed the subject of the lectures which he gave during his travels. There can be little doubt that at his house in Paris he would have been the chief talker and his 'religion of Nature' the chief topic.

The picture of Wordsworth's life in Paris which emerges from all this is not very clear, but the main lines of it would seem to be that Wordsworth had some connection with Girondist circles through Watt, who was more important and much better known in these circles than Wordsworth, and who possibly left Paris in October or November not long after Wordsworth returned there; that Wordsworth may well have known other Englishmen of Watt's radical and Unitarian

---

[1] T. De Quincey, *Collected Works*, vii, p. 8; xii, pp. 59–60; *DNB*, xviii, p. 1218.

[2] *Philosophical Transactions*, lxvii (1777), i, p. 6 and ii, p. 465, where Stewart's account of Tibet was first printed. The British Museum Catalogue confirms the identification.

[3] *DNB*, xviii, pp. 1215–18.

type; but that his involvement in French circles and French politics was not so deep that it did not leave him with evenings to spend at Stewart's house listening to Stewart's talk. In short, Wordsworth's role was probably that of a spectator and listener in the various houses to which he was invited.

There are then three groups to be distinguished among Wordsworth's acquaintance of this period and it is interesting that the doctrine of living nature was current in all three. The first group is the Unitarians, the only group whose influence extended on into the time spent in London. It should be noted that though Wordsworth's only religious observance at this time seems to have been attendance at a Unitarian chapel, yet he never seems to have become an adherent and that when 'living nature' appeared in Wordsworth's poetry in 1794, it was in a more pantheistic dress than the Unitarians gave it. Nevertheless he could hardly have escaped hearing their doctrine.

The second group is the Girondists. Here we have the evidence of Garat for the popularity of the new pantheism in Girondist circles, while among possible influences from this current of thought we can number Beaupuy whose family library was lined with the works of the Encyclopaedists.[1] To this period too can plausibly be assigned Wordsworth's first acquaintance with two books in which Professor J. Warren Beach has found a number of parallels to Wordsworth's words and phrases.[2] These are d'Holbach's *Système de la Nature*, which was in Wordsworth's library at his death, and which argues that apparently inanimate objects are not 'dead' but act by their own forces, and Volney's *Les Ruines des Empires*, which was in 1792 at the height of its enormous popularity, and which expresses a pantheistic doctrine in such phrases as

[1] E. Legouis, *Early Life of William Wordsworth*, p. 203.

[2] J. W. Beach, *The Concept of Nature in Nineteenth Century English Poetry*, pp. 118–20. While noticing the possible influence of these books, Professor Beach is inclined to put more weight on earlier English writers such as Cudworth, Berkeley and Hale, whose works were in Wordsworth's library at his death. It seems much more probable that these were purchases of Wordsworth's orthodox period; they seem very unlikely reading for him in 1792–4.

'âme universelle des êtres', 'moteur mystérieux de la nature' and 'puissance mystérieux qui anime l'univers'. If Wordsworth was influenced by these in forming his philosophy of nature then this would have been the time when they attracted him. Even apart from the possibilities of direct debt which Professor Beach suggests, these books formed an important part of the intellectual atmosphere during Wordsworth's sojourn in France.

Of the persons whom he might have met at Stewart's house, only Bailie can be identified, but this hardly matters, for on those evenings Stewart himself would certainly have held the floor and indeed De Quincey has recorded Wordsworth's own statement about this eloquence.[1] There can be little doubt as to the subject of this eloquence, for Stewart, to the end of his life, was the indefatigable preacher of a 'religion of Nature', set out in a score of volumes published at his own expense, the first of which had appeared the year before Wordsworth met him. These he implored his friends to bury safely for future ages and he asked De Quincey to translate the system into Latin so that it might survive the decay of the English language.[2]

De Quincey described this religion as Spinozan and on another occasion compared Stewart's system of ideas with Schelling's:[3] on the other hand it has been called materialist and an account of his life later formed the first of a series of twopenny tracts on materialism.[4] In fact, when stripped of its bizarre extravagances, it turns out to be a system very close to those which have just been considered. Stewart believed, like Diderot, that atoms experienced 'sufferings and enjoyments' and that a multiplied state of these formed 'the patient feeling of a whole system' or 'mode'—i.e. an organized body;[5] hence 'all matter or nature' was 'co-equal, co-interested and co-eternal in good and evil'.[6] Man was such a mode or system organized 'to effect sensate good'[7] and mankind

[1] See p. 68, n. 1 above. [2] *DNB*, xviii, pp. 1215–18.
[3] T. De Quincey, *Collected Works*, vii, p. 8; xii, p. 59.
[4] C., J.W. *Phases of Thought No. 1* (London, 1861).
[5] J. Stewart, *The Sophiometer* (1818?), p. 27. [6] id., p. 128. [7] id., p. 129.

were 'the instruments of nature in its moral motion, formed
to procure well-being or happiness to all animated matter'.[1]
Thus Stewart's system differed from the general pattern of
contemporary French 'systems of nature' chiefly in that he
recognized that if all organized forms of nature were in fact
alive and capable of feeling (and among his 'modes' he recognized 'plants, fossils, minerals and other organic and inorganic
masses'[2]) then these forms must be given the moral consideration due to all living beings. Man must 'do no violence to any
part of animate matter' and by this means he 'produces and
eternizes a system of moral harmony . . . which passes through
every part of matter'.[3] Such a thorough going deduction from
a theory of natural philosophy to a rule of conduct is characteristic enough of Stewart's eccentricity but it is understandable that Wordsworth, at least, should have found his eloquence interesting.

To sum up, Wordsworth was in touch during 1792 and 1793
with a number of men who held a doctrine of life in natural
objects very like that which first appeared in his poetry in 1794
and in these men the doctrine went hand in hand with the
radicalism which Wordsworth had now adopted. Of the seven
men whom he can be shown to have known between his arrival
in France in 1791 and his departure from London in 1793,
Beaupuy was a French radical nurtured in the doctrines of
the Encyclopaedists: Watt, Nicholson, Johnson and Fawcett
were English Unitarians; Stewart held a doctrine of nature
related to both these traditions; Bailie alone seems to have no
particular connection with them. The doctrines which these
men held, those which Wordsworth set out in the corrections
to *The Evening Walk* in 1794, and those which Coleridge
expounded in *Joan of Arc* differed from what Abrams describes as 'Isaac Newton's ubiquitous God, constituting duration and space and sustaining by his presence the laws of

---

[1] J. Stewart, *The Apocalypse of Nature* (1790?), p. 143.

[2] *The Sophiometer*, p. 128.

[3] *The Apocalypse of Nature*, p. 143. This attitude to other forms of
being possibly reflects Stewart's long sojourn in the East and his
acquaintance with Eastern religion.

motion and gravitation, and the World-Soul of the ancient Stoics and Platonists . . . dwelling amicably together in the nature-poetry of the eighteenth century'[1] in that the newer doctrine stressed an independent life and sensibility in every organized form of being, even those apparently inanimate, and this opened the way for the possibility, already recognized by Stewart, of a moral relationship between man and natural objects. To see Wordsworth against the background of this tradition explains the close parallelism between the early development of his ideas and that of Coleridge's; while the probability that Wordsworth met the tradition as something subsidiary to, and part of, French radicalism explains the strong pantheism and the lack of connection with revealed religion in his ideas which led Coleridge to call him a semi-atheist.[2] Certainly in this milieu Wordsworth would have found new concepts in which to express and to explain his mystical ecstasies.

The Prelude records that it was during the next year, 1793, that Wordsworth began to have fresh insight into the life of nature,

> That in life's everyday appearances
> I seemed about this period to have sight
> Of a new world, a world, too, that was fit
> To be transmitted and made visible
> To other eyes, as having for its base
> That whence our dignity originates.[3]

This new world entered his poetry for the first time in 1794, in the corrections which he was then making to *An Evening Walk*.

> A heart that vibrates evermore, awake
> To feeling for all forms that Life can take,
> That wider still its sympathy extends
> And sees not any line where being ends;
> Sees sense, through Nature's rudest forms betrayed,
> Tremble obscure in fountain, rock and shade,

---

[1] M. H. Abrams, *The Mirror and the Lamp*, p. 64.
[2] *Collected Letters*, i, p. 216.   [3] *The Prelude* (1805), XII. 369–74.

And while a secret power these forms endears
Their social accent never vainly hears.[1]

These lines might epitomize the whole new creed as it had developed in France. Its key words—Nature, life, sense, forms, secret power—are the favourites both of the later *philosophes* and of the mature Wordsworth. But the lines differ from the philosophers' speculations in two ways. They describe an emotional experience in which the forms are endeared to the beholder, and these forms speak with a social accent—that is, they have some significance for his life among men. Such significance is characteristic of mystical experiences.[2] The lines seem to be not a statement of theory but a description of the experiences which Wordsworth had begun to have in 1793, and which were to shape his interpretation of the doctrine he had met in Paris.

Another of these corrections shows that he was using the word 'forms' as Robinet and other *philosophes* had used it, to mean organized bodies of sentient matter. The correction also shows that Wordsworth then traced his belief in the life of nature more to science than to that fancy which *The Prelude* gives as the only source.

And are there souls whose languid powers unite
No interest to each rural sound or sight. . . .
How different with those favoured souls who, taught
By active Fancy or by patient Thought,
See common forms prolong the endless chain
Of joy and grief, of pleasure and of pain;
But chiefly those to whom the harmonious doors
Of Science have unbarred celestial stores. . . .
With them the sense no trivial object knows,
Oft at its meanest touch their spirit glows,
And proud beyond all limits to aspire
Mounts through the fields of thought on wings of fire.

[1] *Poetical Works*, ed. E. de Selincourt, i, p. 10. The publication of these additions disposes of the suggestion made by C. Cestre, *La Révolution française et les poètes anglais*, and others, that Coleridge was the source of Wordsworth's ideas on the life in Nature.

[2] See E. Aegerter, *Le Mysticisme*, p. 27.

But sure with tenfold pleasure they behold
The powers of Nature in each various mould,
If like the Sun their (   ) love surrounds
The various world to life's remotest bounds,
Yet not extinguishes the warmer fire
Round which the close domestic train retire.[1]

In the Associationist philosophy which was popular in England, the word 'forms' meant those shapes which were perceived as simple ideas, and it might as well refer to a table as a tree. Clearly, Wordsworth's 'common forms' which 'prolong the endless chain Of joy and grief, of pleasure and of pain' do not bear this meaning, nor, in the preceding quotation, do those 'rudest forms' which still possess 'sense' that can 'tremble obscure'. Here 'form' seems to mean any organized natural body, and the implication is that such bodies have life and sensibility. This is the sense of the word 'form' which Diderot employed when, to summarize his belief that every organized body of matter, however small or apparently inanimate, had its own little degree of feeling and perception, he wrote that 'every form has the happiness or the unhappiness which is proper to it',[2] and Robinet was using the word in the same sense when he postulated that 'material forms' are only produced by being 'animated' by the 'active power', 'organic living and animal', which is 'the foundation of the visible world'.[3] Whatever has form in this sense has organized being, independent life and feeling. To contemplate the forms is to contemplate their life and that life of the universe of which it is part.

The years 1793 and 1794 seem to have been those in which Wordsworth absorbed the new philosophy of nature and began to apply it to his own experience. It is quite probable that he had experienced moments of ecstasy in his childhood, but he was now, as he had not been before, equipped with a theory which explained them both in religious and scientific terms as a direct contact with the divine principle of the world. This

[1] *Poetical Works*, i, pp. 12–13.   [2] See pp. 20, 24–5 above.
[3] J. B. R. Robinet, *Considerations philosophiques de la gradation naturelle des formes de l'être*, pp. 5–12.

was perhaps the first time that the new philosophy had reached a poet of original mind who was already a lover of natural scenery and steeped in eighteenth-century nature poetry, so it is not surprising that it should be given a less abstract turn. Moreover, at this time, Wordsworth was a lonely man in a world where events stronger than his will had swept the control of his life out of his hands. Reconciliation to life for him meant the contemplation of Necessity and reconciliation with it. He desperately needed to find a religious system in which to believe.

So far, the ideas which he had adopted explained only the moments of ecstasy. They had not been tested by any attempt to explain the miseries of the world, and to those that mourn they had nothing to say. The impulse to work out his ideas thoroughly seems to have come from the contemplation of suffering and despair, and it was in the years when he was

> oppressed by sense
> Of instability, revolt, decay,
> And change and emptiness.[1]

and learned to overcome it, that Wordsworth elaborated his theories into a quasi-religion.

The moods of ecstatic insight which Wordsworth experienced in his solitary wanderings of 1793, were soon succeeded by the despair which followed his brief conversion to Godwinism and his disillusionment with it. In 1795 he tried to analyse the despairing mind in a fragment, *Incipient Madness*, which recounts a visit to a ruined cottage. The mood, as he described it, was marked by a rebellion against the laws of nature, as the other mood had been by sympathy with nature. In short, the two states were those which he would later have described as the imaginative and the fanciful.

> She said: 'that wagon does not care for us'—
> The words were simple, but her look and voice
> Made up their meaning and bespoke a mind
> Which being long neglected, and denied
> The common food of hope, was now become
> Sick and extravagant,—by strong access

[1] *The Excursion*, III. 137–9.

> Of momentary pangs driven to that state
> In which all past experience melts away,
> And the rebellious heart to its own will
> Fashions the laws of nature.[1]

The visit to this cottage was an experience to which Wordsworth returned often in his later thinking; he made it the subject of *The Ruined Cottage*, and out of material originally written for that poem grew both *The Prelude* and *The Excursion*. For the moment Wordsworth was content to contrast the two states of mind—despair with its fanciful attempts to subject nature to the morbid mind, and ecstasy, subjecting the mind to nature and finding human significance there. This contrast was the theme of his most successful early poem, *Lines left upon a Seat in a Yew-Tree*, written in 1795.

>   he many an hour
> A morbid pleasure nourished, tracing here
> An emblem of his own unfruitful life:
> And, lifting up his head, he then would gaze
> On the more distant scene,—how lovely 'tis
> Thou seest,—and he would gaze till it became
> Far lovelier, and his heart could not sustain
> The beauty, still more beauteous! Nor, that time,
> When Nature had subdued him to herself,
> Would he forget those Beings to whose minds,
> Warm from the labours of benevolence,
> The world, and human life, appeared a scene
> Of kindred loveliness: then he would sigh,
> Inly disturbed, to think that others felt
> What he must never feel: and so, lost Man!
> On visionary views would Fancy feed
> Till his eye streamed with tears . . .
> If Thou be one whose heart the holy forms
> Of young imagination have kept pure,
> Stranger! henceforth be warned; and know that pride,
> Howe'er disguised in its own majesty,
> Is littleness; that he, who feels contempt
> For any living thing, hath faculties
> Which he has never used.[2]

[1] *Incipient Madness*, ll. 56–65.
[2] *Lines left upon a Seat in a Yew-Tree*, ll. 30–54.

Thus Wordsworth's experiences had deepened the philosophical speculations on living nature into a belief in the possibility of real contact with the life in nature—a contact in which the forms of nature made, as it were, a language. But his experience had taught him also that the language could be misunderstood—the forms misread—by a rebellious mind seeking emblems of its own despair. Later, in the Solitary's description of

> a troubled mind:
> That, in a struggling and distempered world,
> Saw a seductive image of herself,

he suggested that there could seem to be two kinds of nature.

> Here Nature was my guide,
> The Nature of the dissolute; but thee,
> O fostering Nature! I rejected—smiled
> At others tears in pity; and in scorn
> At those, which thy soft influence sometimes drew
> From my unguarded heart.[1]

But the Solitary was the *advocatus diaboli* of *The Excursion*, or as near as Wordsworth could come to such a figure. Wordsworth himself continued to distinguish the two moods as those of the rebellious spirit and the spirit subdued to Nature.

> A plastic power
> Abode with me, a forming hand, at times
> Rebellious, acting in a devious mood,
> A local spirit of its own, at war
> With general tendency, but for the most
> Subservient strictly to the external things
> With which it communed.[2]

In *The Excursion* he elaborated this to show five different responses to the same natural scene. First the Wanderer describes his response, which is imaginative, recognizing 'a semblance strange of power intelligent' and

> Measuring through all degrees, until the scale
> Of time and conscious nature disappear,
> Lost in unsearchable eternity![3]

[1] *The Excursion*, III. 808–12.
[2] *The Prelude* (1805), II. 381–7.   [3] *The Excursion*, III. 110–12.

Then the Solitary describes two responses, that of the Fancy, 'beguiling harmlessly the listless hours' by tracing humorous resemblances, and that of the same mind oppressed by sense of change and emptiness, when the contemplation feeds 'Pity and scorn and melancholy pride'. He then points out the different response of the botanist or mineralogist and the Wanderer in turn points to the child, 'Dame Nature's pupil of the lowest form'. This careful elaboration is an interesting example of the continuity of Wordsworth's thought, and of its dependence on his earlier experiences.

What Wordsworth meant at this time by the forms of nature and their 'social accents' is less clear, though the subject occupied his mind in the following years. It would seem that he regarded the natural forms as outward and visible expressions of the spiritual force in nature. A fragment written at Alfoxden reads

> And never for each other shall we feel
> As we may feel, till we have sympathy
> With nature in her forms inanimate,
> With objects such as have no power to hold
> Articulate language. In all forms of things
> There is a mind.[1]

The Excursion says the same thing more clearly.

> There is an active principle alive
> In all things, in all natures, in the flowers
> And in the trees
>
> . . .
>
> All beings have their properties which spread
> Beyond themselves, a power by which they make
> Some other being conscious of their life,
> Spirit that knows no insulated spot,
> No chasm, no solitude; from link to link
> It circulates, the Soul of all the worlds.[2]

Thus the Spirit makes its life known through the Forms, and the whole doctrine rests on an emotional, and perhaps mystical

---

[1] *Poetical Works*, v, p. 340.

[2] *The Excursion*, IX. 1–15 and app. crit. The lines are quoted in the form they had in MS 18A, written in 1798–9.

response to them. When this response is made in submission
to Nature, and with a sense of her laws and purposes, then
'an auxiliar light' comes from the mind, adding beauty and
human meaning to the landscape.

Wordsworth then had come to some of his most important
beliefs long before Coleridge visited Alfoxden in June 1797.
Those beliefs had a good deal in common with the ones which
Coleridge had reached on his own account. It is interesting
that one of the first results of the meeting was a note from
Wordsworth to Joseph Cottle, asking the bookseller to send a
copy of Darwin's *Zoonomia* post-haste, and telling him that
a copy could be borrowed, if necessary, from Tom Wedgwood's library. It is impossible to say which poet was introducing the other to this book, for its doctrine of living force in
matter was one which they both believed.

Nevertheless each poet had something to add to the other's
theories. Coleridge believed that the influence of nature (and
hence of God in nature) worked by education, often involving
terror. Following Hartley he believed that the purpose of this
education was a knowledge of the divine[1] and that the period
of direct influence (until the coming Apocalypse) was the
childhood of the man or of the race.[2] On the other hand
Wordsworth believed in the possibility of direct communion
with Nature and of direct insight into her life.

Again, for Coleridge, Nature was symbolical, by which he
meant that its appearances were designed to impress the mind
of man and to bring him to know God. For Wordsworth the
forms of nature were expressive of an independent life which
was to be known and loved for its own sake and this love
brought with it illumination and benevolence towards all life.
The theory which emerged from the discussions between the
two poets took account of both sets of views.

The word around which the emerging theory crystallized
was Imagination. Each poet had at first rested his views of

---

[1] *Religious Musings*, ll. 40–4 and note.
[2] *The Destiny of Nations*, ll. 18–23 and app. crit., 77–86; *Religious Musings*, ll. 208–12.

the natural world chiefly on science. For Wordsworth the
'favoured souls' were

> chiefly those to whom the harmonious doors
> Of science have unbarred celestial stores . . .[1]

while Coleridge's elaborate mathematical arguments in *Joan
of Arc* and his attention to Darwin's science and Priestley's
experiments have already been noticed. The request for
Zoonomia would indicate that the scientific basis of their ideas
remained but each had also named 'Fancy' as an important
agent of knowledge. For Coleridge

> Fancy is the power
> That first unsensualizes the dark mind,[2]

while Wordsworth's favoured soul could be taught

> By active Fancy or by patient Thought,[3]

More recently, in the *Lines on a Seat in a Yew-Tree* Wordsworth had used the word Imagination to describe the power
of true response to Nature and, in doing so, he had brought
into the discussion what was already a potent word. Many of
the points of Coleridge's later theory are to be found scattered
throughout eighteenth-century writings and the imagination
had already been described in different places as intuitive,
superior to reason, and creative.[4] These suggestions of supra-
rational power, and also the part which the word played in
theories seeking to explain the mind's contact with the external
world, made it a very suitable word for all that Wordsworth
and Coleridge were now trying to clarify.

At this point the emergence of the theory of the Imagination
can be traced most easily in Coleridge's writing. During the
Wordsworths' visit to Stowey, later in the same month of
June, he wrote his first 'Wordsworthian' poem, *This Lime-
Tree Bower my Prison*. In it he accepted the idea that the
Universal Spirit may reveal himself directly:

[1] *Poetical Works*, ed. E. de Selincourt, i, pp. 12–13 app. crit.
[2] *The Destiny of Nations*, ll. 80–1.   [3] *Poetical Works*, i, pp. 12–13.
[4] Wilma L. Kennedy, *The English Heritage of Coleridge of Bristol*,
pp. 91–2.

> Struck with joy's deepest calm, and gazing round
> On the wide view, may gaze till all doth seem
> Less gross than bodily, a living Thing
> That acts upon the mind, and with such hues
> As cloathe the Almighty Spirit when he makes
> Spirits perceive his presence.[1]

The peculiar phrasing of 'gazing . . . may gaze till . . .' reveals that the experience here is that described in *Lines left upon a Seat in a Yew-Tree* which had now become his favourite poem.[2] Until now Coleridge had believed with Hartley that development lay away from sense towards concept: the mind had to be 'unsensualized'. This view is interestingly shown in a note in Coleridge's hand in the back fly-leaf of his copy of Hartley's *Observations* (now in the British Museum):

Ideas may become as vivid and distinct, and the feelings accompanying them as vivid, as the original sense-impressions—and thus finally make a man independent of his senses—one use of poetry.

Now he had accepted the opposite idea of a direct revelation in sense-experience and with it the belief that the forms of nature have a quite direct influence on the gazer:

> A Delight
> Comes sudden on my heart, and I am glad
> As I myself were there. Nor in this bower
> Want I sweet sounds or pleasing shapes . . .
> . . . Henceforth I shall know

[1] *Collected Letters*, i, p. 335. In a note to the lines quoted Coleridge wrote, 'You remember, I am a *Berkleian*.' He may have equated Wordsworth's spirit of the universe with Berkeley's *animus mundi*, but if the note was meant as a claim to originality, then the phrasing of 'gazing . . . may gaze till . . .' betrays his debt to Wordsworth.

The poem is Wordsworthian in that it involves the idea of a direct contact with nature. H. J. W. Milley, 'Some Notes on Coleridge's *Eolian Harp*' in *MP* (1939), has suggested that that poem is the stylistic source for the Wordsworthian conversation poem. The further suggestion that it is the source for Wordsworth's ideas is not tenable both because the characteristic Wordsworthian idea of contact and communion with nature was not in *The Eolian Harp* and because its ideas were to be found in Wordsworth's poetry as early as 1794 (see p. 73, n. 1).

[2] He quoted it to Lamb (G. McL. Harper, *William Wordsworth*, p. 237) and to Southey (*Collected Letters*, i, p. 334).

That nature ne'er deserts the wise and pure;
No scene so narrow but may well employ
Each faculty of sense, and keep the heart
Awake to Love and Beauty.[1]

On his part, Wordsworth came to accept Hartley's three ages of man—childhood, youth, and manhood—and to make them the basis of his poetical autobiography. The *Lines left upon a Seat in a Yew-Tree* suggest that the influence of nature in youth already formed part of his ideas, but the first poetic treatment of infancy came early in 1798 in Coleridge's lines on young Hartley at the end of *The Nightingale*. It is a sign of the close interweaving of the two poets' ideas at this time that the first poetic statement of this typically Wordsworthian theme should have been written in Wordsworthian language by Coleridge. It would seem to be through the consideration of this topic of childhood and the 'young imagination' of Wordsworth's *Lines*, which must have formed an important topic of conversation between the two poets, that Coleridge arrived in the October of 1797 at the conception of 'the truth of the Imagination' which was to be so important to English romanticism. On October 16th Coleridge wrote two letters which show that he had formed a theory of the Imagination, closer to Wordsworth's ideas than his later and more celebrated theory, and yet foreshadowing it. In one of these letters, to Poole, he thinks of the Imagination as a power to 'sense' in nature that universal spirit which others can know only by reasoned deduction from simple impressions.

For from my early reading of Fairy Tales, and Genii, etc., etc.,—my mind had been habituated *to the Vast*—and I never regarded *my senses* in any way as the criteria of my belief. I regulated all my creeds by my conceptions not by my *sight*—even at that age. Should children be permitted to read Romances, and Relations of Giants and Magicians, and Genii?—I know all that has been said against it; but I have formed my faith in the affirmative.—I know no other way of giving the mind a love of 'the Great' and 'the Whole'.—Those who have been led to the same truths step by step thro' the constant testimony of their senses, seem to me to want

[1] *Collected Letters*, i, p. 336.

a sense which I possess—They contemplate nothing but *parts*—
and all *parts* are necessarily little . . . They . . . uniformly put the
negation of a power for the possession of a power—and called the
want of imagination Judgement, and the never being moved to
Rapture Philosophy![1]

Wordsworth's own explanation of how the 'young imagination' learns to give human meaning to the forms will be discussed later. Here the important thing is that Coleridge sets
Imagination against Judgement and that he regards the
Imagination as a means of finding the truth, independent of
the Reason and superior to it. The knowledge which the
Imagination gives, in this case of the unity and greatness of
things, is not different from that given by the reason rightly
used, but the Imagination arrives at this knowledge more
quickly and more certainly.

In the other letter, to Thelwall, Coleridge applied this idea
of the Imagination to the Wordsworthian communion with
nature.

My mind feels as if it ached to behold and know something *great*—
something *one* and *indivisible*—and it is only in the faith of this
that rocks or waterfalls, mountains or caverns give me the sense
of sublimity or majesty!—But in this faith *all things* counterfeit
infinity!—

> 'Struck with the deepest calm of joy', I stand
> Silent with swimming sense; and gazing round
> On the wide landscape, gaze till all doth seem
> Less gross than bodily, a living Thing
> Which acts upon the mind, and with such hues
> As cloath th' Almighty Spirit, when he makes
> Spirits perceive his presence.[2]

Coleridge and Wordsworth were both seeking contact with
the Divine in Nature, and for them, at this time, the Imagination was essentially a power of direct knowledge and understanding. It was important poetically not because it was a
power of *poetical* creativeness but because it was an immense
and real enrichment of experience. It opened their experience

[1] id., i, p. 354.   [2] id., i, pp. 349–50.

of nature to all the range of emotions possible between living beings: such emotions were to be captured in poetry but the importance lay in the experience and not in the composition. At this point the main outlines of the Romantic theory of the Imagination, in the form Wordsworth was to continue to hold, were clear, and in this form it entered the stream of English poetry through the two long poems in *Lyrical Ballads*, *The Ancient Mariner* and *Lines written above Tintern Abbey*.

4

Nature and Imagination in
The Ancient Mariner

―――――――――

The scope and purpose of this study make it necessary to treat *The Ancient Mariner* simply as the poetic expression of beliefs and ideas, and, though inevitable, this is unfortunate. It is in the nature of such a treatment that much of the poetry will escape: we shall be examining the bones and sinews of the poem in an academic ossuary instead of contemplating its vivid life and beauty. Yet, perhaps, something may still be gained from a further examination of the intellectual structure of the work. It is true that the poem can be enjoyed simply as a miraculous example of the poetry of the supernatural, as a poem in which we suspend our disbelief in order to enter a world of fantasy where platonic spirits and miraculous interventions make up a traveller's tale, but most readers have felt more in the poem than this. Though the world of *The Ancient Mariner* was one created by a poet, yet we can feel in it a largeness and unity which matches the largeness and unity of the real world. It echoes the real world in the manner of those dreams in which ordinary things take new and mysterious significances. It is a world in which natural forces—heat and cold, wind, seas, rain and lightning—work in strange yet coherent ways towards ends which are not physical but moral. It is a world in which the whole concert of nature plays its part in the mariner's spiritual history. Yet if on the one hand

The Ancient Mariner seems at once to describe and to transform the physical world, on the other hand it seems both to voice and to transform the central belief of the English Romantic poets, the belief that the universe was a unity knowable only through the Imagination. When Wordsworth, or Shelley, or Keats, or even at times Byron, spoke of the unity or significance or truth which their imagination found in the universe, they spoke of the known and waking world, but in *The Ancient Mariner* we find these things in a dream world, and yet we feel their poetic seriousness. It is this aspect of *The Ancient Mariner* which may be brought out by an examination of the ideas in the poem.[1]

The Ancient Mariner has, from this point of view, three sources. The first, springing from Coleridge's Unitarianism and his reading, was his conception of nature as made up of living

---

[1] In my treatment of *The Ancient Mariner* it will be apparent that I both agree and disagree with a number of scholars who have dealt in various ways with the moral of the poem. Thus I agree with the late Humphry House that the moral is:

> He prayeth best who loveth best,
> All things both great and small,
> For the dear God who loveth us,
> He made and loveth all

and that this is 'a moral which has its meaning *because it has been lived*' (*Coleridge*, p. 92), but I suggest that Coleridge (and Wordsworth) had definite theories as to what living this moral implied. I agree with N. P. Stallknecht ('The Moral of *The Ancient Mariner*, *PMLA*, 1932) that the poem deals with the reawakening of the Wordsworthian joy in nature, but I think that he is wrong in looking for his parallels in the biographical account in *The Prelude* of that re-awakening, instead of looking at the doctrinal account which Coleridge already knew in the *Lines left upon a Seat*, and that he therefore misses the exact way in which this doctrine is represented. I agree with Robert Penn Warren (*The Rime of the Ancient Mariner*) that the poem is about the Imagination, though my method does not allow me either to confirm or to deny the psychological values he assigns to various symbols, but I agree also with House (loc. cit.) that in 1798 the poem could not have been written about Coleridge's loss of poetical creativeness, and I would go on to suggest that the poem is not about the problem of the Imagination in literature, which preoccupied Coleridge in 1802, but about the power of the Imagination to understand Nature, which was what concerned both Coleridge and Wordsworth in 1797.

intelligent forces, seen sometimes as parts of a divine mind which transcended them and sometimes as agents of that mind, but always as working to fulfil divine purpose. The second, springing from his conversations with Wordsworth, was his belief in the truth of the Imagination and its power to grasp the nature of the universe. The third, springing from Wordsworth's *Lines left upon a Seat in a Yew-Tree*, was his faith that the Imagination, with its power to see the divine life in nature, had profound importance for the moral life. The first and second of these, as they appear in Coleridge's earlier poems and letters, have been traced in preceding chapters, but some account of Coleridge's interest in the action of the Imagination as a moral force will be necessary if its importance in *The Ancient Mariner* is to be seen.

As early as 1794 Wordsworth had believed that those who recognized the life in nature must love it, even in 'its meanest touch', and that such 'favoured souls' were marked also by their equal capacity for more 'domestic' love.[1] The *Lines left upon a Seat in a Yew-Tree* repeat these ideas in a slightly later form. In this poem those beings whose hearts have been kept pure by 'the holy forms of young imagination' will not 'feel contempt for any living thing'. To them both the world and human life will be scenes of loveliness, and they will be 'warm from the labours of benevolence'. This poem attracted Coleridge: he quoted from it in July, 1797 in a letter to Southey,[2] and its phrase 'the young imagination' seems the probable starting point for those discussions with Wordsworth which led Coleridge to formulate his earliest theory of the Imagination.[3] Certainly the theme of this poem became that of the conclusion to *The Ruined Cottage* when Wordsworth began to turn the latter into the long philosophical poem that Coleridge was urging him to write. Coleridge quoted from that conclusion in a letter to his brother George, in April 1798, to summarize his own ideas, which he gave as:

[1] *Poetical Works*, i, pp. 12–13.
[2] *Collected Letters*, i, p. 334. 'I am as much a Pangloss as ever, only less *contemptuous* than I used to be, when I argue how unwise it is to feel contempt for anything.' [3] See pp. 81–2 above.

I devote myself to such works as encroach not on the anti-social passions—in poetry, to elevate the imagination and set the affections in right tune by the beauty of the inanimate impregnated, as with a living soul, by the presence of Life. . . . I love fields and woods and mountains with almost a visionary fondness. And because I have found benevolence and quietness growing within me as that fondness has increased, therefore I should wish to be the means of implanting it in others, and to destroy the bad passions not by combating them but by keeping them in inaction.

Here Nature and the Imagination, as Coleridge then conceived them, are linked with the right ordering of the affections in a single scheme. The Imagination recognizes the life in Nature —that is to say, the Unitarian God in Nature—and the love for all things which follows this sets the affections 'in right tune'. This statement of Coleridge's purpose in poetry, written just after he had finished *The Ancient Mariner* has more application to that poem than might at first appear.

If we compare Coleridge's poetic purpose as he gave it here with that which had informed *Joan of Arc, Religious Musings,* and *The Destiny of Nations,* the most striking difference was that he now believed the operative power in poetry to be the Imagination. In the early long poems it had been, whether or not Coleridge intended it, the Reason. The material for these poems had been drawn from sermons, works of religious and philosophical controversy, scientific books and interpretations of history; the reader was to be persuaded, if at all, by eloquent argument. Now, though Coleridge's purpose was still the moral one of implanting benevolence, he was prepared to abandon argument and to present imaginatively his way of apprehending the world, and hence of feeling about it and of acting towards it. The reader was to be moved to benevolence not because the poem explained reasons for this but because the poem showed him the world as seen through the Imagination —that is, as 'a living thing Which acts upon the mind'. When Wordsworth proposed to him that they should write a long poem on the sailor who had killed the albatross, Coleridge was ready to approach his subject in quite a different way from that in which he had approached the subjects of his earlier long poems, and though much of the material of those earlier poems was used in *The Ancient Mariner*, it was completely transformed.

As so often in poetry, what counted was the first, and, as it seems afterwards, perhaps the simplest step, the choice of a central symbol. (One remarks in Coleridge at his best his extraordinary power of conveying states of mind through symbols.) The symbolism of *The Ancient Mariner* had its origins in that study of biblical prophecy which had helped to produce the earlier poems. In 1795 Coleridge had been reading, and making jottings from,[1] Sir Isaac Newton's *Prophecies of Holy Writ*, which contained a scheme for the interpretation of prophetic language important to Priestley's interpretation of the French Revolution in terms of The Book of Revelations. One passage he seems to have remarked was 'Riding in clouds [is put] for reigning over much people: . . . the motions of clouds for wars.'[2] By using this to create, instead of to interpret, prophetic language, Coleridge produced the bizarre symbolical passage in *Joan of Arc* in which Oppression riding in an English cloud and Envy in a French one pursue each other over Europe to symbolize the Revolutionary wars. But there was a more pregnant phrase further down Newton's page. 'Rain, if not immoderate, and dew, and living water [is put] for the graces and doctrine of the spirit, and the defect of rain for spiritual barrenness.' Though the two passages occur together in Newton's book, this second symbol differs from the first in that it is a very old and powerful symbol and one that expresses what seems to us a natural way of thinking about spiritual life. When Wordsworth suggested the story of the shooting of the albatross he may have had no more in mind than the old sailor's story of a curse, but from Coleridge's point of view, and indeed from Wordsworth's too, the mariner who so wantonly killed the albatross had committed the very offence which Wordsworth had reproved in the lines Coleridge admired.

[1] *Gutch Memorandum Book* 10 (a); 'Sir I. Newton observes in p. 309 of his *Prophecies of Holy Writ*, Horsley's edition, that riding on beasts is put for reigning over much people.'   [2] I. Newton, *Opera*, v, p. 307.

> He who feels contempt
> For any living thing, has faculties
> Which he hath never used.[1]

That spiritual sin had to be expiated: the mariner had to learn to use these unknown faculties to see the spiritual nature of that physical creation he had so disregarded. Thirst and living water formed a perfect symbol for this, and, moreover, a symbol which brought the physical world into play. Around this symbol Coleridge grouped the forces and regions of nature, tropic and pole and their creatures, and sterile heat, lightning and rain, and, not least, the winds that moved the ship. With few exceptions[2] the agencies which play their part in the story are those of the natural world as Coleridge understood it, for this world whose spiritual nature the mariner came to know was the world of the earlier poems, now treated imaginatively.

It is this, whether realized by the reader or not, which unites the poem and gives the airy texture of the dream world its consistency and strength. Coleridge drew words and images from many different sources but the ideas which those words embody are parts of a single conception. Much of the detail was drawn from those very sources from which Coleridge learned his philosophy of nature, the writings of Priestley and Erasmus Darwin. Professor J. Livingston Lowes[3] has pointed out Darwin's power of 'fecundating' Coleridge's imagination, and shown that the passage describing the Northern Lights, like the similar passage in *The Destiny of Nations*, derives from *The Botanic Garden*, and he has suggested that Coleridge's interest in the polar regions was in some measure stimulated by the same poem. He also mentions Priestley's *Opticks* as a source for the connection between putrescence and the phosphorescence of the waters.[4] But Coleridge's debt to the exponents of the new philosophy of nature was greater than such an account would suggest. The tracing, in *The Road to*

---

[1] *Lines left upon a Seat in a Yew-Tree*, ll. 52–4.
[2] The exceptions are the personifications, Death and Life-in-Death.
[3] J. L. Lowes, *The Road to Xanadu*, pp. 99 and 78–9.
[4] id., pp. 38–41.

Xanadu, of the various sources from which Coleridge drew his vivid phrases—the hooked atoms which linked themselves in the deep well of Coleridge's mind—is elaborate and pains-taking, but what perhaps can be added to it is the suggestion that there was more to the linking of atoms than 'the streamy nature of association'.

The Road to Xanadu is a discussion of what Coleridge was later to call the secondary Imagination—the poet's power over words and symbols—but the fascinating account of that power which it gives is in one respect unsatisfactory; it seems to leave out what Coleridge called the 'irremissive, though gentle and unnoticed, control' of 'the will and understanding'.[1] If Coleridge was trying to present a world which could be under-stood and loved, and through which the real world could be seen with 'visionary fondness', then we might expect more of that coherence which is a sign of control by the will and understanding. In fact, this coherence can be found. To vary Professor Lowes' metaphor, Coleridge's mind, where the 'hooked atoms' were to be found, could be likened to a solu-tion in which his varied reading was dissolved: what caused the crystallization of the images was the introduction (or the birth) of ideas around which they could form. In Coleridge's case a set of symbols and images were to hand which he had already meditated on, with his will and understanding, when he was writing his earlier poems. Moreover, in many cases, what Coleridge had found in his reading in connection with them was not atomized phrases but ideas already organized or images already partly crystallized, ready on the one hand to take their places in the symbolism of the poem, and on the other to attract to themselves phrases drawn from other parts of Coleridge's reading. For instance Darwin's account of the 'ice-islands' 'veiled in mist' and 'thick fog' is part of a con-trast between the polar region, with its 'pale moon-beams', and 'the burning Line'.[2] Moreover, this contrast between tropic and pole occurs again in the last canto of the poem where the North is thus described:

[1] *Biographia Literaria*, ii, p. 12.
[2] *The Botanic Garden*, I. i. 523–46.

> Where leads the northern star his lucid train
> High o'er the snow-clad earth, and icy main,
> With milky light the white horizon streams,
> And to the moon each sparkling mountain gleams.
> Slow o'er the printed snows with silent walk
> Hugh shaggy forms across the twilight stalk;
> And ever and anon with hideous sound
> Burst the thick ribs of ice, and thunder round.[1]

Forty lines earlier there is a description of the tropics:

> When from his golden urn the solstice pours,
> O'er Afric's sable sons the sultry hours;
> When not a gale flits o'er her tawny hills,
> Save where the dry Harmattan breathes and kills;[2]

The rest of this passage must wait until we have discussed the idea around which Coleridge's tropical imagery organized itself, but the note to the last line reads (in part):

The Harmattan is a singular wind blowing from the interior parts of Africa to the Atlantic ocean, sometimes for a few hours, sometimes for several days without regular periods . . . the sun appears through it only about noon, and then of a dilute red . . . this wind or fog is said by Dr. Lind at some seasons to be fatal and malignant to mankind; . . . probably after much preceding wet, when it may become loaded with the exhalations from putrid marshes. The Reverend Mr. Stirling gives an account of a darkness for six or eight hours in Detroit . . . in which the sun appeared as red as blood, and thrice its usual size. . . . He supposes this [the fog to] have been emitted from some distant earthquake or volcano.

Coleridge had already noted this effect of the sun through fog in *Joan of Arc* where, in using allegorically another of Darwin's winds, the Tornado, he had written:

> the unwholesome plain
> Sent up its foulest fogs to meet the morn:
> The sun that rose on Freedom, rose in blood.[3]

[1] id., II. iv. 345–52, 363.   [2] id., II. iv. 325–8.

[3] *The Destiny of Nations*, ll. 448–50. As well as the volcanic miasmata, to which Coleridge's interest later shifted, Darwin also describes miasmata from putrid morasses in a way that could have led Coleridge to associate them with the Tornado; see *The Botanic Garden*, note to I. iv. 82 (the Tornado is described in I. iv. 72–8).

But the Harmattan, like the Reverend Mr. Stirling's 'dark-ness', was eventually described by Darwin as volcanic in origin, and so it would have fitted even better into the apocalyptic scheme which Coleridge had developed in 1796. If we turn now to *The Ancient Mariner* we find that its polar scenes also form part of just such a contrast between the polar region:

> And thro' the drifts the snowy clifts
>   Did send a dismal sheen;
> Ne shapes of men ne beasts we ken—
>   The Ice was all between
>
> . . .
>
> The Ice did split with a Thunder-fit
>
> . . .
>
> Whiles all the night thro' fog-smoke white
>   Glimmered the white moon-shine[1]

and the fatal heat of the tropics at solstice:

> All in a hot and copper sky
>   The bloody sun at noon
> Right up above the mast did stand
>   No bigger than the moon.[2]

This is Darwin's contrast even to individual phrases and, later, to the malignant and fatal effects of the heat heralded by the bloody sun in a *copper* sky.

Though the symbolism of heat and thirst explains why Coleridge took this contrast into the poem, his choice, con-scious or unconscious, of this particular machinery has still to be explained and so too has much else that happens in the

---

[1] *The Rime of the Ancient Mariner*, ll. 55–78 and app. crit.

[2] id., ll. 107–10. Lowes (*The Road to Xanadu*, pp. 158–60) discovers a number of red or bloody-coloured suns in Purchas, *The Natural History of Selborne*, Burnet, Falconer's *Shipwreck* and the Authorized Version of the Bible, all of which may have helped to produce the image in the poem. The chief points about the sun in the Darwin note are that it appears at noon in the tropics in a volcanic mist ('All in a hot and copper sky'), that its heat makes fish rot in the sea, that it is fatal and malignant, that its connection with volcanic action links it with the sun in *Religious Musings* (see p. 94, n. 2) below, and also with Coler-idge's earlier ideas on divine vengeance against mis-doers.

tropics. The rest of Darwin's note on the Harmattan offers some clue:

In many circumstances this wind seems much to resemble the dry fog which covered most parts of Europe for many weeks in the summer of 1780, which has been supposed to have had a volcanic origin. . . . It seems probable that the Harmattan has a similar origin. . . . Nor is it . . . impossible that at some future time contagious miasmata may be thus emitted from subterraneous furnaces, in such abundance as to contaminate the whole atmosphere, and depopulate the earth![1]

Coleridge, from his interest in volcanoes and 'fiery whirlwinds'[2] as means of carrying out divine vengeance and bringing about the Millennium, must have noticed this passage and it would presumably have taken a place in his scheme: that it did so is clear from the fact that in *The Ancient Mariner* the sun shone from a copper sky. Though the rather clumsy volcanoes had themselves disappeared from the reader's view, their heat which made the sun bloody remained as the fire of the Mariner's purgation and brought with it into the poem the contrast of heat and cold of which it formed part in the source.

This heat also leads on to other details in the poem. Darwin's description of the Harmattan continues

---

[1] *The Botanic Garden*, note to II. iv. 328. The note to I. iv. 65, from which Coleridge borrowed Bruce's account of the Simoom, refers the reader to this note for an explanation of the volcanic origin of that wind, and this presumably enabled Coleridge to link the 'fiery whirlwinds' of *Religious Musings* with volcanoes (see next note).

[2] Coleridge seems to have had the whole note in mind in *Religious Musings*, ll. 383–92.

> For who of woman born may paint the hour,
> When seized in his mid-course, the Sun shall wane
> Making noon ghastly! Who of woman born
> May image in the workings of his thought,
> How the black-visaged, red-eyed Fiend outstretched
> Beneath the unsteady feet of Nature groans,
> In fevrous slumbers—destined then to wake,
> When fiery whirlwinds thunder his dread name
> And Angels shout, Destruction!

> Contagion stalks along the briny strand,
> And Ocean rolls his sick'ning shoals to land.[1]

and the note to this, 'Fish killed in the sea by dry summers in Asia', reads in part:

In the island of Sumatra during the November of 1775, the dry monsoons . . . continued . . . much longer than usual . . . and prodigious quantities of sea-fish, dead and dying, were seen floating for leagues on the sea, and driven on the beach by the tides. This was supposed to have been caused by the great evaporation and the deficiency of fresh-water rivers having rendered the sea too salt for its inhabitants. The season then became so sickly as to destroy great numbers of people.

The subject matter of this note, putrefying sea-fish, connects it with another note in the first part of the poem, dealing with putrefraction in African waters. 'It seems possible that fish-slime may become in such a state of incipient putrefaction as to give light.'[2] Thus the heat kills the fish in the depths of the sea, and

> The very deeps did rot: O Christ!
>   That ever this should be!
> Yea, slimy things did crawl with legs
>   Upon the slimy Sea.
>
> About, about, in reel and rout
>   The Death-fires danced at night
> The water, like a witch's oils,
>   Burned green and blue and white.[3]

[1] *The Botanic Garden*, ii. iv. 333–4.

[2] id., Additional note ix to i. i. 192. J. L. Lowes lists passages from Priestley, Father Bourges, Captain Cook, Bartram, Leemius, Hawkins, and Falconer which may have contributed words or phrases to Coleridge's description of the water-snakes. It argues some neglect of Darwin that he missed this passage and the notes to it, which provide a number (though not all) of these suggestions grouped together in a book which Coleridge certainly read, and linked logically with other passages which he used, (particularly as the 'slimy shapes' first appeared in 1795 embedded in a passage drawn from Darwin).

[3] *The Ancient Mariner*, ll. 123–30 and app. crit.

An earlier part of this note dealing with phosphorescence caused by putrefaction reads: 'In some cases, particularly about the coast of Malabar, as the ship floats along it seems during the nights to be surrounded by fire, and to leave a long tract of light behind it.' And the whole is a note to the lines

> Or gild the surge with insect sparks that swarm,
> Round the bright oar, the kindling prow alarm:
> Or arms in waves, electric in his ire,
> The dread gymnotus with etherial fire.
> Onward his course with waving tail he helms
> And mimic lightnings scare the watery realms.

These can still be recognized, though they have been transfigured, in

> But where the ship's huge shadow lay,
> The charmed water burnt alway
>   A still and awful red.

> Beyond the shadow of the ship,
>   I watch'd the water-snakes:
> They mov'd in tracks of shining white,
> And when they rear'd the elfish light
>   Fell off in hoary flakes.

> Within the shadow of the ship
>   I watch'd their rich attire:
> Blue, glossy green, and velvet black,
> They coiled and swam; and every track
>   Was a flash of golden fire.[1]

Thus there is a scheme of ideas running from the wrath of the divine Mind in nature, through the expression of that anger in the fatal heat and blood-red sun of the tropics down to the phosphorescences in which the water-snakes move. The change between the description here of the water-snakes in the phosphorescent sea and the earlier description of the slimy things among the death-fires, also has its place in this scheme. It reflects the change by which the Mariner is moved first to terror and then to holy awe at the manifestations in nature,

[1] id., ll. 269–81.

and by which he is brought later to love of the 'happy living things' (and to the religious act of blessing them). These changes in the Mariner's relation to the natural world, and to the Divine manifested in the natural world, complete the purpose of the whole pattern, just as a similar process of the emotions had formed the completion of the apocalyptic scheme in Coleridge's earlier poetry.

But Coleridge owed Darwin another debt for something which was even closer to the heart of what he had to say. It was for that action of the elements by which the Mariner's ship is carried home from the icy regions of the South. The ship is brought from the South to the tropics by the south wind, and much later in the poem, when the Mariner awakes from his trance, it is brought to harbour in England by the same south wind now blowing away from the equator. But in the intervening time the means are preternatural. While the Mariner is in his trance he learns that as far as the line where the sun is 'right above the mast' the ship has been pushed by the Spirit from the land of mist and snow, and while he is still in his trance the ship is carried along from the line northwards still 'without wave or wind' because the air is cut away before and closes from behind, carrying the ship with it. Coleridge had become interested in the theory of the winds the year before, when he noted Darwin's suggestion that the Millennium might be brought about by, as he noted it, 'progression in meteorology or science of airs and winds'. Darwin outlined his own theory of their action in his Supplementary Note on the Winds in *The Botanic Garden*. There he distinguished between winds blowing towards the equator which were brought about by an increase in the atmosphere at the poles and the consequent pressing of air outwards and the winds blowing away from the equator which were caused by the sudden disappearance of air at the poles and the drawing in of air to fill the vacancy. He wrote:

One fifteenth part of the atmosphere is occasionally destroyed and occasionally reproduced by unknown causes. These causes are brought into immediate action over a large part of the earth at the same time but always act more powerfully to the Northward than to the Southward of any given place [he is speaking of the Northern Hemisphere] and would seem to have their principal effects in the polar circles. Winds generated about the poles are pushed forward towards the tropical line by the pressure from behind. The southwest winds, as the atmosphere is suddenly diminished in the polar regions, are drawn, as it were, into an incipient vacancy. We may still suspect that there exists in the Antarctic circle a bear or dragon as yet unknown to philosophers, which at times drinks up, and at other times vomits out, one-fifteenth part of the atmosphere.[1]

Thus the pushing of the ship to the line by the polar spirit and the drawing of the air from the line to fill the vacancy ahead of it represent the action of the forces which produce the winds. What the Mariner knows in the middle of his voyage is the spirit nature of the winds that blow before and after. Here then is one enlargement of the mariner's faculties—one opening of his mind to the knowledge, as Coleridge saw it, that the physical world was moved by spirit forces akin to his own life.

Something like this is true also of the other spirits in the poem. In *The Ancient Mariner* Coleridge's conception of nature is embodied in spirits who are at once intelligent natural forces and divine agents. He had found confirmation of his beliefs in a number of sources—with Darwin's spirits who punish and bless mankind and Priestley's centres of force which are parts of the divinity, he blended Cudworth's plastic natures,

> Contemplant Spirits! ye that hover o'er
> With untired gaze the immeasurable fount
> Ebullient with creative Deity!
> And ye of plastic power . . .
> (And what if Monads of the infinite mind?)[2]

From Cudworth he had been led on to the neo-platonists whose spirits Cudworth had cited.[3] In November 1796 he

[1] *The Botanic Garden*, additional note XXXIII.

[2] *Religious Musings*, ll. 402–8.

[3] The reason for the appearance in the gloss of Josephus as an authority on spirits may well be that Cudworth mentions Psellus and

purchased the works of Iamblichus and in the glosses which he added to the poem in 1815 he described the spirits in neo-platonic terms. Nevertheless, they are still recognizably the spirits of the earlier poems. The polar spirit, ascribed in the glosses to Josephus and Psellus, loves the bird because, as a spirit of nature, he descends from the monads of that infinite mind which sees the fall of a sparrow but he is also like Darwin's spirit of Frost which reigned at the pole, a natural force producing the winds.

The spirits who descend to work the ship are also natural forces, though they are described, not inconsistently, as angelic spirits in the gloss of 1815. Coleridge was much interested in chemistry. His letters and notebooks have many references to phlogiston and in a letter of 19 November 1796 in which he arranged for the purchase of Iamblichus, he wrote 'I am a so-so chemist and love chemistry'. In January 1798 when he was working at *The Ancient Mariner* he wrote to Estlin, 'I regard every experiment that Priestley made in chemistry as giving wings to his more sublime theological works'. Thus it seems that he would have known Priestley's theory that phlogiston, electricity and light were manifestations of the same force:

May not the light, therefore, emitted from the flame, be part of the phlogiston of the inflammable air, united to the principle of heat, and as light accompanies the electric spark, may not this also be the real ascension of some phlogistic matter, though it is not easy to find the source of it.[1]

He would also have known of the experiments of Beccaria on the measurement of atmospheric electricity and those of Galvani on the electrical stimulation of muscles. Beccaria's

Josephus together on p. 762 of *The True Intellectual System* (1732). A little later (pp. 813 ff.) he gives an account of Psellus as 'a curious enquirer into the nature of spirits'. Lowes (*The Road to Xanadu*, pp. 236–8), who does not use Cudworth as a source-book, finds another source in which Josephus and Psellus are only three pages apart, and that, of course, is quite as probable.

[1] J. Priestley, *Experiments on Air*, iii, p. 107.

work was described at length in Priestley's *History of Electricity*,[1] while Galvanism had created a stir in England as recently as 1793–4[2] and had been discussed in detail in literary and general periodicals.[3] Darwin assumes the identity of heat, light and electricity in his description of the nymphs of fire who

> Dart from the North on pale electric streams,
> Fringing Night's sable robe with transient beams,
> —Or rein the Planets in their swift careers,
> Gilding with borrowed light their twinkling spheres;
> Alarm with comet-blaze the sapphire plain,
> The wan stars glimmering through its silver train;
> Gem the bright Zodiac, stud the glowing pole,
> Or give the Suns phlogistic orb to roll.[4]

As Coleridge had undoubtedly read this passage[5] his acquaintance with the general theory underlying it seems certain.

The spirits who work the ship have all these characteristics of electricity in its different modifications: electrical discharge, atmospheric electricity, galvanism, phlogiston and light. Their arrival is heralded by a display of Northern Lights, an electrical phenomenon:

[1] J. Priestley, *History of Electricity*, pp. 338–42. Priestley seems to concur in Beccaria's opinion that electricity was the common cause of thunder, lightning, hail, rain, snow, and wind.

[2] See F. Baldensperger, '1793–4: Climateric Times for Romantic Tendencies in English Ideology', in *JHI* (1944). Baldensperger also discusses contemporary English interest in theories linking electricity and animal magnetism and thinks of this interest as having its roots in Swedenborg.

[3] e.g. *Analytical Review*, xiii (1792), pp. 470–3; xiv, pp. 350–2; xv, pp. 112, 466–7; xvi (1793), pp. 236–7; xvii, pp. 292–300; xix, pp. 15–19; xx (1794), pp. 179–86.

[4] *The Botanic Garden*, i. i. 129–36.

[5] Coleridge borrowed from the beginning of this verse paragraph in *Joan of Arc* (see p. 41). In *The Ancient Mariner* the wan stars are seen through the Aurora Borealis instead of through the tail of a comet, but Darwin has a note on this passage in which he says, 'small stars are seen undiminished through both the light of the tails of comets, and of the aurora borealis'.

> The upper air burst into life
>> And a hundred fire-flags sheen,
> To and fro, they were hurried about;
> To and fro, and in and out,
>> The wan stars danced between.

They arrive in the wind:

> The strong wind reached the ship: it roar'd
>> And dropp'd down like a stone!
> Beneath the lightning and the moon
>> The dead men gave a groan.

> They groan'd, they stirr'd, they all uprose,
>> Ne spake, ne mov'd their eyes:
> It had been strange, even in a dream,
>> To have seen those dead men rise.

The spirits galvanize the limbs of the corpses:

> The helmsman steer'd, the ship mov'd on;
>> Yet never a breeze up-blew;
> The Mariners all 'gan work the ropes,
>> Where they were wont to do:
> They rais'd their limbs like lifeless tools—
>> We were a ghastly crew.
> The body of my brother's son
>> Stood by me, knee to knee:
> The body and I pulled at one rope,
>> But he said nought to me.

The spirits show themselves as fire.

> They lifted up their stiff right arms,
>> They held them strait and tight;
> And each right arm burned like a torch.

At the last they reveal themselves as 'seraph men', 'all light'.[1]

It should hardly need emphasis that these spirits are not direct representations of nature as those of Darwin's poem are. Nevertheless that they embodied scientific fact (or at least theory) was clear at the time to at least one poet who was also

[1] *The Ancient Mariner*, ll. 313–17, 327–44 and app. crit., 475–80 app. crit., 490.

'a so-so chemist'. In 1814 or 1815, Shelley, who was fond of reciting *The Ancient Mariner* aloud with wild energy, addressed a poem to Coleridge which begins:

> O there are spirits of the air,
> And genii of the evening breeze,
> And gentle ghosts, with eyes as fair
> As star beams among twilight trees:—
> Such lovely ministers to meet
> Oft hast thou turned from men thy lonely feet.
> With mountain winds, and babbling springs,
> And moonlight seas that are the voice
> Of these inexplicable things,
> Thou dids't hold commune, and rejoice
> When they did answer thee.[1]

What I have given as analysis, and what Coleridge's readers understood as imaginative vision, *could* be understood more directly by a poet trained in the same scientific tradition.

Thus while it is true that nature in *The Ancient Mariner* is, in Coleridge's later phrase, supernatural or at least romantic, it is recognizably modelled on the supernatural or romantic aspects of that nature which Coleridge described in full belief in *Joan of Arc* and *Religious Musings*. In the earlier poems Coleridge had expounded history as he thought it had happened or was about to happen and there the natural forces were the historical agents of God's will. Here what is demanded is not belief, but the suspension of disbelief, and natural forces are seen through the eye of the imagination, revealing that divinity which was in them.

---

[1] *Poetical Works*, ed. T. Hutchinson, p. 525. The editor notes (p. 902) Mrs Shelley's statement that the poem was addressed to Coleridge 'in idea', and though various biographers of Shelley have argued (giving different applications) that it was autobiographical, yet there is no need whatsoever to doubt her account. Her story is circumstantial and the poem fits very well with what Shelley might have heard from Southey concerning Coleridge, and, indeed, with Coleridge's own view of his situation as he gives it in *The Blossoming of the Solitary Date-Tree*. It seems a much better account of Coleridge's relations with his wife and Sara than of Shelley's with Harriet and either Cornelia Turner or Mary.

Viewing the poem thus, we can now perhaps see more clearly the intellectual and imaginative unity of *The Ancient Mariner*. Here we must return to the argument of Wordsworth's *Lines left upon a Seat in a Yew-Tree* which Coleridge admired in 1797. Its theme is essentially that which has been put by a modern mystic in the form

Il ne faut jamais oublier que la lumière luit également sur tous les êtres et toutes les choses. Elle est ainsi l'image de la volonté créatrice de Dieu qui supporte également tout ce qui existe. C'est à cette volonté créatrice que notre consentement doit adhérer.

Ce qui permet de contempler la necessité et de l'aimer, c'est la beauté du monde. Sans la beauté ce ne serait pas possible. Car bien que le consentement soit la fonction propre de la partie surnaturelle de l'âme, il ne peut pas en fait s'opérer sans une certaine complicité de la partie naturelle de l'âme et même du corps. La plénitude de cette complicité, c'est la plénitude de la joie; l'extrême malheur au contraire rend cette complicité tout à fait impossible. . . . Et la joie pure n'est pas autre chose que le sentiment de la beauté.[1]

It is our joy in the beauty of the world that enables us to love the Law that governs it. As Wordsworth put it, and as one may interpolate from what he and Coleridge believed, those whose hearts have been kept pure by the imagination, and who submit themselves to nature, will find in the world a strange beauty, that will lead them to love all life and all the living world:

> He prayeth best, who loveth best
> All things both great and small.

On the other hand,

> he, who feels contempt
> For any living thing, hath faculties
> Which he has never used.

As Coleridge's letters show, these faculties were the imagination which could comprehend the life and meaning in what the eighteenth century had thought of as the inanimate world. Now the Mariner had shown contempt for a living thing when

---

[1] S. Weil, *Intuitions Pré-Chrétienne*, p. 157.

he killed the albatross in mere sport. The penance he had to undergo, and the spiritual barrenness which possessed him are symbolized by heat and thirst, inflicted by natural forces that are the spiritual agents of God. When the beauty of the water-snakes moved him to love them, then, as the gloss says: 'By the grace of the Holy Mother, the Mariner is refreshed by rain', which, as we have seen, symbolizes the graces of the spirit. With them came understanding, and in the trance which followed, the Mariner was able to see the world of physical phenomena, not as dead matter moved by mechanical force, but as possessing life, intelligence, beauty and purpose, all the qualities which that 'Newtonian materialism' which Coleridge so hated had banished from the world. For Coleridge as a Unitarian, all these qualities reflected the qualities of a God who at once summed up the physical world and directed it.

As has been suggested throughout this chapter, the substance behind the shadow world of *The Ancient Mariner* is the real world which Coleridge's letters tell us he had come to love 'with an almost visionary fondness'. That real world was not only the world as the science of the late eighteenth century conceived it; it was also the world as Coleridge (and Wordsworth) understood and experienced it. Priestley and Darwin had said that the physical world had the properties of life and Priestley had also said that it was the energy of God: the poets had experienced it in a relationship with a living thing and with an almighty spirit.

The discovery of such a relationship is a form of religious experience and it was natural that Coleridge should use for the framework of the poem a system which he had first developed in connection with the psychology of religious conversion. It has been noticed by D. W. Harding[1] that 'the human experience around which Coleridge centres the poem is surely the depression and the sense of isolation and unworthiness which the Mariner describes in Part IV' and that 'with the sense of worthlessness there is also guilt'. The critic goes on to describe

[1] D. W. Harding, 'The Theme of *The Ancient Mariner*' in *Scrutiny* (1941).

the misery as 'pathological' and the guilt as 'irrational', but, whether this be so or not, this is a state of mind often described in accounts of conversion—the state already described by Coleridge as 'Terror, Mercy's startling prelude'.[1] To attribute the change in the Mariner (and in Coleridge) to 'returning joy in living things' is correct enough but it does not give the full force of the experience in which the joy in living things contains also a sense of relationship with a divine personality, experienced here in every contact with the external world and leading to a deepening of understanding and of trust. It was this which in *Tintern Abbey* lightened 'the burden of the mystery' and 'the heavy and the weary weight of all this unintelligible world', as here it delivers the Mariner from his agony: the psychological unity of *The Ancient Mariner* lies in its full realization of the vital experience which the doctrine of the living universe offered the poet.

[1] *Religious Musings*, ll. 32–4 app. crit.

P. 137.

5

Nature and Imagination in
The Ruined Cottage

While Coleridge was writing *The Ancient Mariner*, Wordsworth was also engaged on a long poem, *The Ruined Cottage*,
from which were eventually to grow his most important poems,
The Prelude and *The Excursion*. A short bare narrative on the
subject of the ruined cottage already existed in June 1797, and
was read to Coleridge on his first visit. What led Wordsworth
to choose this as the starting point for his greatest work was
presumably that the incident on which the short narrative
was based, the visit to a ruined cottage in 1795, was associated
with the period of his greatest despair and with the recovery
that was the turning point of his life. What led him to change
the poem from a simple narrative into an ever-growing philosophical poem was the growth of his thought on the Imagination.

The poem of 1797–8 and the fragments connected with it[1]
contain Wordsworth's first detailed and explicit statements
about the Imagination, and in them can be seen how his ideas
grew out of his beliefs concerning the natural world and how a
system of natural philosophy became a way of living and
feeling. To Wordsworth the Imagination was both a theory
and an experience, and each would have taken a different

[1] E. de Selincourt's edition of the *Poetical Works* has been taken as
the authority for the dating of the various drafts and fragments.

form without the other. His ideas gave the experience its particular significance, and the experience in turn shaped the ideas. Thus the idea of purposiveness in nature demanded that wise passiveness which led to Wordsworth's characteristic experience of nature, the life of nature explained for him his mystical experience of the life of the mind, and both the life and the purposiveness of nature justified that deep meaning which he found in the forms of nature.

The theory of the Imagination at which Wordsworth eventually arrived, by about 1805, is well known from the later books of *The Prelude*, and from other texts, particularly the *Preface* of 1815. These, of course, were written after Coleridge had produced his distinction between Imagination and Fancy (in 1802), as well as after Coleridge had converted Wordsworth from Necessitarianism, and when Transcendentalism had begun to oust Pantheism from Wordsworth's religion.[1] His early thought, in the main, survived these influences for some time, and nowhere more clearly than in the first, fourth, and ninth books of *The Excursion* (which were largely written in 1797–9 as part of *The Ruined Cottage*), but the way in which Wordsworth arrived at his ideas, and the reasons for his confidence in them, can best be seen in the earliest attempts to work out these ideas in poetry.

While Wordsworth was carrying out this first revision of his original narrative he was, of course, in close touch with Coleridge and but for Coleridge the revision would probably not have been undertaken. Nevertheless, though the contributions of the two poets at this time to the theory of the Imagination can probably never be disentangled, this second version of *The Ruined Cottage* is Wordsworth's own statement of his beliefs, and it deals particularly with his own experience and his own problems. The event in Wordsworth's life from which his thought stemmed was his recovery from despair in the years after the Revolution. In that time he learned to contrast his insight into the life of nature, and the reassurance and exaltation it brought, with the mood of rebellion, fashioning

[1] See M. M. Rader, 'Presiding Ideas in Wordsworth's Poetry', Univ. of Washington Publications in Lang. and Lit., No. 2, pp. 121–216.

the laws of nature to its own will and seeing in nature only the emblems of its own despair. In rehandling *The Ruined Cottage* Wordsworth had two aims, to show how the faculty of Imagination is produced by Nature in a favoured being, and to show how the imaginative experience banishes sorrow and despair. To accomplish these aims he made two sets of revisions, first rewriting the early part of the poem dealing with the Pedlar, and then inserting, in the later part of the poem, passages in which he tried to describe directly the imaginative experience and its value to him. Wordsworth began his revision by describing the development of the character of the Pedlar who tells the story and here the description of him as 'a chosen son' is significant. The doctrine of Necessity, like that of Predestination, implies that those who find happiness are specially chosen and as early as 1794 Wordsworth had written of the 'favoured souls' who found ecstasy and moral strength in the contemplation of the life in nature. In the character of the Pedlar he began to explore the making of such a chosen being and the metaphysical grounds for his assurance.

Among the first notes for the character of the Pedlar are some lines which make, in new terms, the distinction that had already appeared in the poems discussed in Chapter III.

> Some men there are who like insects *etc.*
> . . . dart and dart against the mighty stream
> Of tendency . . . others with no vulgar sense
> Of their existence, to no vulgar end
> Calmly float down.

In another attempt on the same idea he wrote

> They rest upon their oars,
> Float down the mighty stream of tendency
> In a calm mood of holy indolence
> A most wise passiveness in which the heart
> Lies open and is well content to feel
> As nature feels and to receive her shapes
> As she has made them.[1]

That the power of nature was a stream of tendency, was one of the fundamental ideas of the new philosophy. Late

[1] *Poetical Works,* v, p. 413, and *The Prelude,* p. 548.

108

eighteenth-century pantheism was, as we have seen, [1] intimately connected with the attempts to formulate a theory of evolution and to explain the world, in all its gradations of existence, as development, not creation. Implied in such a theory was the idea that the whole world process had direction and purpose, and that the end had not yet been attained in this imperfect world. Diderot, though he did not specify the end, thought all nature a tendency aiming at a goal, and later writers were far more sure of the point. For Robinet the end was the spiritualization of matter; for Volney, enlightenment and universal happiness, while Carra plumped boldly for republicanism as the purpose of the evolution of the world. [2]

Wordsworth was not much interested in evolution, though he thought that the 'living Presence' could produce the development of the natural world. [3] Nevertheless, he conceived the life in nature as a force working towards human ends. The passage quoted above appeared at last in *The Excursion* as

> What more than that the severing should confer
> Fresh power to commune with the invisible world,
> And hear the mighty stream of tendency
> Uttering, for elevation of our thought,
> A clear sonorous voice, inaudible
> To the vast multitude; whose doom it is
> To run the giddy round of vain delight,
> Or fret and labour on the Plain below.
>
> But, if to such sublime ascent the hopes
> Of Man may rise, as to a welcome close
> And termination of his mortal course;
> Them only can such hope inspire whose minds
> Have not been starved by absolute neglect;
> Nor bodies crushed by unremitting toil;
> To whom kind Nature, therefore, may afford
> Proof of the sacred love she bears for all. [4]

[1] See pp. 22–5 above.

[2] J. B. R. Robinet, *Considérations philosophiques sur la gradation naturelle* (1768), p. 9; Comte de Volney, *Les Ruines* (1791), p. 81; J. L. Carra, *Système de la raison*, 3rd ed. (1791), p. 81.

[3] See p. 23 above.   [4] *The Excursion*, IX. 85–100.

To Wordsworth, not only was the imaginative experience a natural process, but the human life ascending to such an experience was the end which the life in nature strove to bring about. In submitting himself in wise passiveness to Nature's influences, the Pedlar co-operated with Necessity and with the true process of the world.

Most of the first half of the revised version of *The Ruined Cottage* was given to the Pedlar's development under nature's influences. The account of this shows the influence of Hartley's associationist psychology, to which Wordsworth was probably introduced by Coleridge, but as yet there was no sign of any very detailed reading of Hartley. The elaborate Hartleyan scheme, with its division of life into three ages marked by sensation, fancy and imagination respectively, belongs to the later books of *The Prelude,* written between 1802 and 1805. Here the account is much simpler and the associationist ideas involved are the commonplaces which Hartley got from Locke and which were common property in the eighteenth century. Far more important is the part played by the '*active* universe'.

The description of the Pedlar's earliest childhood makes clear what was meant by the phrase, 'the holy forms of young imagination', used in the *Lines left upon a Seat in a Yew-Tree.* These were natural forms which passed into the child's mind associated with deep feeling.

> deep feelings had impressed
> Great objects on his mind . . .
> He had received
> A previous gift, for as he grew in years
> With these impressions he would still compare
> All his ideal stores, his shapes and forms.[1]

But Wordsworth was not simply trying to explain the growth of the mind on mechanical principles as Hartley had. He was always deeply conscious that the life of the mind was only an extension of a deeper and more pervading life of the universe which was its under-presence and undersoul.[2] The forms are the means by which this universal life becomes the life of the

---

[1] *The Ruined Cottage,* MS B, ll. 81–8.   [2] *The Prelude,* p. 600.

individual mind. The idea that the life of the mind is an extension, through the forms perceived by the senses, of the force of nature is a logical development of the system which Wordsworth had adopted. Such a theory had been developed already by the geologist Hutton in his *Principles of Knowledge* (1794)[1] in which, taking Priestley's position that what we think to be inert matter is really force, Hutton concluded

Having, in an accurate examination of natural bodies, found that magnitude and figure, though commonly esteemed absolute qualities, were in their nature only conditional. . . . I then found that there is nothing in those external things which, strictly speaking, should be considered as absolute volume, or real magnitude and figure; but there were only certain powers by which these conceived qualities may be produced in our mind.[2]

It is unlikely that Wordsworth knew Hutton's book, but his thought, starting from very similar premises, ran on very similar lines. In 1799 he wrote

> All beings have their properties which spread
> Beyond themselves, a power by which they make
> Some other being conscious of their life,
> Spirit that knows no insulated spot,
> No chasm, no solitude; from link to link
> It circulates, the Soul of all the worlds.[3]

In *The Ruined Cottage* the childhood impressions of natural forms on the Pedlar's mind lead on to an experience in which the forms, and the soul which dwells in them, completely possess him and in which his mind becomes one with nature. The scene described seems to be that which Wordsworth saw during the Cambridge vacation, on the morning when he dedicated himself to poetry, but here it was transferred to the Pedlar's ninth year.

[1] Coleridge jotted a quotation from this in the *Gutch Memorandum Book* 47 (b)–48 (a). He later noted in his own copy of the book (now in the British Museum), 'the writer had made an important step beyond Locke, Berkeley and Hartley—and was clearly in the precincts of the Critical Philosophy'. The copy is largely uncut.

[2] J. Hutton, *The Principles of Knowledge*, p. xiv.

[3] *The Excursion*, IX. 10–15 and app. crit.

> Oh! then what soul was his when on the tops
> Of the high mountains he beheld the sun
> Rise up and bathe the world in light. He looked,
> The ocean and the earth beneath him lay
> In gladness and deep joy. The clouds were touched
> And in their silent faces did he read
> Unutterable love. Sound needed none
> Nor any voice of joy: his spirit drank
> The spectacle. Sensation, soul and form
> All melted into him. They swallowed up
> His animal being; in them did he live
> And by them did he live. They were his life.
> In such access of mind, in such high hour
> Of visitation from the living God,
> He did not feel the God; he felt his works;
> Thought was not. In enjoyment it expired.[1]

This experience was clearly of a mystical nature, but Words-worth's explanation is a rational one in terms of his system. The power of nature, 'soul and form', first enters the mind through the senses, and then the mind is swallowed up in the sea from which it was born.

This explanation gives the senses a special function. Through them the mind first grows out of the impressions of nature, and through them, in the 'high hour', the life of the mind and the life of nature become one. Indeed it is only through them that the life of either becomes distinct. The Pedlar lives in and by the sensation, soul and form of nature. They in turn make him conscious of his own life.

> And forms and feelings acting thus, and thus
> Reacting, they shall each acquire
> A living spirit and a character
> Till then unfelt.[2]

The life of nature is made known by the same act of perception and response which gives individual character to the feelings.

The act is creative because the senses perceive not only shape, but also life and meaning in the natural forms. In a

---

[1] *The Ruined Cottage*, MS B, ll. 122–37.
[2] id., Addendum to MS B, ll. 87–90.

fragment of 1797–8 Wordsworth wrote explicitly of the creative power of the senses.

> There is creation in the eye
> Nor less in all the other senses; powers
> They are that colour, model, and combine
> The things perceived with such an absolute
> Essential energy that we may say
> That those most godlike faculties of ours
> At one and the same moment are the mind
> And the mind's minister. In many a walk . . .
> Have we to Nature and her impulses
> Of our whole being made free gift, and when
> Our trance had left us, oft have we, by aid
> Of the impressions which it left behind,
> Looked inward on ourselves, and learned, perhaps
> Something of what we are.[1]

The Pedlar's experience was at once an experience of the one life in nature and man, a creation by the senses of the living spirit and character of each, and an understanding of the meaning of the forms of nature. After it the Pedlar is able to recognize the one life in all being and to understand the language of inarticulate things.

> In all shapes
> He found a secret and mysterious soul
> A fragrance and a spirit of strange meaning.[2]

All this, as well as Hartley's theories, must have been in Wordsworth's mind a few months later when he wrote, in the *Lines composed above Tintern Abbey,* of

> All the mighty world
> Of eye and ear,—both what they half create,
> And what perceive; well pleased to recognise
> In nature and the language of the sense
> The anchor of my purest thoughts, the nurse,
> The guide, the guardian of my heart, and soul
> Of all my moral being.[3]

---

[1] *Poetical Works,* v, p. 343.
[2] *The Ruined Cottage,* MS B, ll. 279–81.   [3] *Tintern Abbey,* ll. 105–11.

It is clear that the theory of the Imagination which Wordsworth was developing here is closely related to that which
Coleridge was outlining in his letters of October 1797. Like
Coleridge, Wordsworth believed that the Imagination gives
the power to escape from the contemplation of parts which
'are necessarily little' and to see infinity in all things.

> All things there
> Looked immortality, revolving life,
> And greatness still revolving, infinite;
> There littleness was not, the least of things
> Seemed infinite.[1]

Like Coleridge he believed that the Imagination could find in
nature what Coleridge called the 'shapes intelligible' of an
'eternal language',[2] and also like Coleridge, he believed that
the growth of the Imagination was fostered by the reading of
fairy tales and romances, but he gives rather fuller and clearer
reasons for this. Coleridge had said only that the reading of
fairy-tales gave him the ability to escape the bondage of the
senses and the judgement and to regulate his creeds by his
conceptions. For Wordsworth, the romances, by association,
gave human significance to natural features and so developed
the power to read the language of the forms.

> Many a tale
> Traditionary round the mountains hung,
> And many a legend peopling the dark woods
> Nourished Imagination in her growth,
> And gave the mind that apprehensive power
> By which she is made quick to recognize
> The moral properties and scope of things.[3]

This important clarification again links the growth of Imagination to the 'forms' and it illustrates that what Wordsworth
was doing, in response to Coleridge's suggestion that he
'deliver upon authority a system of philosophy', was to show
the relationship between the life in nature, the forms which
were its expression, and the development in man of the power

---

[1] *The Ruined Cottage*, MS B, ll. 150–4.
[2] *Frost at Midnight*, ll. 59–62.
[3] *The Ruined Cottage*, MS B, ll. 167–73.

to 'read' these forms and to recognize the character of the life behind them. Despite Coleridge's statement in 1832 that Wordsworth's task was to be that of 'informing the senses out of the mind, and not compounding the mind out of the senses',[1] Wordsworth did neither, but explained both in terms of the 'one life'. His system was based very deeply in the pantheistic 'materialism' of the later eighteenth century: his ideas were an adaption of the new theories to his own experience, particularly his mystical experience, and the validity of these ideas depended wholly on the qualities of life and the purpose which the new 'materialism' found in the physical world. Not only his own belief, but the conviction which he carried to his younger contemporaries, depended on the changed climate of opinion in the physical sciences.

The belief that inanimate objects were in a literal sense alive came nearest to establishing itself as scientific orthodoxy during the years of Wordsworth's most active poetic life. In 1802 Cabanis could write: 'Today we are sufficiently informed about fundamentals to regard as chimerical that distinction which Buffon tried to establish between living and dead matter or between organic and inorganic particles.'[2]

The attitude of orthodox text-books (e.g. *The First Principles of Chemistry* (1792) by Wordsworth's friend William Nicholson, or *The Philosophy of the Human Mind* (1792) by Dugald Stewart),[3] seems to have been one of suspended judgement, but nevertheless the new ideas were championed by a number of distinguished scientists—Priestley, Darwin and Hutton. In radical circles French writers spread the same idea, as *Queen Mab* testifies.[4] In his fundamental belief that the physical world is a 'world of feeling and of life'[5] Wordsworth was neither isolated nor eccentric.

[1] *Table Talk*, 21 July 1832.

[2] P. J. G. Cabanis, *Rapports du Physique et du Moral de l'homme* (1802), ii, p. 362.

[3] W. Nicholson, *The First Principles of Chemistry*, 2nd ed. (1792), p. 74; Dugald Stewart, *Elements of the Philosophy of the Human Mind* (1792), i, p. 86.

[4] *Queen Mab*, ii. 225–43; iii. 214–40; iv. 138–50; and note to vii. 13.

[5] *The Ruined Cottage*, Addendum to ms B, l. 74.

The importance which Wordsworth attached to natural forms is not so often found in other writers of the period but it was a reasonable corollary of the new system. Once the idea of solidity as the fundamental attribute of matter had been given up for, or blended with, the attributes of energy and sensibility, then form and organization took on a special importance. For Diderot and his successors whatever had organization had independent life and a degree of consciousness depending on the complexity of the organization. From this it is only a step to the position that form has a special significance as a function or expression of this life or energy. This step was taken by Robinet and Hutton as well as by Wordsworth.

The most important effect of the new climate of opinion was that it made it easier to see the Imagination as the organ of truth instead of the Judgement. The new philosophy, developed mainly to account for biological phenomena, was deeply imbued with the idea of purposeful development in natural process. It was no coincidence that the two poets most immediately affected by *The Excursion*, Shelley and Keats, were believers in evolution. Coleridge's early ideas have been described in Chapter II, and, though not evolutionary, they were apocalyptic and involved the purposeful working of natural forces towards cosmic ends. Even his later ideas are strongly teleological and have been described by Dr Alice Snyder in these words:

Strictly speaking, Coleridge's scheme of cosmogony, based on the fundamental principle of counter-balancing forces, was not an evolutionary scheme, for it was not essentially a time scheme. But . . . his image of the whole as implicit in every part . . . was the organic conception that needed only to be put in terms of time to give the evolutionary conception of the end as implicit in the beginning.[1]

But if Nature had both an independent life and an independent purpose, then the human *reason* would be unable in the last

[1] Alice D. Snyder, 'Coleridge's Cosmogony' in *SP* (1924), p. 625.

resort to discover this purpose.[1] It could only be communicated by Nature herself, and to a being, through the power of imagination, able to understand the language she used. For Wordsworth at this time the guarantee of 'the truth of the imagination' was that it was a natural and purposive exertion of the divine force in nature and that the meanings it discovered were properties of the forms in which that force expressed itself,

> her shapes
> As she has made them.[2]

The Ruined Cottage was first written out in its new version between January and March 1798. Some three hundred of the seven hundred lines were devoted to the development of Imagination in the Pedlar, but there was as yet nothing to show how the imaginative response to the story of Margaret differed from any other and the poem still had a melancholy close:

> here she died
> Last human tenant of these ruined walls.[3]

Wordsworth immediately set about remedying this defect, and the further changes he made are of great significance. They show both the experience by which Wordsworth's consciousness of a life in nature changed sorrow to cheerful acceptance and the theory which justified that acceptance.

He began by inserting a new passage into the speech by the Pedlar.

> But I have spoken this
> With an ungrateful temper and have read
> The forms of things with an unworthy eye.
> She sleeps in the calm earth and peace is here.
> I well remember that those very plumes
> Those weeds and the high spear grass on that wall

---

[1] The essence of the objections which both Coleridge and Wordsworth made to the Judgement was that it could deal only with parts and not the whole. See p. 83 above and p. 120 below.

[2] *The Prelude*, p. 548.

[3] *The Ruined Cottage*, MS B, ll. 741–2.

> By mist and silent rain-drops silvered o'er,
> As once I passed, did to my mind convey
> So still an image of tranquillity,
> So calm and still, and looked so beautiful,
> Amid the uneasy thoughts which filled my mind,
> That what we feel of sorrow and despair
> From ruin and from change, and all the grief
> That passing shews of being leave behind
> Appeared an idle dream that could not live
> Where meditation was.[1]

He rejected this, and next tried a direct description of his experience, in which

> the cottage and the elms,
> The road, the pathway, and the garden wall
> Which old and loose and mossy o'er the road
> Hung bellying, all appeared, I know not how
> But to some eye within me all appeared
> Colours and forms of a strange discipline.
> The trouble which they sent into my thought
> Was sweet, I looked and looked again, and to myself
> I seemed a better and a wiser man.[2]

The first correction had spoken only the result of the experience. The second had described the experience without explaining it. Wordsworth now returned to the first and swept it up in a long explanatory passage which made a new close to the poem and which, after later revision, occupied a central place in *The Excursion.*

This passage was a summary of Wordsworth's beliefs, bringing together the extension of the love of nature to the love of all being, the language of the forms of nature, the powerlessness of the analytic reason, the life of the forms and the necessity of good when man's mind is possessed by the soul of things. It begins

> Not useless do I deem
> These quiet sympathies with things that hold
> An inarticulate language.[3]

---

[1] id., app. crit. to 366–7.

[2] *Poetical Works*, v, p. 400.

[3] *The Ruined Cottage*, addendum to MS B, ll. 1–3.

The most obvious value of these sympathies is that they lead
to a love of all being and to a state of mind in which execration
and contempt are impossible. But furthermore these forms
bear a relation to man. This seems to have been in part
natural to them and in part the result of association. Earlier
the traditionary tales had nourished the power 'to recognise
the moral properties and scope of things'; in various corrections leading to the addendum now under discussion, 'the
pathway and the garden wall' had appeared 'colours and
forms of a strange discipline' and had also been 'consecrated'
by the Pedlar's tale; and now 'general laws and local accidents
shall tend alike'. The importance of association seems to be
that it develops the habit of looking for moral significance in
natural forms.

> We shall acquire
> The (   ) habit by which sense is made
> Subservient still to moral purposes
> A vital essence and a saving power.
> Nor shall we meet an object but may read
> Some sweet and tender lesson to our minds
> Of human suffering or of human joy.
> All things shall speak of Man, and we shall read
> Our duties in all forms, and general laws
> And local accidents shall tend alike
> To quicken and to rouse, and give the will
> And power by which a (   ) chain of good
> Shall link us to our kind.[1]

This was not the picture of the world presented by orthodox
science,[2] but the objection of both Wordsworth and Coleridge

[1] id., ll. 29–41.

[2] G. R. Potter, in *PQ* (1938), xvii, suggests that Wordsworth was
attacking the doctrines of Lavoisier's *Traité elementaire de chimie*.
Potter's further suggestion that Wordsworth got his own ideas from
Humphry Davy is unsatisfactory because Wordsworth had not yet
met Davy. On the other hand, Davy may well have got some ideas from
Wordsworth. A passage from his *Discourse* (1802) seems to echo Wordsworth's beliefs on the formation and nourishment of the mind.

The germ of power is indeed nature: but it can only be nourished by
the forms of the external world. The food of the imagination is

to the Reason was that it could see nothing but parts,

> In disconnection dead and spiritless[1]

and that there was a whole, and a life of the whole, which it could not grasp. Nature has significance.

> Was it ever meant
> That this majestic imagery, the clouds
> The ocean and the firmament of heaven
> Should lie a barren picture on the mind?[2]

The world is in truth a 'world of feeling and of life'. Only when it realized this could science serve its true end of ministering, in the cause of order and distinctness, to the higher faculties.

Wordsworth now came to the heart of his doctrine—the existence of a soul of things, and the way in which recognition of it vindicates the goodness of necessity. In 1794 Wordsworth had seen

> common forms prolong the endless chain
> Of joy and grief, of pleasure and of pain.[3]

The knowledge had brought respect for all existence, and had banished contempt and pride. He continued to believe in the one life that was joy, but he was now interested in the processes by which knowledge of that life was gained, and in the reassurance the knowledge could give as to the ultimate goodness of the universe.

> supplied by the senses, and all ideas existing in the human mind are representations of parts of nature, accurately delineated by the memory, or tinged with the glow of passion and formed into new combinations by fancy. . . . The appearances of the greater number of natural objects is originally delightful to us, and becomes more so when the laws by which they are governed is known, and when they are associated with ideas of order and utility (pp. 23–4).

With Davy's 'delineated', 'tinged', and 'combinations', compare e.g. Wordsworth's 'colour model and combine' (p. 113 above) and with the whole compare the addendum to MS B of *The Ruined Cottage*, ll. 95–9 and ll. 44–57.

[1] *The Ruined Cottage*, addendum to MS B, l. 62.   [2] id., ll. 68–71.
[3] *Poetical Works*, i, pp. 12–13 (quoted p. 73 above).

In the addendum the world is a world of life, of which the human mind is part, but the *consciousness* of that life comes from the interaction of man and the forms of nature.

> All things shall live in us and we shall live
> In all things that surround us. This I deem
> Our tendency . . .
> And forms and feelings acting thus, and thus
> Reacting, they shall each acquire
> A living spirit and a character
> Till then unfelt, and each be multiplied
> With a variety that knows no end.[1]

But, of course, this life is not subjective. In this process we drink in 'the soul of things'. Wordsworth's ultimate assurance was doubly founded: if we submit to nature's influences, then nature will feed and nourish 'our intellectual soul', and also we shall become part of nature's divine purpose.

> Thus deeply drinking in the soul of things
> We shall be wise perforce, and we shall move
> From strict necessity along the path
> Of order and of good.[2]

The power on which this depends is the Imagination,

> He had discoursed
> Like one who in the slow and silent works,
> The manifold conclusions of his thought,
> Had brooded till Imagination's power
> Condensed them to a passion.[3]

And after this revelation by the Imagination, sorrow and despair become an idle dream. The poem now ends

> casting then a farewell look
> Upon these silent walls we left the shade
> And cheerfully pursued our evening way.[4]

The comparison with *Paradise Lost* which this last line invites is an indication of the importance which Wordsworth placed on this attempt to set down the implications of his faith in the Imagination. Much of the interest of the passage lies in the

[1] *The Ruined Cottage*, addendum to MS B, ll. 79–91.
[2] id., ll. 92–5.   [3] id., ll. 105–9.   [4] id., ll. 145–7.

way it shows the inter-relation between ideas of nature and imaginative experience of nature, as this had developed for Wordsworth between 1794 and 1798. In the first place the whole scheme starts from a real and literal belief in the life of natural objects. When the implications of such a belief are grasped then man's contemplation of natural forms can mean communication with them and eventually communion with the greater life of which they are an expression. In the first experience it is the 'language' of the forms which is important: the features of the landscape have qualities of human person-ality or human feeling to which the observer can respond (the importance of association is that it develops the habit of looking for such qualities) so that he now participates in a 'world of feeling and of life'. But though the recognition of those qualities is a function of the human consciousness, yet the forms themselves have a life which is not that of men; they belong to 'a strange discipline'. The phrase implies both order and purpose in the life of the universe and it is the recognition of this, at once strange to men and yet with meaning for them, that makes sorrow and despair from change and ruin 'an idle dream'. To pass from this communi-cation to communion clearly depends on such a capacity as Wordsworth's for mystical experience, but the coherence of the system depends equally on ideas as to what Nature is, and on the enriched experience which follows when such ideas are imaginatively grasped.

In all this the Imagination meant for Wordsworth quite simply the power to recognize, in his contemplation of them, the life of natural objects and hence to enter into a relationship with them in which all their qualities as living things could be experienced—qualities of character, emotional significance and moral reassurance. When this passage, in its ultimate revision, appeared in *The Excursion* (some years before the publication of *Biographia Literaria*) it was in this sense that its readers, particularly Shelley, Keats and Byron, learned to understand the word Imagination and hence the theories set out in this passage became the most important single source of ideas for the later phase of English Romanticism.

6

Imagination and Fancy

In the years which followed the publication of *Lyrical Ballads* both Wordsworth and Coleridge continued to think about and to discuss the theory of the Imagination, both in the very special sense in which they had been using it and also in its more general sense as denoting a power of artistic creation. In the case of Wordsworth this further thought brought some clarification of his ideas but no very radical changes: both *The Prelude* and *The Excursion* continue, in the main, the ideas to be found in the 1798 version of *The Ruined Cottage* and in the various fragments written at about the same time. Certainly the *Preface* of 1815 shows that he had acquired from Coleridge certain ideas about the Imagination and the Fancy as powers of creating images in poetry but this part of the theory does not appear prominently in his major poems and was not central to his beliefs. In the case of Coleridge, however, this further thought did change vitally his ideas on the Imagination. Between 1800 and 1817 he altered his conception of the One Life and Man's relation to it, he generalized the meaning of the Imagination to cover poetic creation as well as contact with the One Life, he produced his distinction of Imagination and Fancy, and he arrived finally at a Transcendental theory of the Imagination, resting on bases quite different from his Unitarianism of 1797. It was this theory which he published in *Biographia Literaria* in 1817.

In view of its importance in the history of literary criticism, one would expect *Biographia Literaria* to be of much greater importance than *The Excursion* in the formation of the second generation of Romantic poets, but in fact all the evidence indicates that this was not so. The influence of Coleridge's later theories on English poetry must be sought in the Victorian period, not the Romantic. Strangely, Coleridge himself ceased to produce poetry of any importance after the spring of 1802—that is, at the time when he changed his conception of the nature of the One Life and well before he made the distinction which is so fundamental to his later theory of Imagination. Wordsworth, it is true, incorporated the distinction into some of the later books of *The Prelude* and attempted to set it out in his *Preface* of 1815, but it receives little mention in *The Excursion* and it had little importance in his system as a whole. Byron, Shelley and Keats ignore the distinction completely, and I have not been able to find in their poetry[1] any traces of the Transcendental theory of the Imagination, or of Transcendental philosophy generally: indeed, the ideas of Shelley and Byron were fairly well formed before 1817. Therefore I shall not attempt to follow in any detail the changes in Coleridge's ideas after 1802 (and to do so would be an unnecessary labour in view of the extensive treatment his later ideas have received), but the developments which took place between 1799 and 1802 are interesting because they show the growth of the differences between Wordsworth and Coleridge and also because they cast additional light on the original conception of the Imagination which the two poets shared. A second matter of interest is that the particular form which the discussions took provided the source of the later Romantic use of classical mythology.

In order to follow these developments it is important to notice that up to this point the theory of the Imagination had been for Wordsworth and Coleridge a theory about their experience of the world and not a theory about literary expression. In 1797 and 1798 Wordsworth and Coleridge both wrote many poems to express their view of the nature of the world

[1] The influence of Coleridge's theory appears in prose in Shelley's *Defence of Poetry* (1822).

and of the importance of the Imagination which could grasp the nature of the world, but they gave no sign that they thought that the Imagination played a special part in the production of language and imagery, despite the history of the word, nor do they seem, even in the Advertisement to *Lyrical Ballads*, to have given any special thought to the Imagination conceived as a power of creating literary expressions. But after 1798 Coleridge was deeply concerned with the problem of expression. His struggle to finish *Christabel*, his eventual failure to do so, and his sense of waning poetic creativeness, must all have turned his attention in that direction, and, as we should expect, it was Coleridge who developed in this direction the original theory of the Imagination which he and Wordsworth had produced. Wordsworth followed slowly. Even the Imagination-Fancy distinction is applied in *The Prelude* only to the experience of nature and not to literary creation, and though in the *Preface* of 1815 the discussion of the distinction as applied to literature shows that Wordsworth had given long thought to it, yet this was his first written reference to the subject. At the same time he continued to believe in the existence of mute poets, men who had the faculty of Imagination without any power of expressing themselves in poetry.[1] This difference is important in the steps which led up to Coleridge's distinction of Imagination and Fancy, the more so as the discussions which Coleridge had with Wordsworth at the time, and the immediate problem out of which the distinction sprang, were both concerned with expression. Any account of the Imagination as a power of literary conception, and of the distinction between Imagination and Fancy must begin earlier than 1802. Although Coleridge claimed to be first to 'desynonymise' the two words, he claimed (as Wordsworth did also) to base this on a distinction in usage, and the two words had in fact drawn apart in the eighteenth century, 'imagination' becoming the higher word.[2] Moreover the Imagination had already, at different times, been credited with most of the powers which Coleridge later claimed

[1] *The Excursion*, I. 77–80, *The Prelude* (1805), XII. 264–77.
[2] See Wilma L. Kennedy, *The English Heritage of Coleridge of Bristol*.

for it (though *not* with the power of recognizing the life in nature).

By uncovering and reasserting for his century a self-directing power in the mind superior to the reasoning, George Berkeley offered a basis for recognition of an autonomous faculty of imagination associated with reason. By asserting the proneness of the understanding to error and noting the laboriousness of its operations as compared with those of the intuitive reason, David Hume challenged the right of the understanding to dominate imagination. William Collins made the important association of imagination with truth and revealed unmistakably that creativeness is more than combination of images . . . Joshua Reynolds . . . recognized . . . 'a kind of intuition' by which the man of imagination is guided, understood the creativeness of Michael Angelo, knew the imagination as 'residence of truth' and therefore autonomous. . . .[1]

The uses of the word obviously varied and it was in the general sense of a power of intuitive understanding that Coleridge and Wordsworth had adopted the word in 1797.

In the use of the term 'imagination' in literary and artistic criticism, later eighteenth century usage seems occasionally to have made a differentiation between 'imagination' and 'fancy' in which the former had the connotation of conceiving and creating in art, where the latter suggested rather the power of variegating and decorating. In the seventeen-eighties Sir Joshua Reynolds made a contrast between the genius and imagination of Michelangelo and the taste and fancy of Raphael, which Fuseli explained (in 1801) as follows: 'When Reynolds said that M. Agnolo had more *imagination* and Raffaelo more *fancy*, he meant to say, that the one had more sublimity and elemental fire; the other was richer in social imagery, in genial conceits, and artificial variety.'[2]

In 1792 Dugald Stewart, in his *Elements of the Philosophy of the Human Mind*, had drawn a distinction which he claimed was based on the usage of 'our best writers' and in which

---

[1] id., pp. 91–2. But see pp. 14–15 above for certain qualifications to this view.

[2] *Lectures on Painting, Second Series* (1830), pp. 109–10. The lectures were delivered in 1801. The passage is quoted in S. H. Monk, *The Sublime*.

imagination was 'the power which gives birth to the productions of the poet and the painter', while fancy was the power of 'illustrating and embellishing a subject' with 'resembling or analogous ideas'. As Wordsworth also claimed (in the *Preface* of 1815) that ordinary usage distinguished between the two words, it would appear that the kind of differentiation suggested by Fuseli and Stewart was at least half-established by the turn of the century.

Before 1797 neither Wordsworth nor Coleridge paid much heed to any distinction between the two words. Coleridge treated them as synonyms, and when he spoke of the highest poetic power he used 'fancy'.

My fancy met thee in her shaping hour.[1]

Wordsworth did not use 'imagination' in any of his extant works before 1795 or 1796, and then he used it for the power of forming images. 'His imagination is powerful, being strengthened by the habit of picturing possible forms of society where his crimes would no longer be crimes.'[2] But imagination in its sense of receiving or forming images was at the root of Wordsworth's system. It was natural that he should use it for the very special kind of perception he intended, and when he spoke of 'young imagination' in the *Lines left upon a Seat in a Yew-Tree* he fixed the term that would be employed in his discussions with Coleridge. It was, moreover, a suitable term from the point of view of common use both because of its implications of intuitive understanding and because this power of seizing and perceiving the whole in nature was not unlike the artist's power of conceiving a new work. However, this use by the two poets of 'imagination' did not carry with it any contrast with 'fancy'. In Coleridge's letters of 1797 and

[1] *To Richard Brinsley Sheridan*, draft of line 3.
[2] *Preface to The Borderers*. The use of the word here may owe something to Godwin's use of it in *Political Justice* (1793), i, pp. 176–7: 'There is indeed no species of composition, in which the seeds of a morality too perfect for our present improvements in science, may more reasonably be expected to show themselves, than in works of imagination.' In a footnote Godwin discusses Romances from this point of view.

in *The Ruined Cottage*, 'imagination' was not contrasted with 'fancy' but with 'judgement' and if any special sense can be traced in Wordsworth's uses of the word 'fancy' between 1795 and 1800 it is that of 'self-deluding' or 'not subdued to the nature of things'.[1]

In *The Ruined Cottage* the Imagination meant the power 'to apprehend the moral properties and scope of things' and hence to see the whole life and spirit of Nature. Deep feeling played an important part in the growth of this power, for it helped to fasten the forms of nature on the developing mind, and out of this came the power to 'read' these forms. Moreover Imagination itself produced deep feeling in the form of sympathetic understanding and love of Nature and of Man. When Wordsworth first came to use 'imagination' as a term of literary criticism, in the second edition of *Lyrical Ballads* in 1800, he used it in a sense derived from this. In the preface he spoke of casting a certain colouring of Imagination over his tales of rustic life, and what he meant by this is apparent

---

[1] I have traced five occurrences of the word:

> Here will I dwell in peace, so Fancy wrought
> Roaming the illimitable waters round . . .
> To break my dream the vessel reached its bound.
> > *Guilt and Sorrow*, 362–7.

> Even such a man my fancy bodied forth
> From the first moment that I loved the maid . . .
> It may not be—I am cut off from man.
> > *The Borderers*, 1321–7.

> On visionary views would fancy feed
> Till his eye streamed with tears.
> > *Lines left upon a Seat in a Yew-Tree*, 45–6.

> And when at length the silence of my grief
> By some irregular fancy from within
> Or by some chance impression from without
> Was first disturbed . . .
> > Rejected addition to *The Ruined Cottage*.

> In him will admiration be no weak
> Fantastic quality that doth betray
> Its owner, but a firm support . . .
> > *The Prelude*, p. 594.

from the Pedlar's treatment of the tale of Margaret.[1] But more interesting than this is the note to *The Thorn*, where he first distinguishes between imagination and fancy.

Superstitious men are almost always men of slow faculties and deep feelings; their minds are not loose but adhesive; they have a reasonable share of the imagination, by which I mean the faculty that produces impressive effects out of simple elements; but they are utterly destitute of fancy, the power by which pleasure and surprise are excited by sudden varieties of situation and accumulated imagery.

Wordsworth's stress on feeling in this note is in keeping with the ideas of *The Ruined Cottage*. There the significance which he recognized in the forms of nature was an emotional significance. It was developed by the association of the forms with deep feeling, and the life of nature was recognized in the interaction of form and feeling. Thus the man of deep feeling possessed the creative faculty.

> they build up greatest things
> From least suggestions, ever on the watch
> Willing to work, and to be wrought upon.[2]

On the other hand, however necessary quick faculties might be to anyone who was to be more than a 'mute poet', their purpose was expression rather than artistic conception. Here 'fancy' seems to mean the power of varying and embellishing, and from the evidence of Reynolds, Fuseli and Stewart it would seem that Wordsworth was distinguishing Imagination from Fancy in the way in which ordinary usage distinguished

[1] O. J. Campbell and P. Mueschke in 'Wordsworth's Aesthetic Development 1795–1802', Univ. of Mich. Publications in Lang. and Lit., discuss (pp. 33 ff.) how the 'half-mystical aesthetic experience' recorded in *Tintern Abbey* makes possible the great poems of the later editions of *Lyrical Ballads*, marked by pathos and the influence of sensations of nature on conduct. Unfortunately they regard the account of the 'half-mystical aesthetic experience' as a direct expression, 'not translated into any religious system or philosophical code', and so their discussion of the connection lacks detail.

[2] *The Prelude* (1805), XIII. 97–100. Compare the addition to *An Evening Walk* quoted on p. 73 above.

them, but that he was giving something of his own interpretation of the power of the Imagination.

Though Wordsworth in this note contrasted the Imagination and the Fancy as they apply to literary production, yet he does not seem to have found any activity of the Fancy to correspond to, or to contrast with, the activity of the Imagination in the experience of nature. In *The Prelude*, Book II, written in 1799, he distinguished again between the moods of rebelliousness and of wise passivity in the creative power, and in addition he distinguished from the creative power another toil

> Than analytic industry to me
> More pleasing, and whose character I deem
> Is more poetic as resembling more
> Creative agency. I mean to speak
> Of that interminable building rear'd
> By observation of affinities
> In objects where no brotherhood exists
> To common minds.[1]

But he did not call this power the Fancy.

This, then, was as far as any distinction between the two words had gone before Coleridge settled at Keswick near the Wordsworths, at the time when the second edition of *Lyrical Ballads* was in the press. The next two years were to be as decisive for Coleridge the philosopher as the years 1797 and 1798 had been for Coleridge the poet, and it will be necessary to follow closely the way in which he reconsidered firstly the current doctrine of the association of ideas, then the place of mind in the world, and finally his own doctrines of Imagination and of Nature. In 1800 Coleridge was still engaged in the struggle to finish *Christabel*, and it may have been the effort to match in the Second Part the tone and the quality of suggestion of the First Part that set him thinking about the relation between feelings and the words that express them. His consideration of this topic, which was to remain important in his subsequent thinking, led him to the belief that emotion,

---

[1] id., II. 398–405.

not the mechanical factors listed by Hartley, was the important factor in associating ideas. The implications of this break with Hartley's system were important. On 22 September 1800, he wrote to Godwin,

I yet cannot frame myself to the thought that you should cease to appear as a *bold* moral thinker. I wish you to write a book on the power of words, and the processes by which human feelings form affinities with them. In short, I wish you to *philosophize* Horne Tooke's system, and to solve the great Questions, whether there be reason to hold that an action bearing all the *semblance* of predesigning consciousness may yet be simply organic, and whether a *series* of such actions are possible? And close on the heels of this question would follow the old, Is Logic the *Essence* of thinking? In other words Is *thinking* impossible without arbitrary signs? And how far is the word 'arbitrary' a misnomer? Are not words, etc., parts and germinations of the plant? And what is the Law of their Growth? In something of this order I would endeavour to destroy the old antithesis of *Words* and *Things*, elevating, as it were, Words into Things and living Things too. All the nonsense of vibrations etc., you would of course dismiss.

The system of the philologist Horne Tooke was one in which the original words of any language were taken to be the names of things, either things at rest (nouns) or things in motion (verbs). Tooke deduced all the rest of grammar and all the development of abstract ideas from man's use and development of words; truth for instance being defined as 'what a man troweth' and right as 'what has been ruled'. In Tooke's view, Locke was wrong to talk of 'the composition of ideas', but should have seen that they were 'merely a contrivance of language', and Tooke suggests that a new turn could be given to Locke's remark that 'The consideration of Ideas and words . . . would afford us *another sort* of *Logick* and *Critick* than what we have hitherto been acquainted with'.[1]

Coleridge's phrase 'to philosophize Horne Tooke' implies that he did not intend to follow Tooke's own thorough-going nominalist philosophy. What seems to have been in his mind was a consideration of the powers in man which thus developed

[1] Horne Tooke, *Diversions of Purley* (1829), pp. 19, 30, 36.

131

the senses of words and shaped ideas. A letter of 7 August 1803 to Southey shows what he thought this power to be.

I hold that association depends in a much greater degree on the recurrence of resembling states of feeling than on trains of ideas, that the recollection of early childhood in latest old age depends on and is explicable by this, and if this be true, Hartley's system totters. If I were asked how it is that very old people remember *visually* only the events of early childhood . . . I should think it a perfectly philosophical answer that old age remembers childhood by becoming 'a second childhood' . . . I almost think that ideas *never* recall ideas . . . any more than leaves in a forest create each other's motion. The breeze it is that runs through them—it is the soul, the state of feeling.

It can be seen that this is implicit in the earlier letter to Godwin, and that in 1800 Coleridge had taken two important steps. By declaring that 'the soul, the state of feeling' associates ideas and shapes the associated ideas, he had placed the source of knowledge in the soul itself, instead of in nature acting on the mind, while by making words and ideas the outgrowth of inner feelings he brought the process by which ideas are formed close to the process of poetic creation. In a letter to Davy on 3 February 1801, he reaffirmed the importance of his new line of thought.

My heart within me *burns* to . . . *concenter* my free mind to the affinities of the Feelings with Words and Ideas under the title of 'Concerning Poetry and the nature of the Pleasures derived from it'. I have faith that I do understand the subject, and I am sure that, if I write what I ought to do on it, the work should supersede all the Books of Metaphysics . . . and all the Books of Morals too.

This change in Coleridge's metaphysical approach was soon reinforced by that study of Kant's work which was to lead him to his own line in philosophy. He began this study in February 1801,[1] and transcendentalist ideas soon began to enter his correspondence. In March he wrote to Poole that he had 'completely extricated the notions of time and space' and had overthrown the doctrine of association as taught by

[1] *Letters of S. T. Coleridge*, ed. E. H. Coleridge (1895), i, p. 351 note.

Hartley and with it the doctrine of necessity. 'At Words-worth's advice, or rather fervent entreaty', he intermitted the pursuit in order to save his health, but a week later he returned to the subject to attack his old enemy Newton[1] in a letter of 23 March. This letter indicates that the Kantian influence to be seen in the talk of extricating 'the ideas of space and time' was not the whole story, and that his ideas were undergoing continuous modification and alteration rather than abrupt change. (The main influence of his German reading came much later.) The letter shows both the extent of the change in his ideas and also the continuity that still remained between his new ideas and those he had variously held in 1797 and 1800. He began by repeating the attack on the Judgement, as only able to grasp particulars, which he had made in 1797. 'Be not afraid that I shall join the Little-ists. I believe that I shall delight you by my detection of their artifices. *Now Mr. Locke was the founder of this sect, himself a perfect Little-ist.*' He then goes on to assert, as he had the year before, that deep feeling is the operative power in understanding, and he then ends by linking this power with something that sounds very like the Kantian (or Primary) Imagination.

My opinion is this—that deep Thinking is attainable only by a man of deep Feeling, and that all Truth is a species of Revelation. The more I understand of Sir Isaac Newton's works, the more boldly I dare utter to my own mind, and therefore to *you*, that I believe the souls of five hundred Sir Isaac Newtons would go to the making up of a Shakespere or a Milton . . . Newton was a mere materialist—*Mind* in his system is always passive—a lazy Looker-on on an external World. If the mind be not *passive*, if it indeed be made in God's Image, and that too in the sublimest sense, the Image of the *Creator*, there is ground for suspicion that any system built on the passiveness of the mind must be false, as a system. . . . I assure, solemnly assure you, that you and Wordsworth are the only men on Earth to whom I would have uttered a word on this subject.

[1] One constant thing through Coleridge's changes was that he regarded Newton as the chief enemy, whether from the point of view of Baxter (see p. 38 above) or of Berkeley (*Gutch Memorandum Book* 29 (a)), or, as here, of Transcendentalism.

At this point Coleridge's doctrine seems to have been that 'the soul, the state of feeling', equated here with Mind, both shapes our ideas and creates the external world. In *Biographia Literaria* these functions were distributed between the Secondary and the Primary Imagination, but here these seem to be one, and on them the external world, as we know it, depends.

This doctrine has very obvious implications for the soul's relation to that One Life[1] which the Imagination found in Nature, and when Coleridge wrote *Dejection: an Ode* in the spring of 1802 he brought out these implications very clearly. The themes of the poem are his love for Sara Hutchinson, the unhappiness of his marriage and the failure of his 'shaping spirit of Imagination'. In the passages dealing with this last theme, the references to Wordsworth's ideas and Wordsworth's poetry are clear.[2] Sara was a member of Wordsworth's circle and how closely Coleridge had Wordsworth in mind in this part of the poem is shown for instance by the fact that in addressing a draft to Wordsworth he changed

> Thus thus should'st thou rejoice,

addressed to Sara, into

> Thus thus dost thou rejoice,

addressed to William, with the corresponding alteration of

> To thee would all things live

to

> To thee do all things live.

It was with Wordsworth that Coleridge was by implication contrasting himself here, even in the original version.

Equally clear in this section of the poem is the subjective interpretation which Coleridge now put on the life which he and Wordsworth found in nature.

> I may not hope from outward forms to win
> The passion and the life whose fountains are within.
> O Wordsworth we receive but what we give
> And in our life alone does nature live;
>
> . . .

---

[1] At about this time Coleridge lost his faith in Unitarianism. See *Collected Letters*, ii, p. 807.   [2] H. House, *Coleridge*, pp. 136, 166.

And would we aught behold of higher worth,
Than the inanimate, cold world, *allowed*
To the poor loveless ever-anxious crowd,
Ah! from the soul itself must issue forth,
A light, a glory, a fair luminous cloud
   Enveloping the earth!
And from the soul itself there must be sent
A sweet and powerful voice of its own birth,
Of all sweet sounds the life and element!
O pure of heart! thou need'st not ask of me
What this strong music of the soul may be?
. . .
Joy blameless poet! joy that ne'er was given
Save to the pure and in their purest hour.
. . .
O Wordsworth! friend of my devoutest choice
Great son of genius! full of light and love,
   Thus, thus dost thou rejoice.
To thee do all things live, from pole to pole,
Their life the eddying of thy living soul.[1]

The change in ideas will be seen if this is contrasted with any of the passages in which Wordsworth had described Nature as a teacher, for instance,

   But he had felt the power
Of Nature, and already was prepared
By his intense conceptions to receive
Deeply the lesson deep of love, which he
Whom Nature by whatever means has taught
To feel intensely, cannot but receive.[2]

Many passages in Wordsworth's earlier poetry say, as *Dejection* does, that joy and passion in some sense create the One Life[3] but none say, as it does, that the One Life depends on that joy and is a reflection of it. For Wordsworth the One Life was pre-existent—'a soul divine which we participate': for Coleridge it was the product of the creative soul (though that soul

---

[1] Version addressed to Wordsworth, *Collected Letters*, ii, pp. 817–18.
[2] *The Ruined Cottage*, MS B, ll. 113–18.
[3] e.g. *The Prelude* (1805), II. 418–34; v. 10–48; and cf. *Frost at Midnight*, ll. 54–60.

or state of feeling was, of course, the image of the Creator). Joy is the condition of creativeness in both but for different reasons. In the earlier system, to which Wordsworth still held, joy was necessary because otherwise there was a barrier between Man and Nature, and this barrier could be described in terms of rebellion against nature or wise passiveness towards her. In Coleridge's new system joy was necessary because the soul itself was creative and could only create life in nature when it was itself healthy and fully alive.

It is pointless now to discuss which of the two metaphysical views was true; it is sufficient to note that they were different, and that the differences, though they may seem small, issued from what were now fundamentally different concepts of the relationship of Nature to man's soul. Some disagreement between the two poets on the concept of Nature was inevitable and that it took place is shown by one of Coleridge's note-book entries.

Dear William . . . avoid becoming a pedant yourself in a bad cause. . . . But, surely, always to look at the superficies of objects for the purpose of taking delight in their beauty, and sympathy with their real or imagined life, is as deleterious to the health and manhood of the intellect as always to be peering and unravelling contrivance may be to the simplicity of the affection and the grandeur and unity of the imagination. O dearest William. Would Ray or Durham have spoken of God as you spoke of Nature?[1]

It is perhaps worth adding that whatever personal bars to poetic creativeness may be found in Coleridge's own history at this time, yet, when he could speak in this manner of 'the real or imagined life' of natural objects, then the theme of *The Ancient Mariner* was lost to him. The difference between the two concepts is the difference between contact with another being and contact with one's own reflection in a mirror: however interesting the new status of the One Life, as a reflection of the observer's soul, might be to a philosopher, it was unlikely to exercise 'the passion of a great poet' in any but such a minor and personal poem as *Dejection* is.

Of course, in spite of this fundamental difference, the two

[1] *Anima Poetae*, pp. 35–6.

poets still had much common ground for they were still trying to describe the same experience, though in terms of different metaphysical systems. For Coleridge, the soul created the One Life in nature, but in doing so it acted in imitation of the Creator, and the innocent and joyful soul ought naturally to act in this way. Hence he could agree at most points with Wordsworth who found in nature the One Life of which the soul was part, and which the wisely passive soul could discover there through the power of its feelings. Nevertheless there was a difference, and Coleridge, preoccupied with the creative nature of the soul and with his loss of poetic power, became more concerned with the Imagination as an activity of the mind (in its widest sense) exercised in literature, where Wordsworth continued to see it as a natural phenomenon occurring in the life of a chosen being.

The distinction of Imagination and Fancy came out of Coleridge's effort to translate Gessner's *Das Erste Schiffer*, which made him reconsider the use of mythology in poetry, and out of arguments with Wordsworth on poetic diction and the creativeness of passion. A letter of 13 July 1802 to Sotheby describes the problem he found in Gessner's poem and also illustrates his loose use of 'imagination' and 'fancy' as critical terms at this date.[1]

The first conception is noble, so very good that I am spiteful enough to hope that I shall discover it not to have been original in Gessner,—he has so abominably maltreated it. . . . But the machinery is so superlatively contemptible and commonplace; as if a young man could not dream of a tale which had deeply impressed him without Cupid, or have a fair wind all the way to an island within sight of the shore without Æolus. Æolus himself is a god devoted and dedicated, I should have thought, to the Muse of Travestie. His speech in Gessner is not deficient in fancy, but it is a girlish fancy, and the god of the wind, exceedingly disquieted with *animal* love, makes a very ridiculous figure in my imagination.

In the same letter he recounted his difference of opinion with Wordsworth on the subject of poetic diction. The discussion

[1] Compare also *Dejection: an Ode*, stanza VI, where 'fancy' is placed on the same level as 'hope'.

had turned on the way in which passion justified the poetic license of personifying a river, in this case Drayton's Ouse. Wordsworth's arguments were not given, but his position at this time was clear enough. For him the creativeness of human passion would have justified the license, because it would have given a real life to the river. He had just written, in his last revision of *The Ruined Cottage*, made during the winter of 1801–2,

> The Poets, in their elegies and songs
> Lamenting the departed, call the groves,
> They call upon the hills and streams to mourn,
> And senseless rocks: nor idly; for they speak
> In these their invocations, with a voice
> Obedient to the strong creative power
> Of human passion.[1]

But he would not have extended the license to later poets who merely imitated it as a trick of style.

Coleridge on the other hand was interested in the natural affinities between emotions and words, and he gave passion a wider meaning and he thought of creation here as literary creation.

In my opinion, every phrase, every metaphor, every personification, should have its justifying cause in some *passion*, either of the poet's mind or of the characters described by the poet. But *metre itself* implies a *passion*, that is a state of excitement both in the poet's mind, and is expected in that of the reader; and, though I stated this to Wordsworth, and he has in some sort stated it in his preface, yet he has not done justice to it, nor has he, in my opinion, sufficiently answered it. In my opinion, poetry justifies as *Poetry*, independent of any other passion, some new combinations of language and *commands* the omission of many others allowable in other compositions. . . . Indeed, we have had lately some little controversy on the subject, and we begin to suspect that there is somewhere or other a *radical* difference in our opinions.

The fundamental divergence is clear enough. Wordsworth thought of passion as creating or bringing to the level of consciousness a real life which the poetry described: Coleridge

[1] *The Excursion*, i. 475–81.

thought of passion as having particular affinities with the words which were 'the parts and germinations of the plant', and hence as justifying a particular use of language.[1]

This obviously bore on the subject of mythology, as the personification of natural objects, and on its poetic use. Coleridge must have meditated the matter for some weeks. Succeeding letters show that he was thinking about the nature of poetry, his discussions with Wordsworth, and the difference between the imagination of Gessner and that of the Old Testament poets. Finally in another letter to Sotheby, on 10 September 1802, he arrived at his distinction between the Imagination and the Fancy, illustrating it from poetry and mythology. The letter shows that in its origin the distinction was an attempt to apply to literature the theory of the Imagination which Wordsworth had developed in relation to the experience of Nature, and to explain the less fundamental and less successful treatment of Nature to be found in some other poets as being the result of a lesser power, the Fancy.

He began by distinguishing between the poet of Imagination and the poet of Fancy. His premise is that 'Nature has her proper interest and he will know what it is who . . . feels that everything has a life of its own and that we are all *one Life*'. The great poet will have his heart and his intellect intimately combined and unified with the great appearances of nature. He is the poet of passion, distinguished by the Imagination, the modifying and coadunating (unifying) faculty. Bowles, on the other hand, sees in nature only analogies with a moral application (Wordsworth later gave this as the characteristic of the Fancy in the last book of *The Prelude*). His heart and intellect are merely held in loose mixture with the appearances of nature by means of formal similes. Such tricks of style have their place, and there are moods when they please, but these are not the highest and most appropriate moods of the poet.

[1] Coleridge continued his side of this debate in *Biographia Literaria*. Of course the idea that passion demands figurative language was a common one. 'I know indeed that critics have asserted figurative diction to be natural to persons labouring under strong emotions' (Aikin, *Letters from a Father to his Son*, p. 74).

Such a poet as Bowles has the sensibility but not the passion of a great poet, and is distinguished by the Fancy, the aggregating faculty of the mind.

Coleridge illustrated this distinction by a comparison of Hebrew poetry, exemplifying the Imagination, with the Greek which has only the Fancy. 'In the Hebrew Poets each Thing has a Life of its own, and yet they are all our Life. In God they move and live and *have* their being; not *had* as the cold System of Newtonian Theology represents, but *have*.' While for the Greeks, 'All natural Objects were *dead*, mere hollow Statues, but there was a Godkin or a Godessling *included* in each.'[1] In short, the poet of Imagination and passion participates in the *One Life*, and exhibits it in his poetry; the poet of Fancy and mere sensibility does not, and so nature supplies him only with accidental analogies and purely formal similes.

This letter is the culmination of Coleridge's line of thought during the preceding two years. The distinction of Imagination and Fancy is, in the first place, an attempt to apply to literature the theory of the Imagination which had been developed in relation to the experience of nature. In essence, the application Coleridge makes is simple enough, that imaginative poetry is poetry which expresses imaginative experience, but it is complicated by the fact that of all the possible experiences which we might call imaginative, he and Wordsworth had used the word Imagination only for the experience of the One Life in nature. Until now the new faith had been a creed to be expressed in poetry. Coleridge was moving on to

[1] Wordsworth transmitted the essence of this comparison between the two mythologies in *The Excursion*, iv. 707–62, but in this passage he confined the Fancy to Greek Sculpture and his defence of the imaginativeness of Greek religion had a great effect upon the younger poets. In another passage, iv. 847–87, Wordsworth gave examples of Fancy from Greek mythology, but the poet most affected by this passage, Keats, never made any distinction between Imagination and Fancy, and so that passage too contributed to making Greek mythology the type of imaginative creation. It is interesting to wonder what would have happened had Wordsworth followed Coleridge more closely in exalting Hebrew poetry at the expense of Greek. Would Keats have written an *Exodus* instead of *Endymion*?

say that only poetry which expressed this creed could be called poetry of the Imagination, even though this meant condemning Greek poetry.[1]

Further, for Coleridge the soul or the state of feeling shaped both words and ideas. It gave knowledge and it gave expression by the way in which it associated and modified, and hence the Imagination was described as the coadunating and modifying faculty. An analysis of the way in which the Imagination deals with images was also for Coleridge an analysis of the way in which the mind acquires knowledge, and hence came the superiority of the Imagination over the Fancy, which, undirected by feeling, did not unify and modify but merely aggregated. This reason for the Imagination's superiority is fundamental in all his later thinking and, as his reading of German philosophers progressed and his attachment to Transcendental Idealism grew, he transposed his distinction into that system.

Unfortunately, when Coleridge came to publish the distinction in the unfinished chapter of *Biographia Literaria*, he gave it in such a concise form that it is merely a definition[2]

[1] He did not, so far as I know, repeat this condemnation in later writings, but its appearance in *The Excursion* indicates that he must have held the view for some time. His more mature view of the relation of Greek poetry to Greek religion is to be found in *Literary Remains*, II. 73.

> The Greeks were polytheists; their religion was local; almost the only object of all their knowledge, art and taste, was their gods; and, accordingly, their productions were, if the expression may be allowed, statuesque. . . . The Greeks reared a structure which . . . fitted the mind with the calm and elevated impression of perfect beauty and symmetrical proportion.

[2] Both Shawcross (in his edition of *Biographia Literaria*, i, p. lxix) and House (*Coleridge*, p. 149) agree, though for different reasons, that the *Biographia* definition of Imagination does not represent Coleridge's thought satisfactorily. Shawcross thinks that the definition keeps too close to Schelling, and he prefers the account in *On Poesy or Art*: I have tried to show that the two accounts are not inconsistent and that they supplement one another. House regards the definition as too concise (a view in which I concur) and, quoting Coleridge on the part played in association by the affections, he stresses that for Coleridge the exercise of the Imagination involved 'the whole man'. He treats Coleridge's

141

and the passage gives no indication of his full thought on the subject. In the *Biographia*, nature dropped out altogether: the secondary Imagination now simply unified conceptions to make fresh artistic conceptions, and there was no further particular suggestion as to why this unification and modification should be specially important. This account needs to be supplemented from his lecture of 1818 *On Poesy or Art*.

theory almost wholly in terms of introspective psychology and does not quote either *On Poesy or Art* or the important letter to Godwin (22 September 1800). But Coleridge's introspections involved a metaphysical theory of the structure of the mind, and I have tried to stress that his theory of Imagination was at least as much epistemological as psychological (it was intended to overthrow Locke) and that it was the basis of his transcendental metaphysics. No special originality is claimed for the account in this chapter, which is compounded out of those of Shawcross, House and Basil Willey (*Coleridge on Imagination and Fancy*). It is intended simply as an account of the steps which led Coleridge away from his earlier position and it should be read in conjunction with the Epilogue to this book.

R. L. Brett's attempt (*E & S*, 1949) to show that Coleridge's theory, as expressed in *Biographia Literaria* and *On Poesy or Art*, was derived from Cudworth is unsatisfactory because it rests on a series of misdatings. In Brett's view, Coleridge became interested in Cudworth as defender of the established church. (See p. 30, n. 6 above, for the defects of this, which can be indicated quickly by saying that Brett couples Hobbes and Hartley together.) He considers that Coleridge learned from Cudworth to see the mind as active in knowing, but there is nothing in the Cudworth passages he cites except ordinary Platonism, and the Coleridge passage he cites (which is also Platonic) was written before Coleridge had read Cudworth. (See p. 30, n. 6.) Brett then fails to realize that Coleridge's account of hearing Wordsworth read a poem 'in my twenty-fourth year' is at best a conflation of three separate events, the first meeting in 1795, Coleridge's reading of *Guilt and Sorrow* in 1796, and Wordsworth's readings to Coleridge in 1797 (see Margoliouth, *Wordsworth and Coleridge*, pp. 2–4), and so he confidently dates Coleridge's first interest in the Imagination back into 1795–6, that is to say nearer the first reading of Cudworth and before the period of intimacy with Wordsworth (and, one might add, in the period of *Religious Musings* and the revised *Joan of Arc*). Finally Brett rests his argument on an analogy between the action of the plastic power in material creation and the activity of the esemplastic (which he seems to regard as meaning 'shaping'!) power in poetry. ('If we substitute the poet for God in this account of the creation', etc.) This, of course,

Here we learn that the two kinds of imagination, primary and secondary, are, in effect, the one faculty working to produce first the external world and secondly poetic creations based on that world. The results of artistic creation are valid because the external world on which it works has already been created by the Imagination, and so already has qualities of mind in it, and already shares the One Life of the consciousness that created it.

Not to acquire cold notions—lifeless technical rules—but living and life-producing ideas, which shall contain their own evidence, the certainty that they are essentially one with the germinal causes in nature—his consciousness being focus and mirror of both—for this does the artist for a time abandon the external real in order to return to it with a complete sympathy with its internal and actual. For of all we see, hear, feel and touch the substance is and must be in ourselves; and therefore there is no alternative between the dreary (and thank heaven! almost impossible) belief that everything around us is but a phantom, or that the life which is in us is in them likewise.[1]

For this reason, the qualities of the human consciousness will be found as half-realized strivings in all nature, and the artist of genius will synthesize and develop into full thought these incomplete strivings, and thus make actual in consciousness what is already potential in nature.

In the objects of nature are presented, as in a mirror, all the possible elements, steps and processes of intellect antecedent to

is only an analogy and one that might be applied to almost any account of the creation, but in any case Brett thinks that *The Destiny of Nations* was first written in 1797, and so he does not realize that Coleridge had written of the Monads of the all-conscious Spirit before he had read Cudworth. (Indeed, even Erasmus Darwin writes of 'Nature's plastic power'.) Without the support of his mis-datings, Brett's argument is reduced to a loose analogy between imaginative creation and a not unusual account of material creation.

[1] *Literary Remains*, i, p. 224. The passage continues, a few lines later, in a way which relates this life discussed here to the spirit of nature: 'The artist must imitate that which is within the thing, that which is active through form and figure, and discourses to us by symbols—the *Natur-geist* or spirit of nature.'

consciousness, and therefore to the full development of the intelligential act; and man's mind is the very focus of all the rays of intellect which are scattered throughout the images of nature. Now so to place these images, totalized, and fitted to the limits of the human mind, as to elicit from, and to super-induce upon, the forms themselves the moral reflexions to which they approximate, to make the external internal, the internal external, to make nature thought, and thought nature,—this is the mystery of genius in the Fine Arts.[1]

This line of thought makes all nature, as well as works of art, dependent on the Imagination, and it allows as imaginative, in the artistic sense, a much larger class of ideas than simply those which asserted the One Life and its consequences. Coleridge was giving the word back some of the more generalized use it had had in common usage, while still maintaining for this more general use the claim to the essential truth of the Imagination.

From all this, the word 'imagination' developed a wide range of meaning in the Romantic vocabulary. The extremes of the range can be illustrated by Wordsworth's description of the Imagination in terms of literary criticism only in the *Preface* of 1815 and, at the other end, by

> Imagination—here the power so called
> Through sad incompetence of human speech[2]

in *The Prelude*. In their uses of the word in criticism Coleridge and Wordsworth hardly differed, but the highest applications they gave to the word differed as their views on the natural world differed. For Coleridge, the natural world was itself a product of the Imagination; 'substance is and must be in ourselves' and therefore the life which is in us is in it. Because nature thus shared and reflected the qualities of the Imagination which created it, the Imagination could modify and unify these 'rays of intellect scattered throughout the images of nature' and produce genuine creations, while the Fancy worked only on chance material and chance resemblances.

---

[1] id., i, pp. 222–3. Cf. *Aids to Reflection*, Aphorism xxxvi.
[2] *The Prelude* (1805), vi. 592–3.

For Wordsworth the life in nature was not a partial or scattered suggestion of the human, but a 'strange discipline', an independent and different life.

> And 'tis my faith, that every flower
> Enjoys the air it breathes.[1]

This life merged with Man's only through the Imagination. It was in man that this life rose to consciousness,[2] but the voice which became audible in imaginative experience was the 'clear sonorous voice' of the stream of tendency itself.

But the views had enough in common for this fundamental divergence to be, for the most part, ignored by the two poets. Wordsworth immediately adopted the distinction between Imagination and Fancy, though it was not nearly so fundamental to his system as it was to Coleridge's. It had its greatest prominence in his poetry in the later books of *The Prelude*. Wordsworth had begun his poetic autobiography in 1799, withdrawing from *The Ruined Cottage* some passages dealing with the early life of the Pedlar and incorporating them into two books describing his own childhood. In these the power whose growth is described is the poetic or creative spirit, at times rebellious but for the most part subdued to the things it communed with. When Wordsworth continued the poem in 1804–5, he did not alter this account in the first two books, but in the later books he made an explicit distinction between the Imagination and the Fancy. In Book VIII, retracing the stages of development described in Book II, he wrote

> But when that first poetic Faculty
> Of plain Imagination and severe,
> No longer a mute Influence on the soul,
> An Element of Nature's inner self,
> Began to have some promptings to put on
> A visible shape, and to the works of art,
> The notions and the images of books

[1] *Lines Written in Early Spring*, ll. 11–12.

[2] Man's intercourse with Nature was established by the divine intellect but the conscious expression of it, in poetry or philosophy, only by man. See *The Prelude* (1805), v. 10–48.

> Did knowingly conform itself, by these
> Enflamed, and proud of that her new delight,
> There came among these shapes of human life
> A wilfulness of fancy and conceit
> That gave them new importance to the mind;
> And nature and her objects beautified
> These fictions, as in some sort in their turn
> They burnish'd her.[1]

The next eighty lines of this book have many examples of the Fancy, but there was no set description of the power until the last book. There it closely follows Coleridge's letter to Sotheby, and describes the Fancy as finding moral illustrations in nature and as providing a delight in which

> meditation cannot come, which thought
> Could never heighten.[2]

The hundred lines in Book VIII and the twenty lines of the last book are the only places in the poem where Fancy made any important appearance. It was at best only a refinement in Wordsworth's system, and in *The Excursion* it was even less important than in *The Prelude*.

The most important parts of *The Excursion*—Book I, the dissertation on the forms and the creativeness of the Imagination in Book IV, and that on the active principle and the stream of tendency in Book IX—were conceived in 1798 or 1799. These embody the original conception of the One Life as something independent of man and capable of offering to him, through the Imagination, an enriching, and indeed a saving, relationship. To this account of the Imagination as the power to recognize the life in Nature, Wordsworth added, in Book IV Coleridge's very important idea that ancient religion and mythology could embody earlier examples of the imaginative (or in some cases fanciful) recognition of that life. In these three books Wordsworth's contemporaries found the fullest and clearest exposition of his beliefs and it was from this point that the younger poets who were to take the English Romantic tradition to its next stage began the development of their own germinal ideas.

[1] *The Prelude* (1805), VIII. 510–24. [2] id., XIII. 305–6.

7

The Influence of
The Excursion:
Spirit and Form

The debt of the younger Romantic poets to Wordsworth was well recognized even by their contemporaries. To attempt to trace it in some detail is not to deny their own great originality which Shelley rightly protested in his preface to *The Revolt of Islam*: it is simply that this study is less concerned with that originality than with certain of the common elements which form the unity of the movement. There are 'such things as fountains in the world' but we are concerned with the stream and for our purposes the next important turn in its course came with the publication of *The Excursion* in 1814.

The Excursion grew from *The Ruined Cottage* by a process of expansion and addition. The original narrative of Margaret's life became the first book, stating, as it were, the problem. The theme of the Addendum was expanded, to make Books II–IV, by the introduction of a new character, the Solitary, through whom Wordsworth illustrated his contrast between the rebellious, despondent approach to the world and the imaginative one. Book IV which is the heart of the poem, deals with the Imagination and rises to that passage on the forms of nature and their relation to man which first appeared in the Addendum. In Book V another character, the Pastor, is introduced, and Books V–VII are an attempt to fit the Church of England into Wordsworth's system and vice-versa. However interesting as an example of the poet's growing orthodoxy, these books are of little importance to the present study, and they may be dismissed with a quotation to illustrate their method.

> 'No' the philosophic Priest
> Continued, ''tis not in the vital seat
> Of feeling to produce them, without aid
> From the pure soul, the soul sublime and pure;
> With her two faculties of eye and ear,
> The one by which a creature, whom his sins
> Have rendered prone, can upward look to heaven;
> The other that empowers him to perceive
> The voice of Deity, on height and plain
> Whispering those truths in stillness, which the W O R D,
> To the four quarters of the winds, proclaims.
> Not without such assistance could the use
> Of these benign observances prevail:
> Thus are they born, thus fostered, thus maintained;
> And by the care prospective of our wise
> Forefathers, who, to guard against the shocks,
> The fluctuation and decay of things,
> Embodied and established these high truths
> In solemn institutions.[1]

In Book VIII the Wanderer turns to society and the effect of the Industrial Revolution. The tone of this book is Victorian in its combination of pride in progress with dislike of urban industrialism as an outrage on Nature.

> Can the mother thrive
> By the destruction of her innocent sons
> In whom a premature necessity
> Blocks out the forms of nature, preconsumes
> The reason, famishes the heart.[2]

Book IX turns from Industry to the agricultural labourer. Though this book ends in orthodox pieties, the first part of it was conceived before the turn of the century and it contains

---

[1] *The Excursion*, v. 983–1001. [2] id., VIII. 285–9.

much that was central to Wordsworth's system. In it the Wanderer affirms his belief in an active principle animating the forms of nature, and in a stream of tendency in nature working towards imaginative communion of man with nature as the 'sublime ascent' of man's life. All this was contained or implied in the drafts of 1798–9. In the later part of the book the Wanderer goes on to ask what hinders the actual country labourer from reaching this supreme good and decides that what is wanted is free universal education.

The mixed nature of *The Excursion* is apparent from this summary.[1] One part, conceived in 1797–9, continued a religion of personal salvation through Nature and was the part that influenced Shelley and Keats. The rest, written in 1809–12, discussed the application of that system to society, and attempted to reconcile it with the established church. This latter part contained ideas of great importance in the Victorian era, but it was the work of a conservative wishing to preserve the framework of society, and so it had little appeal to the more radical younger poets.

The parts of Wordsworth's system which had the greatest and most immediate effect on English poetry were those which asserted that there was an active principle in each natural form and in the whole of nature, that through the power of the Imagination the poet in contemplating the forms of Nature communes with this spirit, and that the Chaldean, Persian, Hebrew and Greek religions were the results of such imaginative experience of Nature. In 1815 and 1816 this combination of ideas made its appearance in the poetry of Shelley, Keats and Byron (though only the Greek religion was significant for Keats). In each case these ideas changed, permanently for Shelley and Keats and temporarily for Byron, the younger writer's conception of the Poet's task and his themes, turning him to imaginative communion with Nature,

---

[1] Cf. Shelley's comment in *Peter Bell the Third*, ll. 565–8.

> He was no Whig, he was no Tory;
> No deist and no Christian he;—
> He got so subtle, that to be
> Nothing was all his glory.

conceived animistically or pantheistically or both, and to myth as the means of expressing this.

The effect of these ideas can be seen most simply in the poetry of Keats. Though Shelley's reading of Wordsworth was the cause of that all-important difference between *Alastor* and *Queen Mab*, yet he had already read the *philosophes*, and in his poetry their ideas were entangled with Wordsworth's development of them; while the influence of Wordsworth on Byron was only an episode in the latter's career. On the other hand, Keats read *The Excursion* when he was just forming his poetic ideas, and though many other literary influences can be traced in his work, Wordsworth was the source of those ideas of the poet's task and the poet's vision, of Imagination and Beauty, and of time and the timeless, which were to dominate Keats' poetry.

Keats must have read *The Excursion* in 1815 or 1816; certainly his enthusiasm for Wordsworth was well established by November 1816, when he wrote 'Great Spirits now on Earth are sojourning', and the continuing effect on him is shown by the letter he wrote a year later to Haydon—'I am convinced that there are three things to rejoice at in this Age —The Excursion, Your Pictures and Hazlitt's depth of Taste'.[1] The influence of the poem was most immediately apparent in his treatment of mythology. Hazlitt's review of *The Excursion* for *The Examiner*[2] gave great prominence to the passage in Book IV dealing with the Greek myths, quoting it in full and adding:

The foregoing is one of a succession of splendid passages, equally enriched with philosophy and poetry, tracing the fictions of Eastern mythology to the immediate intercourse of the imagination with Nature, and to the habitual propensity of the human mind to endow the outward forms of being with life and conscious motion. With this expansive and animating principle, Mr. Wordsworth has forcibly, but somewhat severely, contrasted the cold, narrow, lifeless spirit of modern philosophy.

[1] *The Letters of John Keats*, ed. M. B. Forman (hereafter noted as *Letters*), p. 78.
[2] W. Hazlitt, *Complete Works*, ed. P. P. Howe, iv, p. 115.

The point about 'cold philosophy' was probably not lost on
Keats: the point about mythology certainly was not. In fact,
Wordsworth's passage on Greek mythology described the
operation of the Fancy but, in failing to grasp or even to
notice the distinction between it and the Imagination, Hazlitt
was at one with Keats and Shelley. Keats' affection for the
passage is well known[1] and when Leigh Hunt, who must have
discussed the subject with Keats himself, came to review the
latter's first volume of poems he pointed out how the use of
mythology in *I stood tiptoe* (the 'first Endymion') was
inspired by Wordsworth's justification of it: 'The first poem
consists of a piece of luxury in a rural spot with an allusion
to the story of Endymion and to the other lovely tales of
mythology on the ground suggested by Mr. Wordsworth in a
beautiful passage of his Excursion.'[2] Nevertheless though
Keats did, as we shall see, derive his ideas on the poetic purposes of mythology from Wordsworth's views on the creativeness of passion, on the language of the forms of nature, and on
the mythology as an embodiment of this, yet he gave his own
individual interpretation to the doctrines. This was natural
enough; each poet who attempted to 'commune with the
forms of nature' as Wordsworth recommended[3] was to interpret the result in accordance with his own interests and his

[1] Wordsworth, *Poetical Works*, ed. E. de Selincourt, v, p. 427.

[2] *The Examiner*, July 1817.

[3] *The Excursion*, IV. 1207–75. In the case of Keats the word 'empathy'
has been much used in this connection. (For a defence of its use see
N. F. Ford, 'The Meaning of "Fellowship with Essence" in *Endymion*'
in *PMLA* (1947): 'the percipient *has the impression* of fusing with and
losing his identity in the aesthetic object'.) If this word means that
Keats' actual experience of natural objects did not go beyond the first
stage of Wordsworth's experience, which Coleridge called 'to look at
the superficies of objects for the purpose of taking delight in their
beauty, and sympathy with their real or imagined life' (p. 136 above),
and that Keats did not in fact reach a mystical union, then the word is
useful but it should not obscure the fact that Keats did reach this
first stage, and that he did at one time expect it to lead on to the further
stage; the fact that, as N. F. Ford points out, he used 'fellowship
divine' as a synonym for 'blending pleasurable' (cf. p. 164, n. 1) is an
argument for this and not against it.

own bias, and hence to interpret the whole concept of this 'inarticulate language' differently.

Here a better idea of the range of interpretation can be got by considering the slightly later versions to be found in Browning and Ruskin as well as those of Shelley and Keats. Shelley may have adopted the idea in 1815 or 1816:

> my human mind, which passively
> Now renders and receives fast influencings,
> Holding an unremitting interchange
> With the clear universe of things around;[1]

but, if he did so, he soon Platonized it and it is in a dress very much more Platonic than Wordsworthian that the idea appears in *Prometheus Unbound*[2] and *Adonais*[3]:

> Rome's azure sky,
> Flowers, ruins, statues, music, words, are weak
> The glory they transfuse with fitting truth to speak.[3]

Browning, interested more in the human personality, stressed the power of the forms to speak of man rather than the power of the human spirit to drink in the soul of things, and his view is more Coleridgean in that the significance comes from man rather than from Nature herself:

> man, once descried, imprints for ever
> His presence on all lifeless things: the winds
> Are henceforth voices, wailing or a shout,
> A querulous mutter or a quick gay laugh,
> Never a senseless gust now man is born.
> The herded pines commune and have deep thoughts . . .
> The morn has enterprise, deep quiet droops
> With evening, triumph takes the sunset hour,
> Voluptuous transport ripens with the corn
> Beneath a warm moon like a happy face:
> —And this to fill us with regard for man.
> . . . All tended to mankind,
> And, man produced, all has its end thus far:
> But in completed man begins anew
> A tendency to God.[4]

---

[1] *Mont Blanc*, ll. 37–40. [2] *Prometheus Unbound*, i. 740–9.
[3] *Adonais*, ll. 466–8. [4] *Paracelsus*, v. 719–73.

Ruskin, interested in form from the point of view of the plastic arts, decided that the test of the beauty of any form was whether or not it was the result of an informing energy or spirit. His theory, again, might be taken as a summary of *The Excursion* as he understood it.

This force, now properly called life, or breathing, or spirit, is continually creating its own shells of definite shape out of the wreck around it. . . . For the mere force of junction is not spirit; but the power that catches out of chaos charcoal, water, lime, or what not, and fastens them down into a given form, is properly called 'spirit'; and we shall not diminish, but strengthen our conception of this creative energy by recognising its presence in lower states of matter than our own;—such recognition being enforced upon us by a delight we instinctively receive from all the forms of matter which manifest it. . . .

There is developed a series of changing forms, in clouds, plants, and animals, all of which have reference, in their action, or nature, to the human intelligence that perceives them; and on which, in their aspects of horror and beauty, there is engraved a series of myths, or words of the forming power, which, according to the true passion and energy of the human race, they have been enabled to read into religion. And this forming power has been by all nations partly confused with the breath or air through which it acts, and partly understood as a creative wisdom, proceeding from the Supreme Deity. And whatever intellectual results may be in modern days obtained by regarding this effluence only as a motion or vibration, every formative human art hitherto, and the best states of human happiness and order, have depended on the apprehension of its mystery (which is certain), and of its personality (which is probable).[1]

Ruskin's theory was meant to be taken literally. When he found that an architectural moulding which he had attacked as ugly, could in fact be found in certain rare crystalline forms, he was at pains to make the exception prove the rule.

The forms of things which are hidden in caverns of the earth or in the anatomy of animal frames, are evidently not intended by their Maker to bear the habitual gaze of man. . . . The first so-called ornament, then, which I would attack is that Greek fret . . .

[1] J. Ruskin, *Works*, xix, pp. 356-7, 378.

which is exactly a case in point. It so happens that in crystals of
bismuth, formed by the unagitated cooling of the melted metal,
there occurs a natural resemblance of it almost perfect. But
crystals of bismuth are not only of unusual occurrence in every-
day life, but their form is, as far as I know, unique among minerals;
and not only unique, but only attainable by an artificial process,
the metal itself never being found pure. . . . On this ground therefore, I allege that ornament to be ugly; or, in the literal sense of
the word, monstrous; different from anything which it is the nature
of man to admire: and I think an uncarved fillet or plinth infinitely
preferable to one covered with this vile concatenation of straight
lines.[1]

To Ruskin the natural forms said 'I am beautiful', and if one
of them lied, it was a disreputable member of the family whom
Nature had done her best to keep silent.

To Keats the language of the forms meant something
different again, though something that may well be implied
in Wordsworth's recognition of 'the language of the sense' as
the 'soul of all my moral being'. Keats' conception, which he
expressed in *I stood tiptoe*, was that this language corres-
ponded to, *and was the source of*, the different emotions embodied in literature.

> For what has made the sage or poet write
> But the fair paradise of Nature's light?
> In the calm grandeur of a sober line,
> We see the waving of the mountain pine;
> And when a tale is beautifully staid,
> We feel the safety of a hawthorn glade:
> When it is moving on luxurious wings,
> The soul is lost in pleasant smotherings:
> Fair dewy roses brush against our faces. . . .[2]

This fits in with Keats' theory of mythology in poetry, also
derived, as Leigh Hunt pointed out, from *The Excursion*.

> In that fair clime, the lonely herdsman, stretched
> On the soft grass through half a summer's day,
> . . . his fancy fetched,

[1] id., viii, pp. 142–4.

[2] *I stood tip-toe*, ll. 125–33; cf. *Sleep and Poetry*, ll. 63–71, and
ll. 122–54.

Even from the blazing chariot of the sun,
A beardless Youth, who touched a golden lute,
And filled the illumined groves with ravishment.
The nightly hunter, lifting up his eyes
Towards the crescent moon, with grateful heart
Called on the lovely wanderer who bestowed
That timely light, to share his joyous sport.
And hence a beaming Goddess with her Nymphs,
Across the lawn and through the darksome grove,
Not unaccompanied with tuneful notes
By echo multiplied from rock or cave,
Swept in the storm of chase; as moon and stars
Glance rapidly along the clouded heaven,
When winds are blowing strong. The traveller slaked
His thirst from rill or gushing fount, and thanked
The Naiad. . . .
The Zephyrs fanning, as they passed, their wings,
Lacked not, for love, fair objects whom they wooed
With gentle whisper. Withered boughs grotesque,
Stripped of their leaves and twigs by hoary age. . . .
These were the lurking Satyrs, a wild brood
Of gamesome Deities; or Pan himself,
The simple shepherd's awe-inspiring God![1]

The passage quoted earlier from *I stood tiptoe* goes on to describe the origins of the Greek myths in terms of the correspondences which Keats found between natural forms and human emotions. Here, when the poet reveals the essence of a natural object, he expresses this essence, and the emotion it conveys to him, not simply by personifying it but by inventing a mythological story. Two of the examples which Keats gives are his own—the luxurious story of Psyche which expresses the dewy roses and the other plants and fruits of the garden, and the story of Narcissus and Echo which expresses the lonely pool and the flower 'deaf to light Zephyrus'. The other two are drawn from the passage in *The Excursion*. The first describes how

he . . . who pulled the boughs aside,
That we might look into a forest wide
To catch a glimpse of Fauns and Dryades,[2]

---

[1] *The Excursion*, IV. 851–87.
[2] *I stood tip-toe*, ll. 151–3; cf. *The Excursion*, IV. 879–87.

told this in the 'sweet desolation' of the story of Pan and
Syrinx, while the last example (for this poem is 'the first
Endymion') tells of the poet, 'sure a lover too',

> Coming ever to bless
> The wanderer by moonlight? to him bringing
> Shapes from the invisible world, unearthly singing
> From out the middle air, from flowery nests,
> And from the pillowy silkiness that rests
> Full in the speculation of the stars.
> Ah! surely he had burst our mortal bars;
> Into some wond'rous region he had gone,
> To search for thee, divine Endymion![1]

In each case the emotion is first inspired by the contemplation
of nature and then captured by the poet in a story. Poetry
here is the inarticulate language of nature, translated into
human speech and telling of human life. In thus making the
'language' narrative, Keats may have thought he was following Wordsworth:

> they shall meet no object but may teach
> Some acceptable lesson to their minds
> Of human suffering, or of human joy.
> For them shall all things speak of Man. . . .[2]

but it is equally likely that he would have been biased towards
this interpretation by his love of Spenser and by his own
ambition towards 'the chief attempt in the Drama—the
playing of different Natures with Joy and Sorrow'.[3]

In *Sleep and Poetry*, written later but before the end of 1816,
further elements of Keats' debt to Wordsworth become
apparent. In this poem the 'high Imagination'[4] makes its first
appearance in Keats' writings as a charioteer, in a passage full
of borrowings from the Cynthia passage of *The Excursion*.

> And can I ever bid these joys farewell?
> Yes, I must pass them for a nobler life,
> Where I may find the agonies, the strife
> Of human hearts: for lo! I see afar,
> O'er-sailing the blue cragginess, a car

---

[1] *I stood tip-toe*, ll. 184–9. [2] *The Excursion*, IV. 1236–9.
[3] *Letters*, p. 91. [4] *Sleep and Poetry*, ll. 163–4.

And steeds with streaming manes—the charioteer
Looks out upon the winds with glorious fear: . . .
The charioteer with wond'rous gesture talks
To the trees and mountains; and there soon appear
Shapes of delight, and mystery, and fear,
Passing along before a dusky space
Made by some mighty oaks: as they would chase
Some ever-fleeting music on they sweep . . .
Flit onward—now a lovely wreath of girls
Dancing their sleek hair into tangled curls
And now broad wings. Most awfully intent
The driver of these steeds is forward bent,
And seems to listen: O that I might know
All that he writes with such a hurrying glow.[1]

The echoes here are obvious[2] but it is also characteristically Wordsworthian that this passage in which the Imagination communes with the trees and the mountains does not deal with the simple pleasures of nature ('the realm of Flora and old Pan') but with 'the strife, the agonies of human hearts'.

Keats' contrast, in *Sleep and Poetry*, between simple pleasure in nature and deep feeling for humanity, his belief that the poet must pass from one to the other, and the linking of the imaginative contemplation of nature to the second, not the first, were all inspired by *Tintern Abbey* and *The Excursion*. The former poem, of course, contrasts Wordsworth's youthful pleasures in nature,

> That had no need of a remoter charm,

with his mature feeling for the same scene,

> hearing oftentimes
> The still, sad music of humanity.

The Excursion, IV. 1187–251 has the same progression. There 'Nature's humbler power', seen in 'her blooming bowers and spacious fields', leads men, through the contemplation of 'these forms in the relation which they bear to man', to the point

[1] id., ll. 122–54.
[2] With *Sleep and Poetry*, ll. 137–40, 148–51; cf. *The Excursion*, IV. 865–9, 873–7.

> When they shall meet no object but may teach
> Some acceptable lesson to their minds
> Of human suffering, or of human joy.

When Man has reached that point,

> that change shall clothe
> The naked spirit, ceasing to deplore
> The burthen of existence,

just as 'the burden of the mystery' is lightened in *Tintern Abbey*. Keats knew that he had not reached this point—he was still conscious of this when he wrote a year later of 'the chamber of maiden thought' and of the point beyond it to which 'was Wordsworth come when he wrote *Tintern Abbey*'[1] but he was setting out deliberately in search of it with the Imagination as his guide.

Of course, for all his importance as a source of ideas and particularly of the concept of Imagination, Wordsworth was far from being the most important *literary* influence on Keats. Indeed, the way in which Keats interpreted Wordsworth's theory of mythology in terms of narrative poetry points immediately to the influence of Spenser (and of Leigh Hunt, 'for knightly Spenser to Libertas told it'[2]) and Keats immediately applied the theory to the Elizabethans.

> Is there so small a range
> In the present strength of manhood, that the high
> Imagination cannot freely fly
> As she was wont of old? prepare her steeds,
> Paw up against the light, and do strange deeds
> Upon the clouds? Has she not shown us all?
> From the clear space of ether, to the small
> Breath of new buds unfolding? From the meaning
> Of Jove's large eyebrow, to the tender greening
> Of April meadows? Here her altar shone,
> E'en in this isle; and who could paragon
> The fervid choir. . . .[3]

[1] *Letters*, p. 143. See also E. C. Pettet, *On the Poetry of Keats*, pp. 127, 130.

[2] *Epistle to my brother George*, l. 24.

[3] *Sleep and Poetry*, ll. 162–73.

Keats' reading in poetry and prose entered largely into both the style and the matter of his poetry, and, in his later years, the influence of Wordsworth must be traced mainly in fundamental ideas, found in 1816 among borrowings that indicate their source, but developed later by Keats into the characteristic forms they take in his greater poetry.

Many of Keats' characteristic ideas on poetry were gathered up in his sonnet *The Poet*,[1] probably written in 1815–16, and one may see how many of these are also Wordsworthian. The sonnet reads:

> At morn, at noon, at Eve, and Middle Night
> > He passes forth into the charmed air,
> > With talisman to call up spirits rare

[1] See the articles in *MLN* (1952), in which E. L. Brooks and E. R. Wasserman debate the authenticity of the sonnet. Brooks prints an inferior version of the poem from *The London Magazine*, October 1821, iv, p. 417, and argues that it could not be by Keats. Wasserman suggests that this is 'a hurried first draft' and points out the number of typically Keatsian ideas to be found in the better version. The *London Magazine* version differs chiefly in line 5, which begins 'From flower, tree, heath . . .' and in the sestet which reads:

> The Poet's sympathies are not confined
> To kindred, country, climate, class and kind,
> And yet they glow intense.—Oh! were he wise,
> Duly to commune with his destined skies,
> Then, as of old, might inspiration shed
> A visible glory round his hallowed head.

For line 5, see p. 160 below. If, as suggested there, the octave of this poem owes much to *The Excursion*, then for the reference of the sestet we have only to look at Wordsworth's *Thanksgiving Ode* and the other poems on Waterloo which he published along with it in 1816. (*Feelings of a French Royalist*, 'Intrepid sons of Albion', *Occasioned by the Battle of Waterloo* and *Ode*, 1815) to realize that the cap fits Wordsworth very well. A possible explanation of the poor workmanship of the *London Magazine* version, which Wasserman significantly calls hurried, could be found in the habit of the Hunt circle of writing sonnets in competition against the clock. The *Sonnet to the Nile* and presumably the sonnet 'Minutes are flying swiftly' are examples of this: in *The Poet* the alliteration of line 10 suggests this method of composition. The publication of the *London Magazine* version over the signature S might easily be the result of the confusion of manuscripts which such a competition could produce.

> From plant, cave, rock, and fountain.—To his sight
> The husk[1] of natural objects opens quite
>   To the core: and every secret essence there
>   Reveals the elements of good and fair;
> Making him see, where Learning hath no light.
>
> Sometimes above the gross and palpable things
>   Of this diurnal sphere, his spirit flies
>   On awful wing; and with its destined skies
> Holds premature and mystic communings:
>   Till such unearthly intercourses shed
>   A visible halo round his mortal head.

That the poet communicates with the spirit in Nature is Wordsworth's main doctrine; the 'secret essence' is the 'active principle' of *The Excursion*, Book IX:

> To every Form of being is assigned . . .
> An *active* Principle:—howe'er removed
> From sense and observation, it subsists
> In all things, in all natures; in the stars
> Of azure heaven, the unenduring clouds,
> In flower and tree, in every pebbly stone
> That paves the brooks, the stationary rocks. . . .[2]

In what is presumably the first draft of *The Poet*, the 'plant, cave, rock', of the fourth line are instead 'flower, tree, heath'. E. L. Brooks has called attention to the weakness of this, 'flower' and 'tree' belonging to the same class;[3] the explanation would seem to lie in their use by Wordsworth. The word 'essence' is an obvious enough synonym for 'active principle' and Wordsworth, Shelley and Byron all used it for the spirit in natural objects[4] (though Keats would not have seen those passages). That this soul of nature is good was another

---

[1] The Woodhouse transcript reads 'hush', an obvious mis-transcription, though it should be noticed that in 1947 N. F. Ford regarded 'hush' as implying 'that to the poet natural objects speak a language' and compared it with *Where's the Poet* (*PMLA* (1947)).

[2] *The Excursion*, IX. 1–8.

[3] E. L. Brooks, '"The Poet", a mistake in the Keats canon?' in *MLN* (1952).

[4] *The Prelude* (1805), II. 344; *Manfred*, I. i. 32; *Queen Mab*, III. 215. See also p. 162, n. 1.

Wordsworthian belief, as was the superiority of the poet's vision to 'cold philosophy'.[1] In the sestet the phrase 'gross and palpable' is Shakespearean but, as applied to the physical world, it may owe something to 'the gross and visible frame of things' which loses its hold on the sense when the Wanderer, a few lines later in Book IX, is placed above it 'to commune with the invisible world'.[2] That such communion was premature in the sense that it was an 'intimation of immortality' was a point made by the greatest of Wordsworth's Odes—a point taken up by Shelley and Byron as well as Keats.[3]

These ideas all had their importance for *Endymion* and the later poems,[4] but on returning to *Sleep and Poetry* we can find one characteristic idea, or rather conflict of ideas, which came as much from what Keats did not accept in Wordsworth as from what he did. When Keats accepted 'the truth of the Imagination' he does not seem to have accepted entirely the view of nature on which it was based, and for him the Imagination and 'the sense of real things' were in perpetual contradiction.

> The visions are all fled—the car is fled
> Into the light of heaven, and in their stead
> A sense of real things comes doubly strong,
> And like a muddy stream, would bear along
> My soul to nothingness; but I will strive
> Against all doubtings, and will keep alive
> The thought of that same chariot and the strange
> Journey it went.[5]

This conflict was to be of more importance later. At the moment, a change which took place in Keats' ideas while he was writing *Endymion* may be taken as an indication that he no longer regarded Wordsworth's view of nature as essential to the Imagination. In *Endymion*, Keats' beliefs about poetry lost the almost startling simplicity and consistency they had had in 'the first *Endymion*', and instead of leading all beauty

---

[1] *The Excursion*, IV. 941–55, 1251–63. [2] id., IX. 63–6, 85–6.
[3] See pp. 184–5 below.
[4] E. R. Wasserman, 'Keats' sonnet "The Poet"' in *MLN* (1952).
[5] *Sleep and Poetry*, ll. 155–62.

back to 'Nature and the language of the sense', he now
recognized a beauty to be found in abstract conceptions. In
the list of things of beauty at the beginning of the poem occurs
'the grandeur of the dooms we have imagined for the mighty
dead'[1] and this grandeur is not connected with the Imagination's contemplation of natural objects, as 'the strifes, the
agonies of human hearts' had been in *Sleep and Poetry*. Keats
was still working out Wordsworth's idea that the love of
nature leads to the love of man, but he now made human
emotions a second, and separate, step after the beauty of
nature. This step led on again to the highest ecstasy which
Wordsworth himself had found through the direct contemplation of nature. By this means Keats made a simple
Platonic ladder, but it fitted ill with the Wordsworthian
system and it very much confused the meaning of 'essence'.

> Wherein lies happiness? in that which becks
> Our ready minds to fellowship divine,
> A fellowship with essence; till we shine,
> Full alchemiz'd, and free of space. Behold
> The clear religion of heaven! Fold
> A rose leaf round thy finger's taperness,
> And soothe thy lips: hist, when the airy stress
> Of music's kiss impregnates the free winds,
> And with a sympathetic touch unbinds
> Æolian magic from their lucid wombs:
> Then old songs waken from enclouded tombs. . . .
> And, from the turf, a lullaby doth pass
> In every place where infant Orpheus slept.
> Feel we these things?—that moment have we stept
> Into a sort of oneness, and our state
> Is like a floating spirit's. But there are
> Richer entanglements, enthralments far
> More self-destroying, leading, by degrees,
> To the chief intensity: the crown of these
> Is made of love and friendship.[2]

[1] *Endymion*, i. 20–1.

[2] id., i. 777–801. This passage is a key one in any interpretation of
Endymion. E. C. Pettet, *On the Poetry of Keats*, ch. iv *passim*, argues
very cogently against the various interpretations of the poem as neo-
platonic allegory, particularly on the grounds of the strong sensuous

Keats took great pains with this passage, which was the foundation of his allegory.

I assure you that, when I wrote it, it was a regular stepping of the Imagination towards a Truth. My having written that Argument will perhaps be of the greatest Service to me of anything I ever did. It set before me at once the gradations of Happiness, even like a kind of Pleasure-Thermometer, and is my first Step towards the chief attempt in the Drama—the playing of different Natures with Joy and Sorrow.[1]

As the letter suggests, this is different from the system of his earlier poems. Though the later description of what this and, indeed, sensual element in the poem, and of the difficulties in the meaning of the word 'essence'. N. F. Ford, 'The Meaning of "Fellowship with Essence" in *Endymion*' in *PMLA* (1947), makes the point that a neo-platonic interpretation conflicts with Keats' strong interest in sensuous experience (p. 1065) and makes an analysis of 17 occurrences of the word in Keats' poetry: he comes to the conclusion that 'essence' is simply a synonym for 'thing' (p. 1074). This seems a little hard in view of the importance which Keats attached to the passage, which he considered the foundation of the allegory. It would certainly seem from the letter to Taylor (*Letters*, p. 91) that Keats himself would have been on the side of the allegorists (though not necessarily of the neo-platonists) and that he worded the passage with great care. The difficulty may be that Ford assumes the choice to lie between 'things' and '*transcendental* essences' (p. 1069, my italics). The Wordsworthian 'active principle' was not transcendental; the knowledge of it came through passion and it was grasped in sense-experience in imaginative contact with nature—it was grasped by Keats as Beauty:

> What the imagination seizes as Beauty must be truth . . . all our Passions . . . are all in their sublime, creative of essential Beauty . . . we shall enjoy ourselves hereafter by having what we called happiness on Earth repeated. . . . And yet such a fate can only befall those who delight in sensation rather than hunger as you do after Truth. (*Letters*, pp. 67–8.)

For Wordsworth this led on to an ecstatic blending with Nature (e.g. *The Excursion*, I. 206–10). What Keats has done is to extend this to abstractions and to expect the same process in the experience of other human hearts in friendship and love: hence the pleasure-thermometer and the triple allegory of the search for this experience in natural beauty, friendship, love. This can be called Platonism but it has little in common with true Platonism or neo-platonism.

[1] *Letters*, p. 91.

'fellowship with essence' means is Wordsworthian,[1] yet the 'essence' of love and friendship is something different from any meaning which can be assigned to the 'essence' of a rose leaf, and very different from Wordsworth's 'active principle'. From this new position Keats had to work out his own way forward, and to reconcile for himself 'the truth of the Imagination' with that 'sense of real things', which already oppressed him in *Sleep and Poetry*. The story of those strivings, and of the journey of Keats' imagination, is best left to the next chapter.

The influence of *The Excursion* on Shelley links two other great influences on his work—that of the French 'materialists' in his early years and that of Plato in his later. As Professor Grabo has shown,[2] many of the ideas which Shelley picked up

Of Ford's list of occurrences of the word 'essence', the instances in poetry after *Endymion* come from Milton (*Poems of John Keats*, ed. E. de Selincourt, p. 603); the sense of soul of an animate being fits his instances 4, 6 and 10; the sense of soul of an inanimate being, a natural object as perceived by the Imagination, fits instances 1, 3, 7, 8 and 9; this same sense extended as suggested above to abstractions fits instance 5 ('Fellowship with Essence'). In the light of this, and of the remarks about 'empathy' above, p. 151, n. 3, Ford's conclusion—that '"fellowship with essence" is not a wedding of finite beings to transcendental reality. The wedding is an earthly "blending", an imaginative "empathic" fusion of a percipient with an aesthetic object'—is one which places the poem firmly in the general scheme described in this book.

[1] Cf. *Endymion*, I. 810–11:

> Melting into radiance, we blend,
> Mingle, and so become a part of it,—

with *The Excursion*, I. 206–10:

> his spirit drank
> The spectacle: sensation, soul and form,
> All melted into him; they swallowed up
> His animal being; in them did he live,
> And by them did he live; they were his life.

[2] C. H. Grabo, *Prometheus Unbound, an interpretation*. Though not entirely convincing, this does at least demonstrate the presence of a number of scientific ideas in *Prometheus Unbound*. (See N. I. White, *Shelley*, ii, pp. 578–9.)

in the course of his early scientific reading remained with him even when his outlook had become thoroughly Platonized. It was his reading of Wordsworth which led him from one system to the other, and it was Wordsworth's influence also which cemented the two sets of ideas into the system which appears in *Prometheus Unbound*.

When Shelley began his poetic career his beliefs were very close to those from which Wordsworth and Coleridge started. He was widely read in the French 'materialist' tradition and had accepted the paradoxical conclusion of that tradition, that matter was spirit. *Queen Mab* borrows from Volney, d'Holbach, Cabanis, Buffon and Erasmus Darwin, and expresses all the leading ideas of the movement—that matter is 'alive', that there is a pervading spirit co-eternal with the universe, that all things are governed by Necessity, and that they work out the will of the pervading spirit in an evolution of nature and man towards perfection. A few quotations will suffice to make this clear.

> Throughout this varied and eternal world
> Soul is the only element: the block
> That for uncounted ages has remained
> The moveless pillar of a mountain's weight
> Is active, living spirit. Every grain
> Is sentient both in unity and part,
> And the minutest atom comprehends
> A world of loves and hatreds.[1]

But although

> No atom of this turbulence fulfils
> A vague and unnecessitated task,
> Or acts but as it must and ought to act.[2]

yet this 'varied and eternal world' is directed by the pervading spirit[3] to produce a millennium.

[1] *Queen Mab*, IV. 139–46.

[2] id., VI. 171–3.

[3] id., note to VII. 13—'There is no God'—which reads: 'This negation must be understood solely to affect a creative deity. The hypothesis of a pervading Spirit co-eternal with the Universe remains unshaken.

> Spirit of Nature! thou
> Life of interminable multitudes;
> Soul of those mighty spheres
> Whose changeless paths through Heaven's deep silence lie;
>
> Soul of that smallest being
> The dwelling of whose life
> Is one faint April sun-gleam;—
> Man, like these passive things,
> Thy will unconsciously fulfilleth:
> Like theirs, his age of endless peace,
> Which time is fast maturing,
> Will swiftly, surely come;
> And the unbounded frame which thou pervadest,
> Will be without a flaw
> Marring its perfect symmetry.[1]

The last lines mark Shelley's faith that this millennium will be a perfection of the physical world as well as of society. The perfecting of society was to be brought about by Godwinian means. For his faith in the perfecting of the physical world he had gone to Erasmus Darwin who suggested that the righting of the earth's inclination to the ecliptic would, in the course of a few centuries, bring back the climatic conditions of the first Paradise. Shelley calculated that this righting might become rapid enough for its conclusion to coincide with the triumph of Rational Benevolence, and assumed that it had been willed by the pervading spirit to that end.[2] The curious resemblance between this system and that which Coleridge expounded in his early poems is very noticeable, but they were quite independent productions. Each was a natural outcome of the apocalyptic and evolutionary tendencies in the thought of the period.

Queen Mab was published in the summer of 1813. During the next eighteen months Shelley began to take a keen interest in Wordsworth,[3] and in 1814 he read the newly published *Excursion*. His first reaction was disappointment that Wordsworth, far from retaining his radical sympathies as Shelley

[1] id., III. 226–40.   [2] id., note to VI. 45–6.
[3] N. I. White, *Shelley*, i, pp. 279, 365.

had imagined,[1] had become conservative in politics and, worse still, orthodox in religion. 'Much disappointed: he is a slave', was Mary's record of Shelley's feelings. But for all that, Shelley took up Wordsworth's ideas of nature and poetry with as much avidity as Keats did, and within six months he had embodied them in his first mature poem *Alastor*. This poem is impregnated with Wordsworthian phrases and is at least an attempt to fit Wordsworth's conception of the Poet to Shelley's case—if, indeed, the Poet here be not Wordsworth himself seen through Shelley's eyes.[2]

Of the many English poets who influenced Shelley's style, Wordsworth was the only one who influenced his ideas in this way. The reason would seem to be that Wordsworth's ideas came as a development and illumination of those which Shelley already held, modifying the system of *Queen Mab* and giving it a different spirit and significance rather than replacing it altogether. The whole effect was revolutionary, but each separate change of idea was superficially slight, and, like Wordsworth's own early progress towards his system, a development of something contained potentially in the conception of a living universe. The 'pervading spirit co-eternal with the universe' became Wordsworth's 'pervading spirit' of nature: Rational Benevolence became love and natural piety: the salvation of Man became an individual quest as well as a universal progress and so on. Volney's thesis that the ancient empires had failed through not observing the natural law was replaced by Wordsworth's belief that certain ancient religions were intuitions of the divine in nature, but this was a minor matter, and ruins were an old interest of his. The only elements which were wholly new to Shelley were the living Presence of Beauty and the Vision,[3] which were destined to lead him on to Plato.

The simplest change was that which Wordsworth produced in Shelley's conception of the Spirit of Nature. In *Queen Mab*

[1] id., i, p. 365.

[2] id., i, p. 170 and E. L. Griggs and P. Mueschke, 'Wordsworth and the Prototype of the Poet in *Alastor*', in *PMLA* (1934).

[3] *Prospectus* in Preface to *The Excursion*, ll. 42, 98.

the spirit, though it made provision for the eventual happiness of Man, took no particular interest in him,

> Spirit of Nature! all-sufficing Power,
> Necessity! thou mother of the world!
> . . .
> No love, no hate thou cherishest; revenge
> And favouritism, and worst desire of fame
> Thou know'st not: all that the wide world contains
> Are but thy passive instruments, and thou
> Regard'st them all with an impartial eye,
> Whose joy or pain thy nature cannot feel,
> Because thou hast not human sense,
> Because thou art not human mind.[1]

Shelley continued to believe that the cause of mind is utterly unlike mind,[2] a point of view which some of Wordsworth's terms in *The Excursion* fitted very well[3] but in *Alastor* the 'Power' became Wordsworth's fostering Nature.

> Earth, ocean, air, beloved brotherhood!
> If our great Mother has imbued my soul
> With aught of natural piety to feel
> Your love, and recompence the boon with mine. . . .[4]

This Power shapes the Poet.

> Every sight
> And sound from the vast earth and ambient air
> Sent to his heart its choicest impulses.[5]

and 'the magnificence and beauty of the external world' are the objects towards which his desires at first point.

---

[1] *Queen Mab*, VI. 198–219.   [2] *On Life*, concluding sentence.
[3] e.g. *The Excursion*, IV. 968–70:

> And if indeed there be
> An all-pervading Spirit, upon whom
> Our dark foundations rest.

and id., IX. 615–17:

> Power inaccessible to human thought,
> Save by degrees and steps which thou hast deigned
> To furnish . . .

and id., III. 112, 'unsearchable eternity'.
[4] *Alastor*, ll. 1–4.   [5] id., ll. 68–70.

Alastor is the tragedy of a poet who hopes to find the embodiment of this beauty in a human partner, and in it Nature is 'that Power which strikes the luminaries of the world with sudden darkness and extinction, by awakening them to too exquisite a perception of its influences'. In this, as Mrs Shelley's note says,

Alastor . . . contains an individual interest only. . . . This is neither the time nor place to speak of the misfortunes that chequered his life . . . inclining him rather to brood over the thoughts and emotions of his own soul than to glance abroad, and to make, as in *Queen Mab*, the whole universe the object and subject of his song.

Nevertheless in this poem Shelley had begun to settle his relation, as a poet, with the Spirit of the Universe. He was aware of the importance of the Vision to Wordsworth, but he himself had not experienced it,

> though ne'er yet
> Thou hast unveiled thy inmost sanctuary.[1]

What he could more easily make his own was the poet's quest for beauty, and Wordsworth's belief that the beauty of the world was an aspect of that 'Presence' he had felt near Tintern Abbey. Wordsworth did not often use the word 'beauty', preferring to stress the 'world of life and feeling', but it does occur very prominently in the *Prospectus* prefixed to *The Excursion*.

> Beauty,—a living Presence of the earth,
> Surpassing the most fair ideal Forms
> Which craft of delicate Spirits hath composed
> From earth's materials—waits upon my steps;
> Pitches her tents before me as I move,
> An hourly neighbour.[2]

It was as this Presence that Shelley now conceived the spirit of the Universe.

A minor effect of Wordsworth's influence was that Shelley adopted his thesis that the ancient religions were intuitions of

[1] id., ll. 37–8. [2] *Prospectus*, ll. 42–7.

this spirit in nature. In *Queen Mab*, Shelley had been inspired by Volney's *Les Ruines*, in which a dreamer is conducted to the ruins of ancient empires by the Spirit of Nature, who explains that the empires fell through not observing nature's regulations for human happiness. A similar visit by the dreamer in *Queen Mab* teaches the same lesson, but when the poet of *Alastor* visits these ruins, he learns instead ancient thought and ancient secrets.

> His wandering step,
> Obedient to high thoughts, has visited
> The awful ruins of the days of old:
> Athens, and Tyre, and Balbec, and the waste
> Where stood Jerusalem, the fallen towers
> Of Babylon, the eternal pyramids,
> Memphis and Thebes, and whatsoe'er of strange . . .
> Dark Aethiopia in her desert hills
> Conceals. Among the ruined temples there,
> Stupendous columns, and wild images
> Of more than man, where marble daemons watch
> The Zodiac's brazen mystery, and dead men
> Hang their mute thoughts on the mute walls around,
> He lingered, poring on memorials
> Of the world's youth, through the long burning day
> Gazed on these speechless shapes, nor, when the moon
> Filled the mysterious halls with floating shades
> Suspended he that task, but ever gazed
> And gazed, till meaning on his vacant mind
> Flashed like strong inspiration, and he saw
> The thrilling secrets of the birth of time.[1]

There are several echoes of Wordsworth here, among which that of *I wandered lonely as a cloud* is most prominent, but the central idea seems to be derived from the Wanderer's discourse on mythology in Book IV of *The Excursion*. In this the Wanderer says that even after the fall of Adam the

> Communications spiritually maintained
> And intuitions moral and divine,[2]

---

[1] *Alastor*, ll. 106–28.   [2] *The Excursion*, IV. 645–6.

which Adam had experienced, had not ceased. 'Solitude was not', and these intuitions were embodied in the religion of the Hebrews, the animism of the Persians,

> the whole circle of the heavens, for him
> A sensitive existence, and a God,[1]

the temples of the Babylonians, the planetary spirits of the Chaldeans and the mythology of the Greeks. This must have been a favourite passage of Shelley's, for echoes of it appeared in Byron's poetry immediately after he had been converted to Wordsworthian 'metaphysics' by Shelley in 1816. Here in *Alastor* the elucidation of the ancient mysteries is described in phrases drawn word for word from *I wandered lonely as a cloud*, and if any meaning should be looked for in the 'memorials of the world's youth' and 'the thrilling secrets of the birth of time', it should be this atavistic Wordsworthianism. Shelley repeated the idea in *The Revolt of Islam*, as he did many of the ideas of *Alastor*, and there

> monuments of less ungentle creeds
> Tell their own tale to him who wisely heeds
> The language which they speak; and now, to me
> The moonlight making pale the blooming weeds,
> The bright stars shining in the breathless sea,
> Interpreted these scrolls of mortal mystery.
>
> Such man has been, and such may yet become!
> Ay wiser, greater, gentler, even than they
> Who on the fragments of yon shattered dome
> Have stamped the sign of power.[2]

Shelley had come to regard ancient myth, at any rate, as having some foundation in the religion of Nature, but he refused to believe that the human intelligence could 'grasp the infinite', or go further beyond the experience of beauty to conceive a 'pervading spirit of the whole illimitible universe'.[3] In 1816 he wrote two poems which summarize his beliefs at

---

[1] id., IV. 678–9.   [2] *The Revolt of Islam*, ll. 760–9.
[3] N. I. White, *Shelley*, i, p. 747.

that time, the *Hymn to Intellectual Beauty* and *Mont Blanc*.
The first rejects all religions (except that of Beauty).

> No voice from some sublimer world hath ever
>> To sage or poet these responses given—
>> Therefore the names of Demon, Ghost, and Heaven,
> Remain the record of the vain endeavour,
> Frail spells—whose uttered charm might not avail to
>> sever
>> From all we hear and all we see,
>> Doubt chance and mutability.[1]

The title suggests Plato, but Wordsworth is an equal influence.
Beauty here is not so much the Platonic abstraction as Words-
worth's 'high hour of visitation from the living God' and his
'Beauty—a living Presence of the earth'.

> The awful shadow of some unseen Power
>> Floats though unseen among us,—visiting
>> This various world with as inconstant wing
> As summer winds that creep from flower to flower,—
> Like moonbeams that behind some piny mountain
>> shower,
>
> . . .
>
> Spirit of BEAUTY, that dost consecrate
>> With thine own hues all thou dost shine upon . . .[2]

Nevertheless the Platonic title points the direction which
Shelley's development of his system was to take.

Mont Blanc expresses that part of his Wordsworthianism,
and of his ideas reaching back to the period before the influence of Wordsworth, which was not to be Platonized. If the
ideas of the *Hymn* were to find expression in the figure of
Asia, representing Intellectual Beauty in *Prometheus Unbound*,
those of *Mont Blanc* were to be represented by Demogorgon.
The poem records the imaginative meaning of the mountain,
and what the Imagination sees in the mountain is the pervading spirit in its other aspect of Power.

> Power dwells apart in its tranquillity,
> Remote, serene, and inaccessible:

[1] *Hymn to Intellectual Beauty*, ll. 25–31.   [2] id., ll. 1–14.

> And *this*, the naked countenance of earth,
> On which I gaze, even these primaeval mountains,
> Teach the adverting mind . . .
> . . . The secret Strength of things
> Which governs thought, and to the infinite dome
> Of Heaven is as a law, inhabits thee!
> And what were thou, and earth, and stars, and sea,
> If to the human mind's imaginings
> Silence and solitude were vacancy?[1]

But it is important to notice that the Imagination sees not only inaccessible Power, but also a moral purposiveness in that power.

> Thou hast a voice, great Mountain, to repeal
> Large codes of fraud and woe; not understood
> By all, but which the wise, and great, and good
> Interpret, or make felt, or deeply feel.[2]

Though Shelley here grounds his belief on the Imagination, this power and purposiveness in nature goes back to *Queen Mab* and forward to *Prometheus Unbound*.

Byron first read Wordsworth seriously at Geneva in 1816, when he was in the company of Shelley, who 'omitted no opportunity to bring the beauties of his favourite poet to the attention of Lord Byron'.[3] Byron's own phrase for it was that

---

[1] *Mont Blanc*, ll. 96–144.

[2] id., ll. 80–4. I. J. Kapstein, 'The Meaning of Shelley's "Mont Blanc"', in *PMLA* (1947), gives an analysis of the poem as showing a state of tension between Shelley's earlier materialism and belief in Necessity and his later idealism and belief in freedom of the will. Very remarkably, he makes no mention whatsoever of Wordsworth or of possible Wordsworthian influence. Nevertheless his article may well serve to bring out the thesis here, that Shelley's Wordsworthianism served to connect Shelley's earlier beliefs with his later by convincing him that communion was possible between the Spirit of the Universe and the poet (cf. Kapstein, p. 1059), that the freedom of the will could be reconciled with Necessity—a belief which Shelley continued to hold (*The Excursion*, IV. 1265–70 and *Prometheus Unbound*, II. ii. 41–56; cf. Kapstein, p. 1045) and that the stream of tendency had goodness as its end (cf. Kapstein, p. 1054).

[3] T. Moore, *Life, Letters and Journals of Lord Byron*. p. 317.

Shelley 'dosed' him with Wordsworth. The results of this reading are all to be found in the poems written in that year— the third canto of *Childe Harold, The Dream,* and *Manfred.* Next year, when Byron sent the fourth canto of *Childe Harold* to Murray, he was able to assure him that 'there are no metaphysics in it—at least I think not' and that 'it treats more of works of art than of nature'.[1] But though Byron's attack of 'metaphysics' was a brief one, and though his recovery from it was complete, it makes an interesting case both because it showed which of Wordsworth's ideas Shelley had so infectively carried, and because some of those ideas were re-transmitted in new forms from Byron to Shelley. This last point will be of particular interest later, in the discussions of *Manfred* and *Prometheus Unbound.*

The spirit in which Byron turned to Nature in 1816 has been discussed often enough since Wordsworth's first indignant comments on his unwanted fellow-worshipper.

> Nor has her gentle beauty power to move
> With genuine rapture and with fervent love
> The soul of Genius, if he dare to take
> Life's rule from passion craved for passion's sake;
> Untaught that meekness is the cherished bent
> Of all the truly great and innocent.[2]

But though Byron turned to the love of nature *instead* of the love of man, the ideas he brought to it were those of Wordsworth. These ideas were again those of the Spirit of Nature and of the active Principle in each natural form, of the ancient religions as founded on Nature and Imagination, and of the creativeness of the Imagination in contact with natural forms. Wordsworth's central experience, that of union through the senses with the life of nature was claimed by Byron,

> I live not in myself, but I become
> Portion of that around me; and to me
> High mountains are a feeling. . . .

.   .   .   .

---

[1] Letter to Murray, 7 August 1817. T. Moore, op. cit., p. 363.
[2] *Not in the lucid intervals of life,* ll. 10–15.

> Are not the mountains, waves, and skies, a part
> Of me and of my Soul, as I of them?
> Is not the love of these deep in my heart
> With a pure passion?[1]

But Byron did not believe, as Wordsworth and Shelley did, that Nature had a purpose. The difference can be seen clearly in Shelley's treatment of the same idea in *Adonais*.

> He is made one with Nature: there is heard
> His voice in all her music . . .
> . . .
> He is a portion of the loveliness
> Which once he made more lovely: he doth bear
> His part, while the one Spirit's plastic stress
> Sweeps through the dull dense world, compelling there,
> All new successions to the forms they wear;
> Torturing the unwilling dross that checks its flight
> To its own likeness, as each mass may bear:
> And bursting in its beauty and its might
> From trees and beasts and men into the Heaven's light.[2]

Byron did not think of Nature as a 'stream of tendency' acting on the human imagination. Instead he regarded imaginative communion with Nature as the intimation of an immortality in which the human spirit would feel directly and without barrier the spirits of nature,

> shall I not
> Feel all I see less dazzling but more warm?
> The bodiless thought? the Spirit of each spot?
> Of which, even now, I share at times the immortal lot?[3]

Whence Byron got this notion, it is impossible to say, but it is curious that Keats should at one time have had much the same idea.

In his descriptions of the 'one life', of the 'language' of nature, and of the creativeness of the imagination, Byron followed *The Excursion* and called in Wordsworth's early

---

[1] *Childe Harold's Pilgrimage*, III. lxxii, lxxv.
[2] *Adonais*, ll. 370–87.
[3] *Childe Harold's Pilgrimage*, III. lxxiv.

Persians and Chaldeans to make his point. In Wordsworth's poem the Persians recognize Nature as 'a sensitive existence'.

> Solitude was not . . .
> Whether the Persian—zealous to reject
> Altar and image, and the inclusive walls
> And roofs of temples built by human hands
> To loftiest heights ascending, from their tops,
> Presented sacrifice to moon and stars,
> And to the winds and mother elements,
> And the whole circle of the heavens, for him
> A sensitive existence, and a God . . .[1]

This re-appears in a passage of *Childe Harold* in which the emphasis on Beauty suggests transmission through Shelley.

> All Heaven and Earth are still: from the high host
> Of stars, to the lulled lake and mountain-coast,
> All is concentered in a life intense,
> Where not a beam, nor air, nor leaf is lost,
> But hath a part of Being, and a sense
> Of that which is of all Creator and Defence.
>
> Then stirs the feeling infinite, so felt
> In solitude, where we are *least* alone;
> A truth which through our being then does melt,
> And purifies from self: it is a tone,
> The soul and source of Music, which makes known
> Eternal harmony, and sheds a charm
> Like to the fabled Cytherea's zone,
> Binding all things with beauty;—'twould disarm
> The spectre Death, had he substantial power to harm,
>
> Not vainly did the early Persian make
> His altar the high places, and the peak
> Of earth-o'ergazing mountains, and thus take
> A fit and unwalled temple, there to seek
> The Spirit, in whose honour shrines are weak,
> Upreared of human hands.[2]

---

[1] *The Excursion*, IV. 650, 671–9.
[2] *Childe Harold's Pilgrimage*, III. lxxxix, xc, xci.

Byron claimed also to have heard the 'language' of natural objects of which Wordsworth spoke a few hundred lines later, but he seemed surer of the importance of what Nature said than of its exact import. Thus in *The Dream* he

> made him friends of mountains: with the stars
> And the quick Spirit of the Universe
> He held his dialogues: and they did teach
> To him the magic of their mysteries;
> To him the book of Night was opened wide
> And voices from the deep abyss revealed
> A marvel and a secret—Be it so.[1]

So it may have been, but one doubts it.

Byron was clearer on the topic of the Imagination. Here his theory began with Wordsworth's Chaldean astronomer-shepherd, for whom 'the imaginative faculty was lord of observations natural'. The Chaldean appears early in the third canto of *Childe Harold*.

> Like the Chaldean, he could watch the stars,
> Till he had peopled them with beings bright
> As their own beams; and earth and earth-born jars,
> And human frailties, were forgotten quite:
> Could he have kept his spirit to that flight
> He had been happy.[2]

This comes close to the conception of the Imagination which Keats at first drew from Wordsworth, but in his development of the conception Byron abandoned nature and came to a much more ordinary view of the matter. For him the Imagination was neither the means for a special communication from the source of all being, nor was it the faculty whose creations were especially founded in the nature of reality. He simply asserted that as all things were creations of the mind, its artistic creations had as much reality as those which we call external nature.

> Is not the past all shadow?—what are they
> Creations of the mind?—The mind can make

---

[1] *The Dream*, ll. 145–51.   [2] *Childe Harold's Pilgrimage*, iii. xiv.

> Substance, and people planets of its own
> With beings brighter than have been, and give
> A breath to forms which can outlive all flesh.[1]

Hence his conception of art as the expression of the artist's self, and not of some deeper reality.

> 'Tis to create, and in creating live
> A being more intense, that we endow
> With form our fancy, gaining as we give
> The life we image, even as I do now.[2]

Something of this may have been in Shelley's mind when he wrote the song of the Fourth Spirit in *Prometheus Unbound*. He was certainly thinking of Byron at the time: the songs of the first and second Spirits are Shelley's answers to those of the First and Second Destinies in *Manfred*. Shelley's poet too creates

> Forms more real than living man,
> Nurslings of immortality.[3]

But Shelley was much closer to Wordsworth. His poet created these forms from 'shapes that haunt thought's wildernesses', in this case 'the lake-reflected sun' and 'the yellow-bees in the ivy-bloom', and his creations are 'nurslings of immortality', a phrase which suggests their dependence on some other power than the poet's skill.

By far the most interesting result of Byron's brief conversion to 'metaphysics' was his discovery, in *Manfred*, of an artistic form particularly fitted to express the new conception of nature. It is true that in *Manfred* Byron's bleeding heart cuts a greater figure than the Universe which acts as chorus to it, but in *Prometheus Unbound* Shelley used the form to produce what is, with *The Prelude*, the greatest poetic celebration of the active universe and its dealings with man. Several things entered into the conception of *Manfred*, among them a hint from Shelley, the hearing of the beginning of Goethe's *Faust* read by 'Monk' Lewis, and the reading of the *Prometheus Vinctus* of Aeschylus. Shelley's suggestion was that the

[1] *The Dream*, ll. 18–22.   [2] *Childe Harold's Pilgrimage*, iii. vi.
[3] *Prometheus Unbound*, i. 748–9.

alpine glaciers were a fit dwelling for Ahriman, the destructive spirit.[1] Out of this Byron made Arimanes,

> Prince of Earth and Air!
> Who walks the clouds and waters—in his hand
> The sceptre of the elements, which tear
> Themselves to chaos at his high command!
> He breatheth—and a tempest shakes the sea;
> He speaketh—and the clouds reply in thunder;
> He gazeth—from his glance the sunbeams flee;
> He moveth—earthquakes rend the world asunder;
> . . .
> To him Death pays his tribute; Life is his,
> With all its Infinite of agonies—
> And his the Spirit of whatever is.[2]

To him, Demogorgon in Shelley's *Prometheus Unbound* was a reply.

Manfred is in outline a Faust story, and its opening scene was obviously inspired by the opening scene of Goethe's play, but, for the speeches of Goethe's Archangels, Byron substituted the songs of the seven spirits of nature. The very names of these spirits show their derivation from Wordsworth's metaphysics as Shelley preached it.

Earth—ocean—air—night—mountains—winds—thy Star.[3] Earth, ocean and air are Shelley's trinity in the opening line

[1] N. I. White, *Shelley*, i, p. 714. Shelley's other remark, that the glaciers suggested Buffon's 'sublime but gloomy theory' that the whole earth would eventually become 'a mass of frost', was presumably responsible for Byron's poem *Darkness*.

[2] *Manfred*, ii. iv. 1–17.

[3] id., i. i. 132. That these spirits represent a Wordsworthian view of nature is further indicated in the invocation which summons them (*Manfred*, i. i. 28–33):

> Mysterious Agency!
> Ye spirits of the unbounded Universe!
> Whom I have sought in darkness and in light—
> Ye, who do compass earth about and dwell
> In subtler essence—ye, to whom the tops
> Of mountains inaccessible are haunts . . .

cf. *The Excursion*, iv. 670–9 and *Childe Harold's Pilgrimage*, iii. xci.

of *Alastor*, and the combination occurs several times in *The Excursion*;[1] night was the time when Byron felt the Wordsworthian unity of nature (see the passage from *Childe Harold* quoted above, page 176); Byron's affection for mountains first appeared in an echo of *Tintern Abbey* in the same canto (quoted on page 174), and his affection for winds presumably also echoes Wordsworth's. Only the star seems to be Byron's own addition, and that may have come from

> The soul that rises with us, our life's star

via the third canto of *Childe Harold*.[2] The idea of giving a soul to these natural phenomena was also part of the Wordsworthianism of the third canto.

> Sky—Mountains—River—Wind—Lake—Lightnings! Ye!
> With night, and clouds, and thunder,—and a Soul
> To make these felt and feeling. . . .[3]

The phrase could be ambiguous, for the capitalized Soul might be the poet's own, but the phrase 'felt and feeling' suggests the full reciprocity of the Wordsworthian contact with the life in Nature, and Byron had already more than once expressed his belief in a 'Spirit of the Universe'.[4]

Byron saw in the spirits of *Faust* a possible means of representing this soul in its different aspects and so providing a dramatic form for the expression of the new philosophy. In the outcome his interest in this proved less than his interest in the expression of his own personality. It was left for Shelley to take full advantage of the dramatic form.

Byron was lavish in his use of spirits, and besides the spirits of nature there were Destinies, conventional demons, and apparitions. Of these Shelley used only those which fitted his metaphysical scheme—the spirits of nature and those representing the workings of necessity—and, of course, he went

---

[1] *Alastor*, l. 1; *The Excursion*, IV. 121 ('earth, sea, air'), IV. 612 ('earth, sky, water'), and I. 191, 201 ('earth, and sky' . . . 'ocean and earth').

[2] See *Poetical Works*, ed. E. H. Coleridge, note to *Childe Harold's Pilgrimage*, III. lxxxviii, which traces the 'star' there to Wordsworth.

[3] id., III. xcvi.   [4] id., III. lxxxix, *The Dream*, l. 146.

back to Byron's source,[1] the *Prometheus Vinctus*. But in many ways *Prometheus Unbound* can be seen as Shelley's answer to Byron's pessimism, and to Byron must go the credit for finding the form in which Shelley's view of the world found its most powerful embodiment.

[1] Letter to Murray, 12 October 1817. T. Moore, *Life, Letters and Journals of Lord Byron*, p. 368.

8

The Influence of
The Excursion:
The 'Stream of Tendency'

One of the great themes of late eighteenth- and early nineteenth-century thought was the doctrine of perfectibility and in most cases this doctrine took an evolutionary form; that is to say, it usually took the form of a belief that man and the universe *must* become steadily more perfect through the working of natural law or divine plan. The period was haunted by the vision of Time moving to an apocalyptic consummation. The strength of this idea in radical political thought is obvious, but it also affected Romantic thought about poetry and even invaded biological science where it can be seen both in those evolutionary theories which assume immanent finality,[1] and in the theories of successive creation. This pervading belief formed the themes of the most important long poems of Shelley and Keats, *Prometheus Unbound* and *Hyperion*, and played an important part in many others, notably in the third book of *Endymion*. Nevertheless, however obvious such a theme may have been in the period, it will be found that the particular form it took in these poems owed much more to

[1] For immanent finality as a leading idea in early nineteenth century evolutionary theory, see Emile Guyenot, *Les Sciences de la vie aux xviie et xviiie siècles: l'idée d'evolution*, p. 420.

182

Wordsworth than to the general spirit of the age. Moreover, as Wordsworth's beliefs were rather different from the general run of 'progressive' theories, these poems need to be analysed carefully if they are not to be misunderstood.

Though the belief in the inevitability of progress did not begin with Wordsworth, he was for younger writers its chief preacher. When Hazlitt wished to quote 'the cant of the day' on the subject, it was Wordsworth's phrase 'the mighty stream of tendency' which he chose as his example, and on another occasion he took, as the finest expression of the doctrine of philosophical necessity, the lines

> A motion and a spirit, that impels
> All thinking things, all objects of all thought.[1]

Wordsworth's expression of the doctrine had all the more force because the word 'spirit' was not a metaphor, as it would have been had Godwin written the lines. Wordsworth's faith that the world was impelled to goodness by an active intelligence, or rather an active force underlying both intelligence and the very forms of being, differentiated him from the rationalist believers in progress, though not, as we have seen[2] from a wider current of late eighteenth-century thought. What set him apart from all others was the goal he set for this progress. The common doctrine of radical thought in the period had been that man was progressing to happiness, and, in some sense or other, heaven on earth. Wordsworth found this happiness in union, through the senses and the Imagination, with the active Principle in nature, and though his heaven was to be found on this earth, it consisted in possession of, and by, the divine. Shelley and Keats might have learnt their belief in progress from many writers: it was from Wordsworth that they learned to see this participation in divinity, this deification, as the goal of the world-process.

Because of this certain characteristic words in the Romantic vocabulary must be treated with care. One of T. E. Hulme's

---

[1] *Tintern Abbey*, ll. 100–1. See also *Poetical Works*, v, pp. 471–2.
[2] See pp. 22–5 above.

complaints against later Romantic poetry was that it over-worked the associations which cluster around the word 'infinity',[1] but in the poetry of Shelley and Keats the use of such words as 'eternity' and 'immortality' is not an appeal to vague associations. The words are used in an exact, if peculiar, sense to mean the possession of the Wordsworthian *summum bonum* in this life.

The arbitrary use of emotive words was perhaps a natural part of the war against orthodox religion, just as attempts to capture such words as 'democracy' are part of the modern political struggle. Certainly Shelley began as early as *Queen Mab* to try to appropriate the word 'eternity' for his own use.

If, therefore, the human mind, by any future improvement of its sensibility, should become conscious of an infinite number of ideas in a minute, that minute would be eternity. I do not hence infer that the actual space between the birth and death of a man will ever be prolonged; but that his sensibility is perfectible, and that the number of ideas which his mind is capable of receiving is indefinite.[2]

When Shelley came under the influence of Wordsworth, his conception became a Wordsworthian one, and in 1816 he applied the word 'immortal' to man's state when in union with the living Presence of beauty.

> Man were immortal, and omnipotent,
> Didst thou, unknown and awful as thou art,
> Keep with thy glorious train firm state within his heart.[3]

Keats at this time gave exactly the same sense to the word.

> O what a wild and harmonized tune
> My spirit struck from all the beautiful!
> On some bright essence could I lean, and lull
> Myself to immortality: I prest
> Nature's soft pillow in a wakeful rest.[4]

Byron's opinion, after his conversations with Shelley in 1816, that contact with Nature's essences in this world was a fore-taste of a future life to be lived in a world of pure essences has

[1] T. E. Hulme, *Speculations*, pp. 127–8.
[2] *Queen Mab*, note to VIII. 203–7.
[3] *Hymn to Intellectual Beauty*, ll. 39–41.   [4] *Endymion*, III. 170–4.

already been dealt with.[1] Keats at one time seems to have shared this idea. 'We shall enjoy ourselves hereafter by having what we called happiness on earth repeated in a finer tone. . . . Adam's dream will do here, and seems to be a conviction that Imagination and its empyreal reflection is the same as human life and its spiritual repetition.'[2] Keats was not sufficiently sure of the after life to develop this particular idea and it plays little part in his poetry, but the application of the Christian words for the highest good to the Wordsworthian union with the active Principle is common both in his poetry and in Shelley's. For the state of 'fellowship with essence', Keats most often used the image of deification. Both *Endymion* and *Hyperion* are stories of such deifications, while Shelley's *Prometheus Unbound* is the story of the attainment by man of that state in which the dead hours

> bear Time to his tomb in eternity,[3]

and the death of Time marks the beginning of new worlds for Nature and for Man.

This particular symbolical use of language indicates the derivation of this theme from Wordsworth's formulation of it in *The Excursion.*[4] Nevertheless, there was an important difference of method. Though it was Wordsworth who set out to write the great philosophical poem, both Shelley and Keats

---

[1] p. 175 above.   [2] *Letters*, p. 68.
[3] *Prometheus Unbound*, IV. 14.
[4] *The Excursion*, I. 211–13, 227–31, 233–4:

> In such access of mind, in such high hour
> Of visitation from the living God,
> Thought was not; in enjoyment it expired.
> . . . all things there
> Breathed immortality, revolving life,
> And greatness still revolving; infinite:
> There littleness was not; the least of things
> Seemed infinite . . .
> What wonder if his being thus became
> Sublime and comprehensive!

The *Immortality Ode* would also have given warrant for the use of the word 'immortality' to describe the Vision.

handled his subject in a more intellectual way than he did; that is to say, both appeared more interested in ideas for their own sake than he was. Wordsworth's greatest poem, *The Prelude*, was inspired by his own experience of the Vision, and by his sense of the loving-kindness of Nature which had chosen and shaped him to receive it. Keats and Shelley, interpreting the Vision by their own lights, were taken rather by the great sweep of Wordsworth's theory, gathering up the world's history and showing the poetic Imagination as the goal. Hence their most ambitious poems deal with the abstract rather than the individual, and with world history rather than any single life.

The interest which the younger poets took in Time was probably the stronger because they grew up when the science of palaeontology was developing, and when the extent of geologic time and the stages through which the world had passed were becoming better known. Wordsworth was not much interested in this, nor in the early nineteenth-century debate on the origin of man

> Here are we, in a bright and breathing world.
> Our origin, what matters it?[1]

It was enough for him that the world was the effect of the living Presence,[2] and that Nature's love for man offered him too a place in the plan. The natural world was perfect and only man still to be perfected. But Shelley and Keats believed not only in the 'grand March of Intellect', but also in the progressive improvement of the whole natural universe. They both held evolutionary ideas in connection with this belief, but in their day the belief itself was scientific orthodoxy. Between the period of literal faith in *The Book of Genesis* and that of modern evolutionary theory, came a half century when orthodox doctrine was that there had been a series of primeval catastrophes, each followed by the creation of successively higher forms of life. The moral drawn by the greatest authority of the period, Cuvier, as well as by most of the

[1] *The Excursion*, III. 237–8.
[2] *The Prelude* (1805), v. 33–6.

popularizers, was that the history of the physical world was a story of progress.[1] The acquaintance of Keats and Shelley with palaeontology, as it then existed, is shown by the passage in *Endymion* describing the ocean floor, and by the description of strata which this passage inspired in *Prometheus Unbound*. The *Endymion* passage occurs near the beginning of the third book, the only book dealing with historic time as opposed to ideal. As Endymion, by entering the ocean, enters allegorically into the element of time, Keats summarizes the world's history in the record of the sea-bed.

> Old rusted anchors, helmets, breast-plates large
> Of gone sea warriors; brazen beaks and targe;
> Rudders that for a hundred years had lost
> The sway of human hand; gold vase emboss'd
> With long-forgotten story, and wherein
> No reveller had ever dipped a chin
> But those of Saturn's vintage; mouldering scrolls
> Writ in the tongue of heaven, by those souls
> Who first were on the earth; and sculptures rude
> In ponderous stone, developing the mood
> Of ancient Nox; then skeletons of man
> Of beast, behemoth, and leviathan,
> And elephant and eagle, and huge jaw
> Of nameless monster. A cold leaden awe
> These secrets struck into him.[2]

Shelley read *Endymion* just before he wrote the last act of *Prometheus Unbound*, and he reproduced there the gist of this passage, with the difference that he described these deposits after they had become strata in the earth.

> The beams flash on
> And make appear the melancholy ruins
> Of cancelled cycles; anchors, beaks of ships;
> Planks turned to marble; quivers, helms and spears,
> And gorgon-headed targes, and the wheels

[1] G. F. Cuvier, *Récherches sur les ossements fossiles*, pp. 346, 405–9. For the popularizers see p. 8, n. 4 above. For Catastrophism see p. 8, n. 3 above.

[2] *Endymion*, III. 123–37.

> Of scythed chariots, and the emblazonry
> Of trophies, standards, and armorial beasts. . . .
> The wrecks beside of many a city vast,
> Whose population which the earth grew over
> Was mortal, but not human; see, they lie,
> Their monstrous works and uncouth skeletons,
> Their statues, homes and fanes; prodigious shapes
> Huddled in grey annihilation, split,
> Jammed in the hard black deep; and over these,
> The anatomies of unknown winged things,
> And fishes which were isles of living scale,
> And serpents, bony chains, twisted around
> The iron crags, or within heaps of dust
> To which the tortuous strength of their last pangs
> Had crushed the iron crags; and over these
> The jagged alligator, and the might
> Of earth-convulsing behemoth, which once
> Were monarch beasts, and on the slimy shores,
> And weed-overgrown continents of earth,
> Increased and multiplied like summer worms
> On an abandoned corpse, till the blue globe
> Wrapped deluge round it like a cloak, and they
> Yelled, gasped, and were abolished; or some God
> Whose throne was in a comet, passed, and cried,
> 'Be not!' And like my words they were no more.[1]

The nature of some of the details which Shelley added (e.g. the fossilized planks and the firm identification of Leviathan with the fossil alligators) suggests that he had access to Keats' source. This source has not been identified but most of the items in the lists can be found separately in the geological literature of the time. The rusted anchors, the prows of ships, and the petrified ships themselves, are mentioned in de Maillet's *Telliamed* (1748), a very early evolutionist work, in which their discovery in inland excavations is adduced as proof that the present strata were formed in the sea.[2] The rude sculptures may be the fossilized carvings discovered in limestone at Guadeloupe in 1805, alongside fossil human skeletons

[1] *Prometheus Unbound*, iv. 287–318.
[2] B. de Maillet, *Telliamed*, pp. 78–80.

which were presented to the British Museum. These attracted considerable notice and were discussed by Cuvier.[1] The giants are in *Telliamed*, in Buffon's *Epoques de la Nature* (1779) and in Bailly's *Lettres sur les Sciences*,[2] the last two of which were quoted by Shelley in the notes to *Queen Mab*; these remains, too, were discussed by Cuvier.[3] The semi-civilized race which was 'mortal but not human' is to be found in Burtin's *Prize Dissertation concerning the Age of the Globe*, reviewed in the *Monthly Review* in 1790.[4] This is an obscure work, but the theory was a way of admitting Pre-adamites without incurring a charge of heresy,[5] so it may well have been taken up elsewhere. The fossil elephants and reptiles are to be found in most geologists after Buffon, and Cuvier's *Récherches sur les ossements fossiles* (1812) contains descriptions and classifications of fossil fish, alligators and dinosaurs, with which last Behemoth is presumably to be identified. Just where the poets might have found all these typical fossils combined in one list, it is impossible to say. The main point is that their arrangement in this order shows that they were understood as the deposits of the earlier epochs or cancelled cycles of the world's existence.

The introduction of these mute memorials at the beginning of the story of Glaucus is not an accident. *Endymion* contains two deifications, that of Glaucus and that of Endymion himself. One of the chief differences between them is that the story of Glaucus is set undersea and that his deification comes about as the result of his release from bondage, when 'Time's creeping' has reached the destined moment. His bondage is to Circe who seems to represent false poetic taste. Endymion represents the poet as a lover of beauty and Glaucus the poet of the early nineteenth century, faced with certain literary problems; the undersea setting serves to mark off the allegory set in time from that which is timeless. Accordingly, the means by which

[1] G. F. Cuvier, *Récherches*, pp. 213–15, 413, 409–12.
[2] B. de Maillet, *Telliamed*, pp. 77–8; G. L. L. Buffon, *Epoques de la Nature*, p. 20. Bailly is quoted in *Queen Mab* note to VI. 45–6.
[3] G. F. Cuvier, *Récherches*, p. 414.
[4] *Monthly Review*, iii, p. 543.   [5] id.

the two deifications are to be achieved are different. Endymion is to begin by seeking the essences of natural objects, typified by the Moon as the most beautiful of them, and from this 'clear religion of heaven' to advance to friendship and love, which lead to the chief intensity.[1] Glaucus' deification comes with his escape from Circe's spell, and in his case the means are a Wordsworthian knowledge of Nature and her active Principles, combined with pious preservation of the great poets of the past.[2]

> If he utterly
> Scans all the depths of magic, and expounds
> The meaning of all motions, shapes and sounds;
> If he explores all forms and substances
> Straight homeward to their symbol-essences;
> He shall not die. Moreover, and in chief,
> He must pursue this task of joy and grief
> Most piously;—all lovers tempest-tost,
> And in the savage overwhelming lost,
> He shall deposit side by side, until
> Time's creeping shall the dreary space fulfil:
> Which done, and all these labours ripened,
> A youth by heavenly power lov'd and led,
> Shall stand before him; whom he shall direct
> How to consummate all.[3]

Here is again that vision of Time moving to an apocalypse which so haunted the thought of the period, and hence the description of the sea's spoils is a poetically appropriate introduction to the undersea world in which Glaucus is to be deified. By summarizing the world's past back to the nameless monsters at the dawn of time, it takes back to its beginnings the long progress which Keats believed would culminate in the perfecting of English poetry.

Though this scheme was inspired by Wordsworth's, it lacks the latter's clarity and strength. To Wordsworth the world of the Imagination was the real world: for Keats the Imagination and the 'sense of real things' were in conflict. For Wordsworth

---

[1] *Endymion*, I. 780–801.
[2] H. C. Nottcutt, *An Interpretation of Keats's Endymion*, pp. 63–4.
[3] *Endymion*, III. 696–710.

good must come because it is the intent of a power which
moulds its favoured children from birth: Keats, though he
believed 'the youth elect' was 'by heavenly power lov'd and
led', treated the whole process as a magical one, and, indeed,
embodied it in a tale of irrational magic. When Keats personified Wordsworth's Spirit of Nature as Pan, it was not as
the shaper of the real world but as a leaven in it.

> Be still the unimaginable lodge
> For solitary thinkings: such as dodge
> Conception to the very bourne of heaven,
> Then leave the naked brain; be still the leaven,
> That spreading in this dull and clodded earth
> Gives it a touch ethereal—a new birth.[1]

Keats thus believed in two parallel and independent worlds,
one a rational world of 'real things' as 'cold philosophy' saw
it, and the other a magical world of essences and powers which
could be perceived by the poetic Imagination.

> A thousand Powers keep religious state,
> In water, fiery realm, and airy bourne;
> . . .
> Yet few of these far majesties, ah few!
> Have bared their operations to this globe—
> Few, who with gorgeous pageantry enrobe
> Our piece of heaven—whose benevolence
> Shakes hand with our own Ceres; every sense
> Filling with spiritual sweets to plenitude. . . .[2]

Endymion belongs wholly to the world of 'the Imagination
and its empyreal reflection', and the absence of the 'sense of
real things' is very noticeable.

The poem in which Keats reconciled these two worlds was
Hyperion, the poem in which he moved furthest from Wordsworth's influence. During 1818 Keats was trying to find his
own way in philosophy. Stung perhaps by Wordsworth's un-
kind cut in describing the *Hymn to Pan* as 'a pretty piece of
paganism', Keats had come to call Wordsworthianism 'a
philosophy engendered in the whims of an egotist'.[3] At the

---

[1] id., I. 293–8.   [2] id., III. 30–9.   [3] *Letters*, p. 96.

same time, the *Epistle to Reynolds* showed that he was dissatisfied with Wordsworth's belief in the goodness of Nature.

> I saw
> Too far into the sea, where every maw
> The greater on the less feeds evermore.—
> But I saw too distinct into the core
> Of an eternal fierce destruction,
> And so from happiness I far was gone.[1]

Nevertheless, when he set out to judge by experience the axioms of philosophy, the axioms he tested were usually those he had learnt from Wordsworth. After comparing the latter's poetry with Milton he wrote, 'It proves there is really a grand march of intellect; it proves that a mighty Providence subdues the mightiest minds to the service of the time being.'[2] He seems to have looked in other places too for evidence of the grand march, and to have found it in the natural world as well as in poetry. As a result, though *Hyperion* has the same themes of deification and the stream of tendency which *Endymion* had, yet it is an original and remarkable treatment of them.

In this poem Keats abandoned the idea that beauty was the touch of some visiting spirit. At the same time he extended the idea of the 'grand march' to nature, and produced an evolutionary theory which held together the two conflicting aspects of things, beauty and the findings of 'cold philosophy'. On the one hand, the evolution of the world in this poem is an evolution in beauty. Each species or kind brings forth a still more beautiful kind which is to supplant it, and even the ancient gods must give way before the more beautiful race to which they have given birth.

> As Heaven and Earth are fairer, fairer far
> Than Chaos and blank Darkness, though once chiefs;
> And as we show beyond that Heaven and Earth
> In form and shape compact and beautiful,
> In will, in action free, companionship,
> And thousand other signs of purer life;

[1] *Epistle to Reynolds*, ll. 93–8. The poem was sent on 25 March 1818, seven weeks after the letter just mentioned.

[2] *Letters*, pp. 144–5.

> So on our heels a fresh perfection treads,
> A power more strong in beauty, born of us
> And fated to excel us, as we pass
> In glory that old Darkness: nor are we
> Thereby more conquer'd, than by us the rule
> Of shapeless Chaos. Say, doth the dull soil
> Quarrel with the proud forests it hath fed,
> And feedeth still, more comely than itself?
> Can it deny the chiefdom of green groves?
> Or shall the tree be envious of the dove
> Because it cooeth, and hath snowy wings
> To wander wherewithal and find its joys?
> We are such forest-trees, and our fair boughs
> Have bred forth, not pale solitary doves
> But eagles golden-feather'd, who do tower
> Above us in their beauty and must reign
> In right thereof;[1]

On the other hand, the new races dispossess the old because they are more powerful as well as more beautiful, and for that reason are fitter to survive. The passage continues,

> for 'tis the eternal law
> That first in beauty should be first in might:
> Yea, by that law, another race may drive
> Our conquerors to mourn as we do now.

These lines make *Hyperion* almost the first recorded statement of the doctrine of evolution by natural selection. Keats possibly got his idea from what seems to have been the earliest statement of the doctrine, published in 1818 by W. C. Wells, a physician and a teacher at Keats' old medical school, for Wells' theory had the same peculiar feature that it made superior beauty the sign of superior intelligence and superior physical organization. Beauty was for Wells the mark of the master races.[2]

That this view now seems absurd, and perhaps tainted with

[1] *Hyperion*, II. 206–28.

[2] H. W. Piper, 'Keats and W. C. Wells' in *RES* (1949). The traditional sources of *Hyperion* (i.e. mainly Milton and the mythology) are clearly correct as far as they go. What requires further explanation is Keats' remarkable (but not quite unique) anticipation of Darwin,

racialism, should not be allowed to obscure the very different appearance which it must have had in 1818. Then it was at least a scientifically reputable view of the world, and, for Keats, a theory which promised to show that the importance of beauty was the result of a law of nature, and that the whole development of the universe had beauty as its purpose. In this poem only, among his longer poems which deal with ideas, there was no open or hidden conflict in his beliefs, and here he could rival the 'Apollonian' quality he admired in Milton.[1] *Endymion* had an air of make-believe about it, while nearly all his greater odes were written out of the conflict of ideas. *Hyperion* has both epic strength of design and certainty of tone.

The poem was modelled very closely on *Paradise Lost* as the Romantics saw it. It had two aims—to 'assert Eternal Providence', and also to paint sympathetically and tragically the fate of the fallen spirits.[2] Of these, it was the second task that Keats failed to complete. He abandoned the fragment at a point corresponding to the first appearance in *Paradise Lost* of God the Father and God the Son. At this point the exposition of the ideas of the poem was complete, and what should have followed was the tragic conflict between the old and the new, in the persons of Hyperion and Apollo. Here Keats had set himself a difficult task for he had to write sympathetically of Hyperion, the older and less beautiful god, when he thought of himself and his contemporaries as, like Apollo, bringing a new godhead in poetry. It would seem from the speech of Oceanus that the whole theme of the poem would have been wider than this, and would have been one of reconciliation with the world of 'real things' and its 'eternal fierce destruction' because that world is bringing forth ever-greater beauty, both physical and mental.

Accept the truth and let it be your balm.[3]

The system which enabled Keats to write with such dramatic detachment was clear and coherent, but it was perhaps too

[1] Lord Houghton, *Life and Letters of John Keats*, p. 165.
[2] See id., p. 163 for Keats' admiration of the character of Satan.
[3] *Hyperion*, ii. 243.

much so to correspond with the tragic complexities of Keats' own life. He abandoned *Hyperion* because the verse 'cannot be written but in an artful, or, rather, artist's humour'.[1] In the same way the system seems to have been one he did not employ except in art. It was indeed one which offered little consolation to a dying poet.

The world of the other poems written at the same time as, and after, *Hyperion* was the divided world which Keats first found after reading *The Excursion*, and first recorded in *Sleep and Poetry*. Though much has been added, the germ of the *Ode to a Nightingale* may be found in the passage on Greek religion in the fourth book of *The Excursion*.

> And, doubtless, sometimes, when the hair was shed
> Upon the flowing stream, a thought arose
> Of Life continuous, Being unimpaired;
> That hath been, is, and where it was and is
> There shall endure,—existence unexposed
> To the blind walk of mortal accident;
> From diminution safe and weakening age;
> While man grows old, and dwindles, and decays;
> And countless generations of mankind
> Depart; and leave no vestige where they trod.[2]

Keats knew the beauty which was the sign of that Life continuous, and he believed that he could perceive that Life through the Imagination, but his trust was never the absolute trust born of Wordsworth's mystical experiences. He had tried, in *Endymion* and *Hyperion*, to attach himself to theories, but in the end it was only the actual and perceptible beauty that he could 'prove on his pulses'. So, in the last of his poems to treat that conflict which had begun with his reading of *The Excursion*, Wordsworth's claim for the whole invisible world perceived by his imagination was made by Keats for that manifestation of it he knew.

> Beauty is truth, truth beauty,—that is all
> Ye know on earth, and all ye need to know.

[1] *Letters*, p. 384.

[2] *The Excursion*, IV. 753–62, and note on the passage in *Poetical Works*, v, p. 427.

While Keats was writing *Hyperion* and the odes, Shelley was engaged on *Prometheus Unbound*, a fuller and more complex statement of a Romantic view of the world. Shelley was more at home than Keats with metaphysics, and, fortified by his earlier reading of the French *philosophes* and his later reading of Plato, he found in Wordsworth's system none of the puzzles and the contradictions with sense that tormented the younger and less educated poet. Shelley's mature beliefs owed much to Godwin and Plato, but they rested ultimately on ideas which he had adopted from *The Excursion* and in these ideas he had complete trust.[1] *Prometheus Unbound*, like *Hyperion*, seems to come from an attempt to state the foundations of the poet's faith, but here the foundations are the ones on which the faith was built, not new underpinnings for an older structure.

The immediate impulse to the writing of the poem is probably to be found in the conversations which Shelley had with Byron in the autumn of 1818, and which he recorded in *Julian and Maddalo*.

> Our talk grew somewhat serious, as may be
> Talk interrupted with such raillery
> As mocks itself . . .
>   'twas forlorn,
> Yet pleasing, such as once, so poets tell
> The devils held within the dales of Hell
> Concerning God, freewill and destiny:
> Of all that earth has been or yet may be . . .
> Or hope can paint or suffering may achieve,
> We descanted.[2]

In this debate Julian (Shelley) and Maddalo (Byron) each took his characteristic side.

>   'it is our will
> That thus enchains us to permitted ill—
> We might be otherwise—we might be all
> We dream of happy, high, majestical.

[1] For Shelley's habit of treating Wordsworthianism (whether his own, Byron's or Wordsworth's) as the natural thought and feeling of his age, see p. 199 below.   [2] *Julian and Maddalo*, ll. 36–46.

Where is the love, beauty, and truth we seek
But in our mind? and if we were not weak
Should we be less in deed than in desire?'

'Ay, if we were not weak—and we aspire
How vainly to be strong!' said Maddalo;
'You talk Utopia.'[1]

In this poem the argument is given an individual, and perhaps personal[2] application through the introduction of the madman. Nevertheless, it is clear that the conversation had a wider scope, and that it turned on matters of faith.

As we have seen, Byron and Shelley had held similar conversations before in Switzerland in 1816. At that time Shelley had persuaded Byron to his own Wordsworthian faith, and the ideas which he induced him to adopt have been traced in the preceding chapter. Since that time Byron had renounced 'metaphysics', and there is no full record of the arguments which he used against Shelley in 1818. Nevertheless in 1816, after Shelley's departure but before his own break with Wordsworthianism, Byron had written his drama *Manfred* in which he used the spirits of nature to express his view that the tendency of the world was not to good but to evil, and that 'the spirit of whatever is' is cruel and unrelenting. Thus this poem put the pessimistic view that Shelley disliked into the context he accepted and when he returned from Venice in the autumn of 1818, he began not only *Julian and Maddalo* but also *Prometheus Unbound*, in which he took the machinery of *Manfred* and transformed it to an expression of his own faith.

The story of *Prometheus Unbound* is a myth with a double interpretation; it is a story of individual regeneration[3] and also a story of the regeneration of the universe. Of these two meanings, the second is the predominant one. Prometheus is clearly stated to be an immortal, which means, in terms of structure, that he is a quasi-allegorical figure of the same order as Jove and Asia. His triumph does represent something

---

[1] id., 170–9.   [2] N. I. White, *Shelley*, ii, pp. 43–9.
[3] For an interpretation of the poem as a story of individual regeneration see C. S. Lewis, *Rehabilitations*.

that will only come at the destined hour. This change in the type of hero from Manfred, a mortal challenging and scorning the universe, to Prometheus who is, in effect, a process in the universe, marks the reason for Shelley's continued optimism in the face of the arguments of Byron and the instance of the madman.

What Shelley took over from *Manfred* was (besides the unconquerable hero), the machinery for his poem. Byron's spirits of nature, the Destinies, Arimanes and the 'overruling infinite' (the last barely mentioned in *Manfred*) became Shelley's spirits of nature, spirits of human thought, Jove and Demogorgon. The first and second spirits of human thought, who come from the battle-trumpet blast of freedom and the sigh of the drowning seaman who gave his plank to an enemy, are point-by-point answers to Byron's two destinies who raise the Usurper for a nation's destruction and save a pirate from the shipwreck, while his spirits who come from the dreams of the sage and the lips of the poet are less direct answers to the destiny who sows plague and panic in human societies.[1] The treatment of Jove is also pointedly different from that of his counterpart Arimanes (though Byron in one line allows an 'overruling infinite'), and Byron's lines

> To him Death pays his tribute; Life is his
> With all its Infinite of agonies—
> And his the Spirit of whatever is[2]

seems to be answered in Demogorgon's dialogue with Asia:

> All spirits are enslaved which serve things evil:
> Thou knowest if Jupiter be such or no.
> ASIA: Whom called'st thou God?
> DEMOGORGON: I spoke but as ye speak,
> For Jove is the supreme of living things.
> ASIA: Who is the master of the slave?
> DEMOGORGON: If the abysm
> Could vomit forth its secrets . . ..But a voice
> Is wanting, the deep truth is imageless.[3]

---

[1] *Manfred*, ii. iii. 16–53; *Prometheus Unbound*, i. 694–750.
[2] *Manfred*, ii. iv. 14–17.   [3] *Prometheus Unbound*, ii. iv. 110–16.

But in the main, *Prometheus Unbound* ignores the details of *Manfred*, and answers Byron by affirming Shelley's own faith.

That faith had developed greatly from the simple Wordsworthianism of 1815. Indeed, Shelley, with his background of reading in radical and scientific works, seems in 1819 to have regarded the Wordsworthian system as the normal thought of the age rather than the product of one mind. He wrote of a review of the *Revolt of Islam*, 'The only remark worth notice in this piece is the assertion that I imitate Wordsworth. It may as well be said that Lord Byron imitates Wordsworth or that Wordsworth imitates Lord Byron, both being great poets, and deriving from the new springs of thought and feeling, which the great events of our age have exposed to view, a similar tone of sentiment, imagery and expression.'[1] This defence, of course, overlooks the very considerable difference between Shelley's *Queen Mab*, where he was affected only by the general spirit of the age, and his later work in which his ideas show the specific influence of Wordsworth, as, indeed, do the relevant poems of Byron. Nevertheless Shelley had altered the system sufficiently to be able to regard it as wholly his own. These alterations particularly affected his ideas of immortality and the 'deification' of humanity, and his concept of nature, both of which became much Platonized.

On the matter of immortality, Shelley held two distinct, but not incompatible ideas. One, going back to his *Queen Mab* days, was that the soul, as part of the pervading spirit of the universe, would inhabit ever-higher forms of being up to the highest.[2] The other belief, which reaches its finest expression in *Adonais*, was that the soul would be united after death to the spirit of the universe. In 1816 Byron, presumably echoing the ideas with which Shelley was 'dosing' him, wrote

> When Elements to Elements conform,
> And dust is as it should be, shall I not
> Feel all I see less dazzling but more warm?
> The bodiless thought? The Spirit of each spot?
> Of which, even now, I share at times the immortal lot?[3]

[1] *Complete Works*, x, pp. 95–6.
[2] id., viii, p. 227. [3] *Childe Harold's Pilgrimage*, III. lxxiv.

Shelley re-expressed this idea in his images of the painted veil and of the dome of many-coloured glass. These images go beyond Byron's relatively simple idea that the spirit of which matter is the embodiment can be known more fully when that embodiment is no longer interposed, and beyond Shelley's own imagery of spirits shining through the vestments which hide them. Matter, 'the shadows which the world calls substance',[1] is only part of what is meant by the veil or the dome of glass. Life also involves a distortion in the moral world and obscures Intellectual Beauty in actions and thoughts as well as in nature, in music and words as well as in flowers and the azure sky.

> The painted veil, by those who were, called life,
> Which mimicked, as with colours idly spread,
> All men believed or hoped. . . .[2]

But it is not only after death that man can penetrate this veil. After Asia, that is Love, has visited Demogorgon, she is transfigured; she goes back beyond birth to the Platonic Heaven of Forms:

> We have passed Age's icy caves,
> And Manhood's dark and tossing waves,
> And Youth's smooth ocean, smiling to betray:
>   Beyond the glassy gulfs we flee
>   Of shadow-peopled Infancy,
> Through Death and Birth, to a diviner day;
>   A paradise of vaulted bowers,
>   Lit by downward-gazing flowers,
>   And watery paths that wind between
>   Wildernesses calm and green,
> Peopled by shapes too bright to see,
> And rest, having beheld; somewhat like thee;
> Which walk upon the sea, and chant melodiously![3]

Wordsworth had used the same combination of the figures of the Platonic Heaven of Forms, the diviner day before birth, and the immortal ocean to explain man's relation with the

---

[1] *Sonnet: The Painted Veil*, draft of line 6.
[2] *Prometheus Unbound*, III. iv. 190–2.   [3] id., II. v. 98–110.

divine in the *Ode: Intimations of Immortality*[1] but in that poem Wordsworth had lost the belief (still preserved in passages of *The Excursion*[2]) that such a diviner day could be man's on earth. Here Shelley is affirming his belief that this perfect relationship is possible on earth and will be established at the destined hour, 'harmonizing this earth with what we feel above'. Therefore, at the end of the third act, the painted veil is torn aside for the living, and Man undergoes an apotheosis which, until that hour, he could only know beyond the grave.

This is more than a highly coloured statement of Godwin's political theories. It is grounded on the metaphysical belief in the 'stream of tendency' which is stated very simply and clearly in *Adonais*:

> the one Spirit's plastic stress
> Sweeps through the dull dense world, compelling there,
> All new successions to the forms they wear;
> Torturing th' unwilling dross that checks its flight
> To its own likeness, as each mass may bear;
> And bursting in its beauty and its might
> From trees and beasts and men into the Heaven's light.[3]

In *Prometheus Unbound* this 'stream of tendency' appears as Demogorgon's law:

> There those enchanted eddies play
>   Of echoes, music-tongued, which draw
>   By Demogorgon's mighty law,
>   With melting rapture, or sweet awe,
> All spirits on that secret way;
>   As inland boats are driven to ocean
> Down streams made strong with mountain-thaw;
>   And first there comes a gentle sound
>   To those in talk or slumber bound,
>   And wakes the destined soft emotion,—
> Attracts, impels them. . . .[4]

It is true that this is both inevitable and the result of the exercise of man's free-will, but the paradox is no greater than

[1] *Ode: Intimations of Immortality*, ll. 58–76, 166–71.
[2] e.g. *The Excursion*, IV. 1229–76.
[3] *Adonais*, ll. 381–7.   [4] *Prometheus Unbound*, II. ii. 41–51.

the orthodox one of free-will and fore-knowledge, and Shelley
accepted it:

> Those who saw
> Say from the breathing earth behind
> There streams a plume-uplifting wind
> Which drives them on their path, while they
> Believe their own swift wings and feet
> The sweet desires within obey.[1]

Demogorgon is identical with the 'one Spirit', at once drawing
by beauty and compelling the 'unwilling dross' to its own
likeness.

Demogorgon, or that 'imageless' truth which he represents,
is the deep foundation of the natural world as well as of human
nature. As we have seen in the preceding chapter, Shelley
always, like Keats and Byron in their Wordsworthian periods,
thought of natural objects as having their own 'life' or
'essences' (though the word which he normally used was
'spirit').

> Ye elemental Genii, who have homes
> From man's high mind even to the central stone
> Of sullen lead; from heaven's star-fretted domes
> To the dull weed some sea-worm battens on:
>
> .   .   .   .
>
> Spirits, whose homes are flesh; ye beasts and birds,
> Ye worms, and fish; ye living leaves and buds;
> Lightning and wind; and ye untameable herds,
> Meteors and mists, which throng air's solitudes.[2]

Even in *Queen Mab* Shelley had believed, on the basis of
chronological calculations, that moral and physical perfection
would coincide. On his present system it was evident that when
the 'one Spirit' had harmonized the moral world to its own
likeness, it would do the same for the physical world. The
evolution which was the progress of this Spirit was to result
in a millennium in which all things 'put their evil nature off',
the earth brings forth no more diseases or poisons, toads
become beautiful, venomous and malicious beasts good, the
ocean perpetually calm and the moon fertile.

[1] id., ii. ii. 51–6.   [2] id., iv. 539–47.

It is this that the last act celebrates. The act begins with the dead hours bearing Time to his tomb in eternity because Time in a sense has stopped. Time is no longer working out an evolution and succession in time no longer has any importance. From a progress Time has become a dance.

> Once the hungry Hours were hounds
>   Which chased the day like a bleeding deer,
> And it limped and stumbled with many wounds
>   Through the nightly dells of the desert year.
>
> But now, oh weave the mystic measure
>   Of music, and dance, and shapes of light,
> Let the Hours, and the spirits of might and pleasure,
>   Like the clouds and sunbeams, unite.[1]

Into the orchestra eventually join all the spirits of nature— the earth (with a glance at its long history buried in the strata), the moon hymning its new fertility, suns, stars, the dead, the elements and living things. It is in relation to a universe living and developing to this consummation that Shelley's views of Man, Imagination, and the reformation of the world must be seen: it is only in relation to such a universe that they are coherent and tenable. The 'abstruse and imaginative theories with regard to the Creation', referred to by Mrs Shelley in her notes to the poem, were the groundwork of his whole faith.

Except for the epic satire *Don Juan*, which lies outside the scope of this study, *Prometheus Unbound* was the last of the great long poems of the Romantic Revival. The list of the poems examined or touched on—*Joan of Arc*, *Religious Musings*, *The Ancient Mariner*, *The Prelude*, *The Excursion*, *Endymion*, *Hyperion* and *Prometheus Unbound*—though it starts with prentice work, covers most of the greatest Romantic achievement in large-scale poetry. Each of these poems is, in a broad sense, religious. Each, like *Paradise Lost*, had as its aim to

> assert Eternal Providence
> And justify the ways of God to men.

[1] id., IV. 73–9.

Each tried to do so by expounding a faith in a living, purposive universe which was (except in the case of *Hyperion*) the outward form of a pervading spirit, and hence the expression to men of that spirit. By reading with his Imagination the significance and beauty of that form, man would come into contact with the one Spirit, be moulded by it, and reach unity with the divine, grace or apotheosis, and happiness.

There was a connection between this saving faith which the Romantics were endeavouring to explore and propagate, and the profusion of great poems of the first rank. The faith was one which could be held sincerely in the light of contemporary knowledge of the natural world, and, however doubtful the metaphysics, it was a large, noble and passionately held faith capable of inspiring and organizing a long major poem. Between the urgency of their mission and the embracing largeness of their creed the poets had to plan greatly and could plan greatly. It is most significant that in the Victorian age, when the Romantic faith had become subjectivism and the Romantic hope mere aspiration, the power to produce large highly organized poems disappeared, and the best long poems took the form of the lyric or narrative cycle. But the Victorian decline was felt, if not so acutely, in short poems as well as in long. Wordsworth's description of the relation of his short poems to his long as that of cells and oratories to a church, is one that holds more widely. The long poems were built for the celebration of a faith which equally inspired the whole practice and theory of the poets who held it.

Epilogue

The Imagination from a Non-Romantic Viewpoint

It is now time to leave the history of the Romantic theory of the Imagination, and to consider its value. Nothing that has been said in the previous chapters depends in any way on what may be said in this, for in them we have not been trying to say what the poets ought to have thought, or could have meant, in terms of later theories, but what they did think and mean in terms of their own world. Nevertheless, this book would be incomplete without some attempt to find whether the Imagination is a mere mirage, visible only from the peculiar standpoint of the Romantics, or whether it is something permanent which other generations, who have left the Romantic Pis-Gah, must chart on any map they use. The word Imagination is one we still employ. If it leads to nothing but self-deceit we are better without it; if it points to something of the first importance, we should know the grounds for our confidence.

Obviously such a discussion must be carried on in terms other than these which represent the metaphysical assumptions of the Romantics, but any confirmation it may bring will be by that much the more valuable.

Before any analysis is made, it will be necessary to recall some important ways in which the Romantic theories of the Imagination and the Romantic use of the word differed from the modern. The most important of these differences is that the Romantics used the word in two senses, or at least in two

205

contexts, only one of which is common modern use. In the first context, the Imagination affects the poet's experience of the natural world; in the second, the sense which has survived more clearly, its activities are apparent in literature. In the first context it was said by Wordsworth 'to recognise the moral properties and scope of things', to 'half-create' as well as to perceive, and to see 'life and greatness' in things, by Shelley, 'to mark the before unapprehended relations of things . . . the same footsteps of Nature impressed on the various subjects of the world', by Keats, to 'talk to the trees and the mountains' and, by Coleridge, to focus 'rays of intellect . . . scattered throughout the images of nature'.[1] All this can perhaps be summed up in Wordsworth's statement that he found in natural forms 'a spirit of strange meaning'.[2] In the second sense, the Imagination is a power exercised in poetry. Its effects are discovered by listening to a poem, not by looking at natural forms. In this context, Wordsworth said that it 'shapes and creates' through its 'conferring, abstracting, and modifying powers',[3] and Coleridge called it 'the esemplastic power' which 'dissolves, diffuses, dissipates in order to create'.[4] What it creates is a new image, made from the materials it has acted upon.

It should be noticed that the Romantics did not always confine the Imagination (in this sense) to poetry. Wordsworth thought that it also worked in prose,[5] and Shelley that 'All the authors of revolutions in opinion are . . . necessarily poets as they are inventors, [and] as their words unveil the permanent analogy of things by images which participate in the life of truth.'[6] Even among the nineteenth-century scientists, Charles Darwin stressed the importance of Imagination in scientific advance.[7]

---

[1] *The Excursion*, I. 167–8; *Tintern Abbey*, ll. 106–7; *The Excursion*, I. 227–8; *The Defence of Poetry*, in *Complete Works*, ed. Ingpen and Peck, vii, p. 111; *Sleep and Poetry*, ll. 136–7; *On Poesy or Art*, quoted in *Biographia Literaria*, ii, pp. 257–8.

[2] *The Ruined Cottage*, MS B, ll. 150–4.   [3] *Preface* of 1815.

[4] *Biographia Literaria*, i, p. 202.   [5] *Preface* of 1815.

[6] *Complete Works*, vii, p. 115.

[7] *The Descent of Man* (1871), I. ii. 45, quoted in *OED*.

The second important difference is that the Romantics believed, as few men do now, in the truth of the Imagination. For Wordsworth it was 'Reason in her most exalted mood'; for Shelley it was 'the storehouse of axioms common to all knowledge'; Keats was 'certain of nothing but . . . the truth of the Imagination'; and for Coleridge it grasped truths to which the judgement had to be led step by step, and it realized and developed into thought the strivings of nature. This faith depended, of course, on the belief that the natural world played its part in the productions of the Imagination.

The first detailed analysis of the operation of the Imagination in poetry is to be found in Wordsworth's *Preface* of 1815. The examples he chooses are all similes or metaphors, and they may be typified by Milton's flying Fiend, who seems

> As when far off at sea a fleet descried
> *Hangs* in the air. . . .

In his analysis he points out how the word 'hangs' coalesces the fleet into a unity and blends it with the figure of Satan. His point in all the examples is this, that by the operation of the Imagination two objects are so modified that they 'unite and coalesce in a just comparison'.

This is a very narrow view of the Imagination, as we can see by comparing it with Ruskin's in *Modern Painters*. Ruskin describes two chief forms of the Imagination, the Associative, and the Penetrative, which goes straight to the heart of the thing without any preliminary operations or coalescences. As instances of this kind of Imagination he gives Dante's description of white-hot flame in Purgatory

> Ed io facea *con l'ombra piu rovente*
> *Parer la fiamma.*[1]

and Macduff's 'he has no children'. The point he makes is a very strong one, for these are lines that most people would accept unhesitatingly as examples of Imagination, even though they are not at all susceptible to the sort of analysis

---

[1] 'And with my shadow I made the flame appear ruddier.' *Il Purgatorio*, XXVI. 7–8.

which Wordsworth applied in his *Preface*. But this line has been little followed up, and for the moment I must leave it on one side and see if a further consideration of the Imagination Associative will throw light on it.

A number of recent studies, ranging from idealist to psychoanalytical, have stressed very strongly the 'fusing' power of the Imagination and used this as the basis for their concepts or definitions of it. This emphasis is perhaps due to the fact that most of these studies start from Coleridge.[1] *Biographia Literaria*, the *locus classicus* for Coleridge's theory of Imagination, divorces that power from life and the experience of nature more completely than does any other Romantic definition or description, even of Coleridge's own.[2] We are thus left to seek our criterion of what is imaginative in the mind (or the sub-conscious) and the only one which seems to present itself is this 'fusing' power. Such a definition lies open to the attack made on it by F. L. Lucas who points out very forcibly in *The Decline and Fall of the Romantic Ideal* that it excludes most of the greatest things in literature, because they are simple, and exalts the complicated and *recherché*.[3]

A way out of metaphysics and metapsychology is offered by J. J. C. Smart's review in *Mind* of D. G. James' book *The Life of Reason*. In this book Dr James employs the terminology of 'ideas' and 'faculties', and using a quotation from *The Merchant of Venice* as an example:

> Your argosies with portly sail
> Like signiors and rich burghers of the flood. . . .

says 'The labour of the Imagination is, so far as it can, to apprehend an idea which somehow consists of the idea of both ship and trader.'

Professor Smart comments,

Professor James wants to supplement the two Augustan faculties of sensation and understanding with a third, Imagination. . . .

[1] e.g. J. L. Lowes, *The Road to Xanadu*; I. A. Richards, *Coleridge on Imagination*.

[2] See p. 141–2 above.

[3] F. L. Lucas, *The Decline and Fall of the Romantic Ideal*, pp. 173–6.

Locke's language gives us no way of talking of such situations as seeing a puzzle picture *as* something or other, and there are important similarities between these and the poetic seeing of a ship *as* a portly merchant.[1]

That the Imagination is a particular case of 'seeing as' is obviously just for all the cases of the Imagination Associative. Our next step then must be to find what is involved in 'seeing one thing as another'.

Wittgenstein has a very interesting discussion of 'seeing as' in his *Philosophical Investigations*.[2] There he starts from certain examples of things which can be seen in two ways, for example, an outline which can be seen as the head of a rabbit or as the head of a duck, and an octagon with the alternate segments shaded which can be seen as a black Maltese cross on a white background or as a white cross on a black background. In these cases, once we have seen the two possibilities, or had them pointed out to us, we can see the diagram as one thing or the other, more or less at will. Wittgenstein points out that in these cases we speak of 'seeing it as a black cross' and not simply 'seeing a black cross', and points out certain other differences that go with this, e.g. that we can 'try to see it as a black cross'.

All these considerations would seem to point to something different from ordinary seeing in these cases, as, too, might the curious sensation which accompanies the change in our seeing. This sensation is perhaps less marked in other instances which Wittgenstein mentions—the case of the face which is seen as like someone else's and that of the right-angled triangle which can be seen as hanging from an invisible wire, or as resting on its base, as having fallen on its side or as pointing in one direction.

In a review of *Philosophical Investigations* in *Mind*,[3] P. F. Strawson points out that under the strain of Wittgenstein's examples the notion that perception can be divided into 'sense data' and 'interpretation' gives way. A return to the

[1] *Mind* (1950), p. 121.
[2] L. Wittgenstein, *Philosophical Investigations*, pp. 193–214.
[3] *Mind* (1954), pp. 70–99.

diagram of the Maltese crosses will make this clear. It will be obvious to anyone who looks that we do not change an interpretation of sense data; we simply see it differently.

Strawson also points out that there is no difference between 'seeing as' and 'seeing'. What happens when the white cross is seen after the black is no different from what happens when a light is switched on in a dark room. Here one might add that what the phrase 'seeing as' marks is not a different *kind* of seeing but an ambiguity, that is, a possibility of seeing the thing in more than one way. Let us take the case of a black feature which can be seen as a rock or a cave. All the features which Wittgenstein noted about 'seeing as' can be found here. We can say, 'Now I am seeing it as a cave', we can try to see it as a rock, and so on. Yet once we discover which it is, say by asking a friend with binoculars, then our seeing it as a cave (if that is what it is) will in no way differ from seeing a cave. All that the forms of expression have indicated is that there was more than one way of seeing it.

Thus we can begin to discuss the statement that the Imagination is 'seeing something as something else' from the two points that 'seeing as' is no more than an expression used to indicate that there is more than one way of seeing something and that seeing cannot be divided into 'sense data plus interpretation'.

At this point the reader may feel moved to object that, whereas Wittgenstein was using the word 'seeing' literally, the same word applied to the Imagination must be used metaphorically: the objects described by the poets are not physically before our eyes, and perhaps never could be. This objection will be less simple and less convincing when we consider Wittgenstein's examples. How far is seeing a pencil line as a drawing of the head of a rabbit a case of simple physical seeing? There is a history of art involved here. Again Wittgenstein's case of seeing a triangle as pointing in a certain direction seems very parallel to the case of seeing argosies as rich burghers. Yet we can think of cases in which physical sight seems of hardly any importance and class them with Shakespeare's argosies as examples of Imagination. Where are the lines to be drawn? Let us try to construct a scale of examples ranging from the most literal cases of 'seeing as' to the most metaphorical, and see then where a line may be drawn. Such a scale could run as follows.

1. The black spot which can be seen as a rock or a cave.

2. (Placed higher because the objects depend on convention.) The diagram of the two Maltese crosses.

3. The outline which can be seen as the head of a duck or as that of a rabbit.

4. The person seen as someone else.

5. The triangle seen as suspended from its apex, resting on its base, fallen over, or pointing.

6. A skull seen as grinning.

7. The case implied in the phrase 'the predatory fork and the calm stupidity of the spoon',[1] where the fork is seen as a predatory animal and the spoon as an expressionless gaping face.

8. The case of a woman who is about to buy a hat until a friend whispers, 'My dear, it's the Taj Mahal', and who then sees it differently.[2]

9. Shakespeare's argosies 'like signiors and rich burghers of the flood'.

10. Milton's Satan, 'as when far off at sea a fleet descried Hangs in the air'.

11. Milton's 'rathe primrose that forsaken dies'.

12. Shakespeare's description of Prince Hal and his companions, in which the 'seeing as' is sometimes closer to and sometimes further from the literal—

> All plumed like estridges that wing the wind;
> Bated like eagles having lately bathed;
> Glittering in golden coats like images;
> As full of spirit as the month of May
> And gorgeous as the sun in mid summer.

13. Wordsworth's 'thy soul was like a star and dwelt apart'.

14. The phrase 'the river of time'.

[1] Example supplied by Dr C. B. Martin.

[2] Example used by J. Wisdom in *Philosophy and Psychoanalysis*, p. 248.

At what point here can we draw a line above which 'seeing as' is a matter of simple physical seeing? One man might exclude the pointing triangle, another the grinning skull, and yet another might draw the line between Shakespeare's estridges and his eagles. All that we can say is that as we go up the scale the circumstances in which we can say, 'I can see it as B', depend less and less on having the object before our eyes (or on visualizing it) until, at the end, physical sight seems of very little importance. While it is possible to make a distinction between the ends of the scale, it will not help us in our investigation of 'seeing as'.

The situation may become clearer if we realize that in all the cases the statement 'I can see B', implies that I know how to go on. If I say 'I see a cave', it means I know how to go on in relation to it, e.g. I know what will happen if I fire a tracer bullet at it. If I say 'I see the drawing of the head of a rabbit', I can go on and, for instance, draw in the body. If I see a pointing triangle, I can draw arrows continuing the direction. If I see a hat as the Taj Mahal, I can go on to buy it for the leading character in a production of *Charley's Aunt*. If I see Milton's soul as a star, I can go on by taking an appropriate attitude to him, and by expecting from him guidance but not intimacy. If I see Time as a river, I can go on to talk coherently about events that happen at different times. While it is true that I could not rightly say 'I see a cave' unless a cave (or a black spot which might be one) were before my eyes, and the change from seeing the spot as a cave to seeing it as a rock is a definite change in our visual experience, and that this is not so at the other end of the scale, nevertheless this implication of being able to go on runs through all the cases. It is this which makes it reasonable to apply the word 'seeing' to things which depend very little upon our eyesight.

If the reader still feels that so practical a matter as seeing a rock can have nothing in common with so airy a one as seeing the primrose that forsaken dies, he might wish to object that the early cases in the list are clear-cut and the later ones vague. In the early cases we can clearly confirm that what is there is a cave or a rock or we can show that there is a black and white cross there to be seen. If someone says he sees a white cross in the diagram we can say 'true', and if he says he sees a white elephant we can say 'false'. From this point of view these will differ from the later cases, where we may feel that the friend might as well have said 'white elephant' as 'Taj Mahal'. We can put this point in another way, and say that in the early cases the object or diagram prompts us, or guides us, to say that we see a cave or a cross. Now the borderline case might be the duck-rabbit which prompts us but might not prompt a primitive man accustomed to drawing ducks and rabbits as X-ray pictures. For a European, the first case where this uncertainty manifests itself might be the case of the pointing triangle. Yet, just as we have learned to see pointing hands, so we might learn to see a triangle as always pointing in the direction of its sharpest angle, and we might then make up diagrams similar to the double Maltese cross, in which an equilateral triangle could be seen as pointing in any of three directions. All that this distinction establishes is the presence of conventional or learnt ways of seeing. So long as the object lends itself we can establish new ways of seeing.

The qualification 'so long as the object lends itself' is important. The new way of seeing is not completely arbitrary. The outline drawing of a duck is conventional, but it has become so through its resemblance to the silhouette of a duck. In the same way, the fork can be seen as predatory and the spoon as stupid, but it seems impossible to see the fork as calm and stupid and the spoon as predatory, any more than it seems possible to see the triangle pointing in the direction of its hypotenuse, or to see Shakespeare's argosies as coalminers. No line can be drawn by suggesting that in the later cases the new way of seeing is unrelated to the object.

Nevertheless, the fact that we want to make some distinction between the cases where there are well-established ways of seeing and those where there are not shows that we do feel a difference between them. To go from one well-established way to another is not the same as going from a well-established way to one we have never considered before. In the one case we already know very well how to go on; we already know how to complete the drawing of a duck's head, and, though we may have some initial difficulty in applying it to the diagram, we feel that the resolution of this difficulty does not give us any fresh understanding. In other cases (which need not be higher up our scale) the resolution of our initial difficulty in 'seeing the thing as B' brings with it knowledge of a fresh way of going on, and we feel that our understanding has been enlarged. In this sense, saying a hat is the Taj Mahal is not the same kind of thing as saying it is a cloche, or a toque or a picture hat, nor is seeing an argosy as a rich burgher the same thing as seeing it as a three-master. We do not use the phrase 'seeing as' of established ways of seeing—that is we do not indicate that there is more than one way of seeing the thing—except in those special and comparatively rare cases where two such ways of seeing are equally possible. We do use 'seeing as' of the Imagination because we presuppose that there is already an old way and that this is a new one.

A last objection that might be made is that in certain of the cases at the beginning of the scale (and in them only) there is a 'visual click', and that in them we do, so to speak, change our focus. If I am seeing the diagram as the head of a duck, then this 'visual click' must occur before I can honestly say, 'Now I am seeing it as the head of a rabbit' and go on in the appropriate way. This seems to happen only when the alternative ways of seeing are well-established ones in which our eyes are trained; that is, it happens with caves, crosses and outline drawings, but does not happen (or does not happen so markedly) in the case of the triangle seen as suspended or as resting on its base. Moreover, it seems to happen only when the alternative ways of seeing differ widely. It occurs when we change from seeing a duck to seeing a rabbit, but not when we change from seeing a hand to seeing a hand pointing. In the latter case, we feel that our attention has been called to a feature of the hand but that, if our seeing has been altered, the change has not been great. That this explains the difference between this and cases like the former one, would seem to be borne out by the fact that we do have the sensation of sudden change when we recognize a face as that of a friend. Here the features that have come to our attention have made us see something very different from an unknown face.

This 'visual click' does not occur then in those cases where there is no great change or when there is no well-drilled way for the eye to 'switch' to, and naturally, it does not occur when the eye is not involved. Yet there is, in most of the latter cases, a sense of well-defined 'switch' in the understanding, at least when we hear the phrase concerned for the first time. It would seem that in these cases we get the new understanding, and see the thing in the new way, just as suddenly and completely as we do in the earlier instances. We realize, as soon as we hear the phrase, that we can go on in the new direction, even though all the steps are not yet laid out in our minds. This sudden access of new power and grasping of new meaning is something the Romantics continually described as characteristic of the Imagination.

We have now reached some important conclusions about what is meant by 'seeing one thing as another', both generally and as it applies to the Imagination. In the first place we have found that the phrase 'seeing as' is only a way of indicating that there is more than one way of seeing a thing. We have also found that seeing cannot be divided into sense data and added interpretation. Thus the statement that Imagination is a matter of seeing one thing as another would be wrong if it implied that we first see a thing correctly and then see it as something else, and it would also be wrong if it implied that the Imagination added a further interpretation to the thing. As it is hard to avoid these implications when using the phrase, it would be better if we said that Imagination is a matter of seeing a thing differently. This different seeing is just as indivisible, and may be just as 'correct', as the original one from which it differs.

> There is creation in the eye
> Nor less in all the other senses; powers
> They are which colour, model, and combine
> The thing perceived with such an absolute

> Essential energy that we may say
> That those most godlike faculties of ours
> At one and the same moment are the mind
> And the mind's ministers.[1]

The next point was that this seeing is not arbitrary. We cannot see everything as anything; rather a new way of seeing is a *discovery*. The object can be seen in some ways, and it cannot be seen in others, because the object must lend itself to a new way of seeing (even the most unexpected), and in some sense suggest it. To quote Wordsworth again

> Forms and feelings acting thus, and thus
> Reacting, they shall each acquire
> A living spirit and a character
> Till then unfelt.[2]

The last point was that the way in which we use the word 'seeing' is very similar to the way in which we use the word 'understanding'. Of course, when the object is before the eyes, there are certain obvious qualifications (which can be summed up by saying that it then has *also* to conform to our use of the word 'descry') but these do not affect the general sense running through all uses of the word. Thus, to see a thing differently is to have a different understanding of it, and we can see why Wordsworth called the Imagination

> another name for absolute power
> And clearest insight, amplitude of mind,
> And Reason in her most exalted mood.[3]

But, of course, it is not Reason in the ordinary sense; it is a commonplace that we do not find a new way of seeing something by a process of formal logic. It comes as a discovery, not as a corollary to an earlier way of seeing. 'Those who have been led to the same truths step by step, through the constant testimony of their senses, seem to me to want a sense which I possess . . . They . . . called the want of imagination, judgement.'[4]

[1] Wordsworth, *Poetical Works*, v, p. 343.
[2] *The Ruined Cottage*, addendum to MS B, ll. 87–90.
[3] *The Prelude*, XIV. 190–2.   [4] Coleridge, *Collected Letters*, i, p. 354.

While all this goes to explain why we can call Imagination a matter of 'seeing as' or of 'seeing differently', it does not explain why some cases of 'seeing as' are called imaginative, some are called fanciful, and some (if they are called anything) prosaic. I think the answer is that these words are used to indicate freshness, interest and value. This can be seen from the employment of the term Fancy. Both Wordsworth and Coleridge use it for cases where there is no new 'seeing' at all, only the drawing of analogies, but Wordsworth also allows that the Fancy can sometimes be creative.[1] When he contrasts an example of this last sort of Fancy with one of Imagination, the tests he applies are of the kind which I have suggested.

I will content myself with placing a conceit . . . in contrast with a passage from the 'Paradise Lost':

> 'The dews of the evening most carefully shun
> They are the tears of the sky for the loss of the sun.'

After the transgression of Adam, Milton, with other appearances of sympathising Nature, thus marks the immediate consequence.

> 'Sky lowered, and, muttering thunder, some sad drops
> Wept at completion of the mortal sin.'

The associating link is the same in each instance; Dew and rain, not distinguishable from the liquid substance of tears, are employed as indications of sorrow. A flash of surprise is the effect in the former case; a flash of surprise, and nothing more; for the nature of things does not sustain the combination. In the latter, the effects from the act, of which this is the immediate consequence and sign, are so momentous, that the mind acknowledges the justice and reasonableness of the sympathy of nature so manifested.

Similarly to distinguish a prosaic instance like the pointing triangle, or a fanciful one like the grinning skull, from

> To every natural form, rock, fruit or flower,
> Even the loose stones that cover the highway,
> I gave a moral life; I saw them feel. . . .

[1] *Preface* of 1815. 'Yet it is not the less true that Fancy, as she is an active, is also, under her own laws and in her own spirit, a creative faculty.'

217

some such criteria as freshness, interest and value must be used. Value, as a test for imaginativeness, is a question-begging word, but here much depends on the subject. It is obvious how the word is to be applied to that stroke of the Imagination that produced Charles Darwin's theory of natural selection, but in poetry the new understanding is in large part emotional, and the implications of the new way of seeing the matter largely concern our ways of feeling.[1] What is essential in all cases is that the creative mind, under pressure, and perhaps baffled by difficulties, makes a sudden leap to a new was of seeing of which the implications, the ways in which it can 'go on', are rich and fruitful. In the magnitude and importance of what has been resolved, and in the satisfaction offered by the new understanding, lies the value of the new seeing, while in the suddenness and completeness of the resolution lies the reason why we feel the Imagination to be miraculous.

All this discussion about the Imagination has told us nothing that was not already implicit in the use of the word by sensible and sensitive men. What it has done is to clear away the misconstructions, the distorting interpretations, and the limitations that result from making our thinking about the Imagination conform to some particular metaphysical theory. We can see the gain when we consider some of the problems left over from the beginning of the discussion. For instance, we can now disentangle the puzzle about the Imagination Associative and the Imagination Penetrative. Ruskin distinguished these because in the latter there is no association; there is no question of seeing one thing *as* another, and there can be no 'coalescing' or 'fusion' of images. But the discussion has suggested that the essence of the Imagination is that it leads us to see something differently—to have a new vision of it or insight into it. Of course this 'fusion' of images is one of the commonest ways in which we do see a thing afresh. The implied comparisons help us to seize those features of the

[1] For an interesting discussion of the emotional implication of poetic imagery see G. Bachelard, *La Psychanalyse du Feu, L'Eau et les Rêves*, and other works by the same author.

thing which are important in the new aspect. To say that the argosies are like 'signiors and rich burghers of the flood' calls our attention to a dozen features of the shape and movement of the vessels, and presents them all at once, so that suddenly we see the ships differently. The new way of seeing cannot be separated from the comparison. Yet a similar result can be got by other means. Take for instance

> Thou wast not born for death, immortal Bird!
> No hungry generations tread thee down;
> The voice I hear this passing night was heard
> In ancient days by emperor and clown.

This does not depend upon comparison. Instead the flash of surprise at the literal untruth of the first line carries us on to see the nightingale as the eternal voice of beauty in a suffering world. There is no coalescence of images, but we see the nightingale with new eyes, and we call this new vision of it imaginative. The process of fusion which writers on the Imagination describe is of great interest to any study of literary technique, but it is of no value as a shibboleth to discover what is imaginative and what is not.

Thinking of the Imagination as 'seeing something as something else' or as 'seeing something differently' also casts light on those Romantic uses of the word which are no longer current. The chief of these are that the Romantics used the word when describing how they saw natural objects, and that they spoke of, and believed in, 'the truth of the Imagination'. Both of these uses will become clearer if we examine them as statements about seeing. Wittgenstein remarked that 'we find certain things about seeing puzzling, because we do not find the whole business of seeing puzzling enough'. Wordsworth did realize how strange the whole business was, and he claimed for his way the same consideration that we give to 'ordinary' seeing. Of course, the ways in which we go on from different 'seeings' are different, even in ordinary instances, and in this way seeing a drawing is not the same as seeing a mark on paper and seeing a rock is not the same as seeing a coloured spot. The way in which Wordsworth saw natural objects, full of life and inarticulate language, was not ordinary.

the clouds were touched,
And in their silent faces could he read
Unutterable love. Sound needed none,
Nor any voice of joy; his spirit drank
The spectacle.

That is, in every sense we have found, imaginative, but the
choice between this and the 'stock' way of seeing clouds is
not one between seeing things fancifully and seeing them 'as
they really are'. Wordsworth's way is one that seizes features
of the object; it is not an hallucination, and one can imagine
cultures in which objects are habitually seen in such a way.
To speak of it as true is not absurd, though, of course, it may
be wrong. How we choose between this and other ways of
seeing the same object is by choosing between the uses we
can make of each and between the metaphysical or logical
systems into which each will fit.

Poetry is read for that surprise and delight which comes
from the imaginative enlargement of understanding, but it is
written by men who seek new vision to satisfy their whole
being. Wordsworth's way of seeing natural forms was sanc-
tioned by current metaphysical theories as to the nature of
things, and his explanations of what he saw became even more
entangled with them. But his insight into the Imagination did
not depend upon metaphysics, and it was from that insight
that the Romantic Revival stemmed. He realized that for the
poet and his readers, imaginative seeing involves the emotions.
'Seeing as' implies 'treating as'; it defines a whole way of
feeling and behaving towards its objects, and, by so doing,
defines and gives 'a living spirit and a character' to the
emotions themselves.[1] The process by which the emotions
express themselves through symbols is only another side to the
process by which the poet charts new regions of feeling in
relation to the world. Much of Wordsworth's greatest poetry,
in *Tintern Abbey*, *The Prelude* and the fourth book of *The
Excursion* was written to point out the implications which his
vision held for the life of the feelings. On the other hand, he
never regarded the Vision as something purely subjective. He

[1] Cf. L. Wittgenstein, *Philosophical Investigations*, p. 178.

held fast to the belief that imaginative seeing was a true communication with the Spirit of the Universe, and a true grasping of the significance of things. The poems which embody that faith reinstated imaginative poetry as a way of understanding the world.

Coleridge's Views on Evolution in 1795

Lines 283–95 of *The Destiny of Nations* are interesting both because of the relationship of the passage to

> Yea, slimy things did crawl with legs
> Upon the slimy sea

and because of the light it casts on Coleridge's ideas at this time on the subject of evolution.

The passage in *Joan of Arc* and in *The Destiny of Nations* runs:

> When Love rose glittering, and his gorgeous wings
> Over the abyss fluttered with such glad noise,
> As what time after long and pestful calms,
> With slimy shapes and miscreated life
> Poisoning the vast Pacific, the fresh breeze
> Wakens the merchant sail uprising. Night
> An heavy unimaginable moan
> Sent forth, when she the Protoplast beheld
> Stand beauteous on Confusion's charmed wave.
> Moaning she fled, and entered the Profound
> That leads with downward windings to the Cave
> Of Darkness palpable, Desert of Death
> Sunk deep beneath Gehenna's massy roots.

The relevant passage in Darwin is *The Botanic Garden*, I. i. 101–4:

> When LOVE DIVINE, with brooding wings unfurled
> Called from the rude abyss the living world
> 'LET THERE BE LIGHT!' proclaim'd the ALMIGHTY LORD,
> Astonished Chaos heard the potent word.

(Another passage on the creation, I. i. 416–17 describes 'IMMORTAL LOVE. . . . O'er the wide waste his gaudy wings unfold'.)
The note to I. i. 101 reads:

From having observed the gradual evolution of the young animal or plant from its egg or seed, and afterwards its successive advances to its more perfect state or maturity; philosophers of all ages seem to have imagined, that the great world itself had likewise its infancy and its gradual progress to maturity, this seems to have given origin to the very antient and sublime allegory of Eros, or Divine Love, producing the world from the egg of Night, as it floated in Chaos.

The note goes on to give evidence for evolution, and ends: 'Perhaps all the supposed monstrous births of Nature are remains of their habits of production in their former less perfect state, or attempts towards greater perfection.'

The later lines of Coleridge's passage refer, of course, to the roots of the Upas-tree (*The Botanic Garden*, II. iii. 236 ff.), but the word 'Protoplast', which is not in *The Botanic Garden* (though it occurs in his notebook immediately after a note on Darwin's Upas-tree (*Gutch Memorandum Book* 4b)), suggests that Coleridge had been following evolution and perhaps spontaneous generation in some other book. The simile of the 'slimy shapes and mis-created life' is intended to illustrate the state of things before the beginnings of organized life, and these slimy forms were apparently produced by heat from organic matter—as they also seem to be in *The Ancient Mariner*. How they acquired legs in the later poem I cannot guess, but there is a description of sea-worms with legs in the note to *The Botanic Garden*, II. i. 266 (on Grass-wrack).

During its time of floating on the sea, numberless animals live on the undersurface of it; and being specifically lighter than the sea water, or being repelled by it, have legs placed as it were on their backs for the purpose of walking under it. As the Scylloea. See Barbut's Genera Vermium.

The whole passage, as it appears in *Joan of Arc*, seems to express a more evolutionary view of the origin of life than the views which Coleridge held later. It is true that in January 1796, after dis-cussion with Erasmus Darwin about Hutton's *Theory of the Earth*, he seems to have regarded theories about the earth's origin as irrelevant: 'What is it to us *how* the earth was made, a thing impossible to be known, and useless if known? (Letter to Wade, 27 January 1796.)'

Nevertheless, theories about the origin of *life* were not so irrelevant to the argument which Coleridge had just been con-ducting with Darwin, for this argument concerned the question, 'whether we be the outcasts of a blind idiot called Nature, or the

children of an all-wise and infinitely good God?' (Letter to Wade.)
G. R. Potter (*PLMA*, 1925) concludes from this letter that Coleridge was opposed to the idea of evolution at this date, but this is
not certain, though it would be true of a later period. All we know
is that Darwin disagreed with Hutton about geology (Coleridge's
own view is neither stated nor implied for Hutton's theory would
favour evolution), and that Coleridge disagreed with Darwin about
Providence. The *Joan of Arc* passage may point to the immediate
subject of their disagreement. Darwin believed in evolution from
original 'living filaments' which developed into different species
by adapting themselves to their environment. Coleridge, in *Joan
of Arc* seems to have believed in spontaneous generation, with the
protoplast appearing among the results of such generation. We
know from *The Friend* that Coleridge used the word 'protoplast'
in an unusual sense (not found in *OED*) to mean 'nisus formativus'
(*The Friend* (1818), Vol. III, p. 213–14). This is a technical term
used in the seventeen-nineties by those who may have agreed with
Darwin about the fact of the evolution of species, but disagreed
with him about the nature of the process. In 1794 a prize of
400 guilders was offered in the *Analytic Review* for an essay on the
following question:

Do the Experiments made by SPALLANZI with Frogs and other animals,
added to the observations of HALLER, furnish sufficient Grounds for
admitting the pre-existence of animal Seeds or Germs, (*pré-existence des
germes*) and thus for considering the propagation of Animals as issuing
forth from certain Seeds or Germs, which have been formed ever since
the existence of the animate creation? Or are there any observations,
which effectively controvert the above mentioned Doctrine of the pre-
existence of animal Seeds, and at the same time establish the contrary
position, viz. that there exists in Nature a Power of Generation or
Formation, described by BLUMENBACH (Nisus formativus) and to which
power the Propagation of Animals may be attributed? (Analytic
Review, xix, p. 112.)

Thus Coleridge may well have been arguing that evolution was an
example of the divine power—'Nature's vast ever-acting Energy'
—acting providentially, while Darwin maintained that evolution
was a mere response to environment on the part of the 'animal
seeds' and, if this were so, Coleridge would be continuing the line
of thought he expressed in *Joan of Arc* and this line of thought
would be consistent with his Unitarianism. However, for Coleridge's views before the end of the century the *Joan of Arc* passage

is the only evidence, and certainly, as Potter demonstrates, though Coleridge continued to think of organic life as the result of an organizing power in nature, he later dropped any idea of evolution *in time*. Indeed, towards the end of his life, he noted against this passage: 'These are very fine lines, tho' I say it, that should not: but, hang me, if I know or ever did know the meaning of them, tho' my own composition.'

APPENDIX B

Hyperion and *The Excursion*

Though Keats was engaged in *Hyperion* on the same problem, of the place of beauty in the world, which had first arisen out of the doctrine of Imagination in *Sleep and Poetry*, and though Robert Gittings (*John Keats; The living year*, p. 18) finds a general stylistic resemblance to *The Excursion*, yet I can only find two passages (one in the revised version only) which seem to indicate borrowing from *The Excursion*. The first passage describes Hyperion's cloud-palace, which shows some debt to the cloud palace ('the revealed abode of Spirits in beatitude'), in *The Excursion*, II. 835–74 (see Douglas Bush, 'Notes on Keats' reading', *PMLA* 1935). Gittings (op. cit., pp. 22, 202) thinks the resemblance very generalized and wishes to derive the image from Milton's sun 'curtained with cloudy red', surely an even more generalized resemblance. *The Excursion* provides not only the conception of a cloud-palace, but also many of the materials and forms—'diamonds and gold,' clouds 'confused, commingled, mutually inflamed, Molten together', 'in fleecy clouds voluminous enwrapped', 'towers and battlements', 'golden domes and silver spires', 'blazing terrace upon terrace' and 'serene pavilions'. Shelley used the same passage in *The Revolt of Islam*, I. 586–616. The second passage is that characterizing the 'dreamer' in *The Fall of Hyperion*. Gittings (op. cit., p. 179) derives this from Beatrice's injunction to Dante at the end of the Purgatorio, to rid himself of fearfulness and shame, 'and speak no more as one who dreams'. But the dreamer in *The Fall of Hyperion* is much more closely characterized than this. We are first told (1–18), in a passage which echoes Wordsworth's doctrine of mute poets (*The Excursion*, I. 77–80), that only poets save imagination from 'dumb enchantment' and enable the dreamer to tell his dreams. Dreamers are of two types, the poet and the fanatic (1–17) and the latter 'weaves a paradise for a sect' (1–2). Later, all dreamers are contrasted with those who 'seek no

226

wonder but the human face; No music but a happy-noted voice',
and Moneta (who does not necessarily represent Keats for her
'black gates were shut against the sunrise', a point I owe to
Professor C. S. Lewis) contrasts the dreamer and the poet. All this
seems fairly close to the ideas of *The Excursion*, III. 290–356, where
the Solitary says that he is not among those 'who in this frame of
human life perceive An object whereunto their souls are tied In
discontented wedlock', and that he prefers the real world to
Arcady. Wordsworth, speaking as the author, agrees:

> if smiles
> Of scornful pity be the just reward
> Of Poesy thus courteously employed
> In framing models to improve the scheme
> Of Man's existence, and recast the world,
> Why should not grave Philosophy be styled,
> Herself, a dreamer of a kindred stock,
> A dreamer yet more spiritless and dull?

and he instances the 'world-excluding groves' of the Epicureans.
Thus we have here Keats' two types of dreamer, we have the contrast between the dreamer and the man who accepts man's existence, and we have the placing of the poet in both of the last two
classes. This suggests that Wordsworth's thought might have
played some part in the revision, and that the burden of Oceanus'
speech, 'Receive the truth, and let it be your balm', might have
been broadened out into a Wordsworthian acceptance of, and joy
in, all being. But there is so little of the revised version that any
remarks about its theme must be utterly conjectural.

Q*

BIBLIOGRAPHY

This bibliography lists books and articles cited in the text together with a small selection of works used but not cited. Sections II and III are each arranged in two parts: (a) Books and Pamphlets; (b) Articles.

I. Texts

BYRON, GEORGE GORDON NOEL, LORD. *Works*, ed. E. H. Coleridge. London, 1904–36.

COLERIDGE, SAMUEL TAYLOR. *The Complete Poetical Works*, ed. E. H. Coleridge. Oxford, 1912.

—— *Biographia Literaria, with his aesthetical essays*, ed. J. Shawcross. Oxford, 1907.

—— *The Friend*, 2nd ed. London, 1818.

—— *Collected Letters*, ed. E. L. Griggs. Oxford, 1956.

—— *Anima Poetae from the unpublished notebooks of Samuel Taylor Coleridge*, ed. E. H. Coleridge. New York, 1895.

—— *Literary Remains*, ed. H. N. Coleridge. London, 1836.

—— *The Notebooks of Samuel Taylor Coleridge*, ed. K. Coburn. London, 1957. Vol. 1.

—— 'Notizbuch aus Jahren 1795–8' (*Gutch Memorandum Book*), *Archiv* 98 (1896).

—— *Table Talk and Omniana*. Oxford, 1917.

KEATS, JOHN. *Poetical Works*, ed. H. W. Garrod. Oxford, 1939.

—— *Poems of John Keats*, ed. E. de Selincourt. 4th ed. London, 1920.

—— *The Letters of John Keats*, ed. M. B. Forman. 4th ed. Oxford, 1952.

SHELLEY, PERCY BYSSHE. *Complete Poetical Works*, ed. T. Hutchinson. London, 1912.

—— *The Complete Works of Percy Bysshe Shelley*, ed. R. Ingpen and W. E. Peck. London, 1929. Vol. v–xii.

WORDSWORTH, WILLIAM. *Poetical Works,* ed. E. de Selincourt and Helen Darbishire. Oxford, 1940–9.

—— *The Prelude, or Growth of a Poet's Mind,* ed. E. de Selincourt. Oxford, 1926.

—— *Early Letters of William and Dorothy Wordsworth (1787–1905),* ed. E. de Selincourt. Oxford, 1935.

II. LITERARY HISTORY, BIOGRAPHY AND CRITICISM

(a) Books and Pamphlets

ABRAMS, MEYER HOWARD. *The Mirror and the Lamp: romantic theory and the critical tradition.* New York, 1953.

AIKIN, JOHN. *Letters from a Father to his Son, on various topics, relative to literature and to the conduct of life.* London, 1793.

BACHELARD, GASTON. *La Psychanalyse du feu.* Paris, 1938.

—— *L'Eau et les Rêves, Essai sur l'imagination de la Matière.* Paris, 1942.

BEACH, JOSEPH WARREN. *The Concept of Nature in Nineteenth Century English Poetry.* New York, 1936.

BOWRA, SIR CECIL MAURICE. *The Romantic Imagination.* London, 1950.

BRANDL, ALOIS. *Samuel Taylor Coleridge and the English Romantic School.* London, 1887.

BUSH, DOUGLAS. *Mythology and the Romantic Tradition in English Poetry.* London, 1932.

CALDWELL, JAMES RALSTON. *John Keats's Fancy.* Ithaca N.Y., 1945.

CESTRE, CHARLES. *La Révolution française et les poètes anglais (1789–1809).* Paris, 1906.

DE QUINCEY, THOMAS. *Works.* Edinburgh, 1862–3. Vols vii, xii.

DONNER, HENRY WOLFGANG. *Thomas Lovell Beddoes. The Making of a Poet.* Oxford, 1935.

FAIRCHILD, HOXIE NEALE. *Religious Trends in English Poetry.* New York, 1939.

FINK, ZERA SILVER (ed.). *The Early Wordsworthian Milieu: a notebook of Christopher Wordsworth with a few entries by William Wordsworth.* Oxford, 1958.

FINNEY, CLAUDE LEE. *The Evolution of Keats' Poetry.* Cambridge, Mass., 1936.

GITTINGS, ROBERT. *John Keats: the living year, 21 September 1818 to 21 September 1819.* Melbourne, 1954.

GRABO, CARL HENRY. *A Newton among Poets: Shelley's use of science in 'Prometheus Unbound'.* Chapel Hill, 1930.

—— *Prometheus Unbound, an interpretation.* Chapel Hill, 1935.

—— *The Magic Plant; the growth of Shelley's thought.* Chapel Hill, 1936.

HANSEN, LAWRENCE. *The Life of S. T. Coleridge: the early years.* London, 1938.

HARPER, GEORGE MCLEAN. *William Wordsworth, his life, works and influence.* 3rd ed. New York, 1929.

—— *Spirit of Delight.* New York, 1928.

HAVENS, RAYMOND DEXTER. *The Mind of a Poet: Wordsworth's thought with particular reference to 'The Prelude'.* Baltimore, 1941.

HAZLITT, WILLIAM. *The Complete Works,* ed. P. P. Howe. London, 1930–4. Vol. iv.

HOUGHTON, RICHARD MONCKTON MILNES, 1st Baron. *Life and Letters of John Keats.* London, 1927.

HOUSE, ARTHUR HUMPHRY. *Coleridge.* London, 1953.

HUGHES, ARTHUR MONTAGUE D'URBAN. *The Nascent Mind of Shelley.* Oxford, 1947.

HULME, THOMAS ERNEST. *Speculations: essays on humanism and the philosophy of art.* 2nd ed. London, 1954.

JAMES, DAVID GWILYM. *Scepticism and Poetry: an essay on the Poetic Imagination,* London, 1937.

—— *The Life of Reason; Hobbes, Locke, Bolingbroke.* London, 1949.

KENNEDY, WILMA L. *The English Heritage of Coleridge of Bristol, 1798. The Basis in Eighteenth-Century English Thought for His Distinction between Imagination and Fancy.* New Haven, 1947.

LAMB, CHARLES. *The Works of Charles Lamb,* ed. W. Macdonald. New York, 1903.

LEGOUIS, ÉMILE. *The Early Life of William Wordsworth, 1770–1798. A Study of 'The Prelude'.* Tr. J. W. Matthews. London, 1897.

LEMONNIER, LEON. *Les Poètes romantiques anglais.* Paris, 1943.

LEWIS, CLIVE STAPLES. *Rehabilitations and Other Essays*. London, 1939.

LOWES, JOHN LIVINGSTON. *The Road to Xanadu: a study in the ways of the imagination*. 2nd ed. London, 1930.

LUCAS, FRANK LAURENCE. *The Decline and Fall of the Romantic Ideal*. Cambridge, 1936.

MARGOLIOUTH, HERSCHEL MAURICE. *Wordsworth and Coleridge 1795–1834*. Oxford, 1953.

MEYER, GEORGE WILBUR. *Wordsworth's Formative Years*. Ann Arbor, 1943.

MONK, SAMUEL HOLT. *The Sublime: a study of critical theories in XVIII-century England*. New York, 1935.

MOORE, THOMAS. *Life, Letters and Journals of Lord Byron*. New ed. London, 1932.

MOORMAN, MARY CAROLINE. *William Wordsworth, a biography*. Vol. I. Oxford, 1957.

NOTCUTT, HENRY CLEMENT. *An Interpretation of Keats's Endymion*. Cape Town, 1919.

PETITJEAN, ARMAND. *Imagination et Realisation*. Paris, 1931.

PETTET, E. C. *On the Poetry of Keats*. Cambridge, 1957.

RICHARDS, IVOR ARMSTRONG. *Coleridge on imagination*. 2nd ed. London, 1950.

RUSKIN, JOHN. *The Works of John Ruskin*, ed. T. Cook and A. Wedderburn. London, 1903–12. Vols. viii, xix.

SARTRE, JEAN PAUL. *L'imagination*. Paris, 1936.

SHERWOOD, MARGARET. *Coleridge's Imaginative Concept of Imagination*. Wellesley, 1937.

STALLKNECHT, NEWTON P. *Strange Seas of Thought: Studies in Wordsworth's philosophy of man and nature*. Durham, North Carolina, 1945.

THORPE, CLARENCE DEWITT. *The Mind of John Keats*. New York, 1926.

WARREN, ROBERT PENN (ed.). *The Rime of the Ancient Mariner*. New York, 1946.

WHITE, NEWMAN IVEY. *Shelley*. London, 1947.

WILLEY, BASIL. *The Eighteenth Century Background. Studies on the Idea of Nature in the Thought of the Period*. London, 1946.

—— *Coleridge on Imagination and Fancy*. Warton Lecture on English Poetry. London, 1946.

—— *Nineteenth Century Studies: Coleridge to Matthew Arnold*. London, 1950.

WORDSWORTH, CHRISTOPHER. *Memoirs of William Wordsworth, poet laureate*. London, 1851.

(b) *Articles*

BALDENSPERGER, F. '1793–4: Climacteric Times for "Romantic" Tendencies in English Ideology'. *JHI*, v (1944), pp. 3–20.

BENZIGER, J. 'Organic Unity: Leibniz to Coleridge.' *PMLA*, lxvi (1951), pp. 24–48.

BERNBAUM, E. 'Is Wordsworth's Nature Poetry Outdated?' *ELH*, vii (1940), pp. 333–46.

BRETT, R. L. 'Coleridge's Theory of the Imagination.' *E & S*, N.S. ii (1949), pp. 79–90.

BROOKS, E. L. '"The Poet" an error in the Keats Canon?' *MLN*, lxvii (1952), pp. 450–4.

BUSH, D. 'Notes on Keats' Reading.' *PMLA*, l (1935), pp. 785–806.

CAMPBELL, O. J. and MUESCHKE, P. 'Wordsworth's "Guilt and Sorrow": a study in the genesis of Wordsworth's aesthetic.' *MP*, xxiii (1936), pp. 293–306.

—— 'Wordsworth's Aesthetic Development: 1795–1802.' Univ. of Michigan Publications in Lang. and Lit. Vol. x. (1933).

CARRITT, E. F. 'Addison, Keats and Wordsworth.' *E & S*, xxii (1936), pp. 26–36.

CLARKE, C. 'Nature's Education of Man: Some remarks on the Philosophy of Wordsworth.' *Philosophy*, xxiii (1948), pp. 302–16.

DUNN, S. G. 'A Note on Wordsworth's Metaphysical System.' *E & S*, xviii (1932), pp. 74–109.

FAIRCHILD, H. N. 'Hartley, Pistorius and Coleridge.' *PMLA*, lxii (1947), pp. 1010–21.

—— 'Keats and the Struggle-for-Existence Tradition.' *PMLA*, lxiv (1949), pp. 98–114.

FORD, NEWELL F. 'The Meaning of "Fellowship with Essence" in *Endymion*.' *PMLA*, lxii (1947), pp. 1061–76.

—— '*Endymion*—a Neo-Platonic Allegory?' *ELH*, xiv (1947), pp. 64–76

GINGERICH, S. F. 'From Necessity to Transcendentalism in Coleridge.' *PMLA*, xxxv (1920), pp. 1–59.

GRIGGS, E. L. and MUESCHKE, P. 'Wordsworth as the Prototype of the Poet in *Alastor*.' *PMLA*, lxix (1934), pp. 229–45.

HARDING, D. W. 'The Theme of *The Ancient Mariner*.' *Scrutiny*, ix (1941), pp. 334–42.

HAVENS, R. D. 'Discontinuity in Literary Development: the case of English Romanticism.' *SP*, xlvii (1950), pp. 102–11

KALLICH, M. 'The Association of Ideas and Akenside's *Pleasures of Imagination*.' *MLN*, lxii (1947), pp. 166–73.

KAPSTEIN, I. J. 'The Meaning of Shelley's "Mont Blanc".' *PMLA*, lxii (1947), pp. 1046–60.

KELLEY, M. W. 'Thomas Cooper and Pantisocracy.' *MLN*, xlv (1930), pp. 218–20.

LOVEJOY, A. O. 'The Meaning of Romanticism for the Historian of Ideas.' *JHI*, ii (1941), pp. 257–78.

—— 'Coleridge and Keats' Two Worlds.' *ELH*, vii (1940), pp. 341–62.

MACGILLIVRAY, J. R. 'The Pantisocracy scheme and its immediate background.' *Studies in English by Members of University College, Toronto* (1931), pp. 131–69.

MAYO, R. D. 'The Contemporaneity of the Lyrical Ballads.' *PMLA*, lxix (1954), pp. 486–522.

MILLEY, H. J. W. 'Some Notes on Coleridge's *Eolian Harp*.' *MP*, xxxvi (1939), pp. 359–75.

PIPER, H. W. 'Keats and W. C. Wells.' *RES*, xxv (1949), pp. 158–9.

POTTER, G. R. 'Coleridge and the Idea of Evolution.' *PMLA*, lx (1925), pp. 379–97.

—— 'Wordsworth and the "Traité elementaire de chimie" of Lavoisier.' *PQ*, xvii (1938), pp. 312–16.

RADER, M. M. 'Presiding Ideas in Wordsworth's Poetry.' Univ. of Washington Publications in Lang. and Lit. Vol. ii, pp. 121–216.

DE SELINCOURT, ERNEST. 'Coleridge's *Dejection: An Ode*.' *E & S*, xxii (1936), pp. 7–25.

SNYDER, A. D. 'Coleridge's Cosmogony.' *SP*, xxi (1924), pp. 616–25.

STALLKNECHT, N. P. 'The Moral of *The Ancient Mariner*.' *PMLA*, xlvii (1932), pp. 559–69.

WASSERMAN, E. R. 'Keats' Sonnet "The Poet".' *MLN*, xlvii (1952), pp. 454–6.

WELLS, G. A. 'Man and Nature: an Elucidation of Coleridge's rejection of Herder's Thought.' *JEGP*, li (1952), pp. 312–25.

III. SCIENTIFIC, PHILOSOPHICAL, AND MISCELLANEOUS WORKS

(*a*) *Books and Pamphlets*

AEGERTER, EMILE. *Le Mysticisme*. Paris, 1952.

BAILIE, GEORGE ALEXANDER. *A history and genealogy of the family of Bailie of north of Ireland*. Augusta, Ga., 1902.

BARBER, WILLIAM HENRY. *Leibniz in France: from Arnauld to Voltaire: a study in French reactions to Leibnizianism: 1670–1760*. Oxford, 1955.

BAXTER, ANDREW. *An Inquiry into the Nature of the Human Soul; wherein the immateriality of the soul is evinced from the principles of reason and philosophy*. 3rd ed. London, 1745.

BEUCHAT, CHARLES. *Histoire du naturalisme francais*. Paris, 1949–50.

BONNET, CHARLES. *Œuvres*. Neufchatel, 1779. Tomes V–VII, 'Considerations sur les corps organisés'; tomes IX–X, 'La contemplation de la Nature', and tomes XV–XVI.

BUFFON, GEORGE LOUIS LECLERC, COMTE DE. *Les Epoques de la Nature*, ed. G. Meunier. Paris, 1894.

CABANIS, PIERRE-JEAN-GEORGES. *Rapports du physique et du moral de l'homme*. Paris, 1802.

CARNEGIE, ANDREW. *James Watt*. New York, 1905.

CARRA, JEAN-LOUIS. *Système de la Raison, ou le Prophète philosophe*. 3rd ed. Paris, 1791.

CONDORCET, JACQUES MARIE DE CARITAT DE. *Esquisse d'un tableau historique des progrès de l'esprit humain*, ed. O. H. Prior. Paris, 1933.

CUDWORTH, RALPH. *The True Intellectual System of the Universe*, 2nd ed. London, 1743.

CUVIER, GEORGES. *Récherches sur les ossements fossiles des quadrupèdes*. 4th ed. Paris, 1834.

DARWIN, ERASMUS. *The Botanic Garden; A Poem in Two Parts. Part I containing The Economy of Vegetation. Part II. The Loves of the Plants. With Philosophical Notes.* London, 1791.
—— *Zoonomia or the laws of Organic Life.* London, 1794–6.

DAVY, SIR HUMPHRY. *A Discourse, introductory to a course of lectures in chemistry, delivered in the theatre of the Royal Institution.* London, 1802.

DIDEROT, DENIS. *Œuvres complètes,* ed. J. Assézat. Paris, 1875–7. Vol. i–iv.

EDEN, WILLIAM, BARON AUCKLAND. *The Journal and Correspondence of William, Lord Auckland,* ed. G. Hogge. London, 1860–2.

FUSELI, HENRY. *Lectures on Painting delivered at the Royal Academy, March 1801.* 2nd ser., ed. J. Knowles. London, 1830.

GARAT, DOMINIQUE-JOSEPH. *Memoires historiques sur la vie de M. Suard, sur ses écrits, et sur la xviiiᵉ siècle.* Paris, 1820.

GODWIN, WILLIAM. *Political Justice.* London, 1793.

GOW, HENRY. *The Unitarians.* London, 1928.

GRIFFITHS, OLIVE M. *Religion and Learning: English Presbyterian thought from 1662 to the foundation of the Unitarian movement.* London, 1935.

GUYENOT, EMILE. *Les Sciences de la vie aux xviiᵉ et xviiiᵉ siècles. L'idée d'evolution.* Paris, 1941.

HARTLEY, DAVID. *Observations on Man, his frame, his duty, and his expectations.* Notes and Additions by H. Pistorius. London, 1791.

HAZARD, PAUL. *European Thought in the Eighteenth Century from Montesquieu to Lessing.* Tr. J. Lewis May. London, 1954.

HOLBACH, PAUL-HENRI-DIETRICH, BARON D'. *Système de la Nature ou des lois du monde physique et du monde morale, par M. Mirabaud.* London, 1770.

HOLT, RAYMOND VINCENT. *The Unitarian Contribution to Social Progress in England.* London, 1952.

HUNT, ROBERT. *The Poetry of Science, or studies in the physical phenomena of nature.* 3rd ed. London, 1854.

HUTTON, JAMES. *Dissertations on different subjects of Natural Philosophy.* Edinburgh, 1792.

—— *An Investigation of the Principles of Knowledge and the Progress of Reason, from Sense to Science and Philosophy.* Edinburgh, 1794.

LEIBNIZ, GOTTFRIED WILHELM. *The Monadology and Other Philosophical Writings,* translated with introduction and notes by Robert Latta. Oxford, 1898.

LITCHFIELD, RICHARD BUCKLEY. *Tom Wedgwood, the first photographer, an account of his life.* London, 1903.

MCCLACHLAN, HERBERT. *The Unitarian Movement in the religious life of England.* London, 1934.

MCCOSH, JAMES and DICKIE, GEORGE. *Typical Forms and Special Ends in the Creation.* Edinburgh, 1856.

MAILLET, BENOIT DE. *Telliamed ou Entretiens d'un philosophe indien avec un missionaire francais sur le dimunition de la mer, la formation de la terre, l'origine de l'homme etc.* Amsterdam, 1748.

MALONE, DUMAS. *The Public Life of Thomas Cooper.* New Haven, 1926.

MARET, HENRI-LOUIS-CHARLES. *Essai sur le panthèisme dans les societés modernes.* Paris, 1840.

MATHIEZ, ALBERT. *La Révolution et les Etrangers.* Paris, 1919.

MAUPERTUIS, PIERRE-LOUIS MOREAU DE. *Essai sur la formation des corps organisés.* Berlin, 1754.

MILLER, HUGH. *Old Red Sandstone, or new walks in an old field.* 7th ed. Edinburgh, 1854.

MONRO, ALEXANDER. *Observations on the Structure and Functions of the Nervous System.* Edinburgh, 1783.

MONTLOSIER, FRANCOIS-DOMINIQUE DE REYNAUD, COMTE DE. *Des Mystères de la Vie Humaine.* Paris, 1829.

MORNET, DANIEL. *La Penseé française au XVIIIe siècle.* 4th ed. Paris, 1936.

MUIRHEAD, JAMES PATRICK. *The Life of James Watt, with selections from his correspondence.* London, 1858.

MUIRHEAD, JOHN HENRY. *Coleridge as a Philosopher.* 2nd imp. London, 1954.

NEWTON, SIR ISAAC. *Isaaci Newtoni Opera,* ed. S. Horsley. London, 1779–85. Vol. v.

NICHOLSON, WILLIAM. *The First Principles of Chemistry.* 2nd ed. London, 1792.

PRIESTLEY, JOSEPH. *Disquisitions relating to Matter and Spirit. To which is added the history of the philosophical doctrine concerning the origin of the soul, and the nature of matter.* London, 1777.

—— *idem.* 2nd ed. enlarged. Birmingham, 1782.

—— (ed.) *Hartley's Theory of the Human Mind. With essays relating to the subject of it.* London, 1775.

—— *Experiments and observations relating to various branches of Natural Philosophy: with a continuation of the observations on air.* London, 1799–86. Vol. iii.

—— *The Conclusion of . . . Dr. Hartley's Observations . . . on the nature of Man . . . illustrated in the events of the present times, with notes.* London, 1794.

—— *The Present State of Europe compared with antient Prophecies; a sermon (on Matt. iii, 2) preached . . . Feb 28, 1794 . . . The day appointed for a general fast. With a preface containing the reasons for the Author's leaving England.* London, 1794.

ROBINET, JEAN-BAPTISTE-RENÉ. *Considérations philosophiques de la gradation naturelle des formes de l'être.* Paris, 1768.

[RUSSEL]. *An Essay on the Nature and Existence of a Material World.* [?], 1781.

STEWART, DUGALD. *Elements of the Philosophy of the Human Mind.* London, 1792–1827. Vol. i.

STEWART, JOHN. *The Apocalypse of Nature, wherein the source of moral motion is discovered and a moral system established, through the evidence and conviction of the senses, to elevate man to intellectual existence and an enlightened state of nature.* London, 1790 (?).

—— *The Sophiometer; or regulator of Mental Power.* London?, 1818?

TOOKE, JOHN HORNE. *The Diversions of Purley.* New ed. revised by R. Taylor. London, 1829.

VOLNEY, CONSTANTIN FRANCOIS CHASSEBOEUF DE. *Les Ruines ou Meditation sur les Révolutions des Empires.* Paris, 1791.

WAKEFIELD, GILBERT. *The Spirit of Christianity compared with the Spirit of the Times in Great Britain.* London, 1794.

WATTS, ALARIC ALFRED. *Alaric Watts, a narrative of his life, by his son.* London, 1884.

WEIL, SIMONE. *Intuitions Pré-Chrétiennes.* Paris, 1951.

WILBUR, EARLE MORSE. *A History of Unitarianism and its antecedents.* Cambridge, Mass., 1946.

WISDOM, ARTHUR JOHN TERENCE DIBBEN. *Philosophy and Psycho-analysis.* Oxford, 1953.

WITTGENSTEIN, LUDWIG. *Philosophical Investigations.* Tr. G. E. M. Anscombe. Oxford, 1953.

ZITTEL, KARL ALFRED VON. *History of Geology and Palaeontology to the end of the nineteenth century.* Tr. M. M. Ogilvie-Gordon. London, 1901.

(*b*) *Articles*

GREGORY, JOSHUA. 'The Animate Model of Physical Process.' *Science Progress*, xx (1925), pp. 298–308.

SCOTT, W. L. 'The Significance of "Hard" Bodies in the History of Scientific Thought.' *Isis* 50 (1959), pp. 199–210.

SMART, J. J. C. Review of D. G. James, *The Life of Reason* in *Mind*, lix (1950), pp. 120–1.

STRAWSON, P. F. Review of L. Wittgenstein, *Philosophical Investigations* in *Mind*, lxiii (1954), pp. 70–99.

INDEX

Abrams, M. H., 3, 5, 71–2
Addison, Joseph, 11, 12–14
Aegerter, E., 62, 73
Aeschylus, 178, 180
Aikin, J., 139
Akenside, Mark, 15
Alembert, J. R. d', 22
Analytical Review, 100, 224

Bachelard, G., 218
Bailie, Mrs C. W. H., 67
Bailie, Thomas, 66–7, 70–1
Bailie, T. M., 67
Bailly, P., 189
Baldensperger, F., 100
Balguy, J., 47
Barber, W. H., 17
Baxter, A., 30, 33–4, 38, 133
Beach, J. W., 63, 69–70
Beaupuy, M., 17, 60, 69, 71
Beccaria, J. W., 99–100
Beddoes, Thomas, 26–7
Berkeley, G., bishop, 13, 16, 44–5, 56–8, 63, 69, 81, 111, 126, 133
Blackmore, R., 15
Blumenbach, J. F., 40, 224
Bohr, N., 17
Bonnet, G., 17, 25
Boscovitch, R. J., 17, 34
Bowles, W. L., 139–40
Bowra, C. M., 15
Brandl, A., 39
Brett, R. L., 30, 142–3
Brooks, E. L., 159–60
Browning, Robert, 142
Bruno, Giordano, 25
Buffon, G. L. C. de, 17, 22–3, 165, 179, 189
Burke, Edmund, 11
Burtin, F. X. de, 189
Bush, D., 226

Byron, Lord, 86, 122, 124, 149–50, 160–1, 173–81, 184, 196–200, 202–3
  Childe Harold's Pilgrimage, 174–180, 199
  Darkness, 179
  Don Juan, 203
  The Dream, 174, 177–8, 180
  Manfred, 160, 174, 178–9, 197–9

Cabanis, P. -J. -G., 17, 25, 115, 165
Campbell, O. J., 129
Carnegie, A., 26
Carra, J. -L., 25, 109
Cestre, C., 73
Chateaubriand, F. R., 50
Christie, T., 64
Clausius, R. J. E., 17
Cobb, J. J., 66
Coleridge, Hartley, 56, 82
Coleridge, Samuel Taylor, 1–4, 11, 15–17, 26, 28, 29–59, 71–3, 79–84, 85–105, 107, 114–17, 123–7, 130, 151–2, 165–6, 222–5
— changes in belief: adopts Unitarianism, 29–32; Hartleyanism, 31; Platonism, 43–6; Berkeleyanism, 56–7; Transcendentalism, 132–5, 141; rejects Unitarianism, 134
— on 'One Life', 36, 39, 41, 43–6, 58, 79, 83, 88, 96, 98, 104–5, 133–139, 144; on Newton, 6, 38, 50, 133, 140; Fancy, 80, 127, 137; Imagination, 82–3, 88, 127–8, 139–44, 206, 208; natural symbols, 57–8, 143
— Imagery: clouds, 89; electricity, 41–2, 99–101; heat, 52–3, 59; 91–93; polar regions, 90–3; putrefaction and phosphorescence, 90,

239